305.90664 RIC

Richards, David A. J.

Identity and the case
for gay rights : race,
CHAVEZ

IDENTITY
AND THE CASE FOR
GAY RIGHTS

IDENTITY
AND THE CASE FOR
GAY
RIGHTS

Race, Gender, Religion
as Analogies

DAVID A. J. RICHARDS

The University of Chicago Press
Chicago and London

David A. J. RICHARDS is the Edwin D. Webb Professor of Law and director of the Program for the Study of Law, Philosophy, and Social Theory at New York University. He is author most recently of *Women, Gays, and the Constitution: The Grounds for Feminism and Gay Rights in Culture and Law* (1998), also published by the University of Chicago Press.

The University of Chicago Press, Chicago 60637
The University of Chicago Press, Ltd., London
© 1999 by The University of Chicago
All rights reserved. Published 1999
Printed in the United States of America
08 07 06 05 04 03 02 01 00 99   1 2 3 4 5

ISBN: 0-226-71208-7 (cloth)
ISBN: 0-226-71209-5 (paper)

Cover illustration: The "Tyrannicides." Roman marble copies of original Greek bronzes (of Harmodios and Aristogeiton) by Kritios and Nesiotes. Height 6 feet 5 inches (1.95 m). 477–476 B.C. (original). National Museum, Naples. "Harmodios and Aristogeiton killed Hipparkhos, the brother of the tyrant Hippias, in 514 B.C., and were regarded in popular tradition as having freed Athens from tyranny. Both Harmodios and Aristogeiton perished in consequence of their act; Harmodios was the eromenos [lover] of Aristogeiton, and Hipparkhos's unsuccessful attempt to seduce him was the start of the quarrel which had such a spectacular political outcome (Thuc. vi 54–9)." K. J. Dover, *Greek Homosexuality* (London: Duckworth, 1978), 41.

Library of Congress Cataloging-in-Publication Data

Richards, David A. J.
    Identity and the case for gay rights : race, gender, religion as analogies / David A. J. Richards.
      p. cm.
    Includes bibliographical references and index.
    ISBN 0-226-71208-7 (cloth : alk. paper).—ISBN 0-226-71209-5 (paper : alk. paper)
      1. Gay rights—United States.   2. Afro-Americans—Civil rights.
  3. Women's rights—United States.   4. Freedom of religion—United States.   5. Gays—United States—Identity.   6. Identity (Psychology)—United States.   I. Title.
  HQ76.8.U5R53   1999
  305.9′0664—dc21   99-32745
                                                                    CIP

⊚ The paper used in this publication meets the minimum requirements of the American National Standard for Information Sciences—Permanence of Paper for Printed Library Materials, ANSI Z39.48-1992.

For Donald Levy

Come, I will make the continent indissoluble,
I will make the most splendid race the sun ever shone upon,
I will make divine magnetic lands,
With the love of comrades,
With the life-long love of comrades.

—Walt Whitman, *Leaves of Grass*

I meant *Leaves of Grass* . . . to be the Poem of Identity, (of *Yours*,
whoever you are, now reading these lines.) . . . For genius must
realize that, precious as it may be, there is something far more
precious, namely, simple Identity, One's-self.

—Walt Whitman, Preface to *Leaves of Grass*

The history of the American Negro is the history of this strife,—
this longing to attain self-conscious manhood, to merge his
double self into a better and truer self. In this merging he wishes
neither of the older selves to be lost. He would not Africanize
America, for America has too much to teach the world and
Africa. He would not bleach his Negro soul in a flood of white
Americanism, for he knows the Negro blood has a message for
the world. He simply wishes to make it possible for a man to be
both a Negro and an American, without being cursed and spit
upon by his fellows, without having the doors of Opportunity
closed roughly in his face.

—W. E. B. Du Bois, *The Souls of Black Folk*

It is my thesis that the core of the problem for women today is
not sexual but a problem of identity—a stunting or evasion of
growth that is perpetuated by the feminine mystique.

—Betty Friedan, *The Feminine Mystique*

CONTENTS

ACKNOWLEDGMENTS

This stimulus to writing this book was an invitation from Dean Robert C. Clark and the faculty of the Harvard Law School to deliver the Shikes lecture in civil liberties at Harvard Law School on April 8, 1998, on the subject of sexual orientation. Prior to that invitation, I had completed work on a long study on the historical and contemporary development of arguments for feminism and gay rights in the United States, published by the University of Chicago Press in 1998 as *Women, Gays, and the Constitution: The Grounds for Feminism and Gay Rights in Culture and Law.* I took the invitation to deliver the Shikes lecture as an opportunity to condense and focus arguments dealing with gay rights in the earlier work, but also critically to state and investigate, much more extensively than I had earlier, each of the main legal analogies associated with arguments for gay rights, and to explore further the nature and implications of an identity-based theory of gay rights. To do justice to this ambition, I wrote as the Shikes lecture not only the lecture I delivered but this longer work, which was distributed to the Harvard Law School faculty as background for the lecture.

I did both my undergraduate and law school work at Harvard and am, for this reason, especially grateful to Dean Clark and the faculty of the Harvard Law School for the invitation extended to their former student and for their gracious and stimulating response to and comments on both the lecture and this work; I am grateful as well for the illuminating conversations I had, while at Harvard, with Professor Janet E. Halley of Stanford Law School, who delivered a related lecture on the subject of gay rights. I am particularly happy to acknowledge my gratitude to Professors Martha Minow and Frank Michelman of Harvard Law School for their comments and warm support of my work both in the past and while I was at Harvard.

I am most grateful also for the support, now and in the past, of my work of Douglas Mitchell, senior editor at the University of Chicago Press, and gratefully acknowledge as well my debt for the illuminating and quite helpful comments on the work from its two readers for the Chicago Press, Professor Katherine E. Franke of Fordham University Law School and Professor Mary E. Becker of the University of Chicago School of Law.

This book was researched and written during a sabbatical leave taken from the New York University School of Law during the academic year 1997–98. Work during both the sabbatical leave and associated summers was made possible by generous research grants from the New York University School of Law Filomen D'Agostino and Max E. Greenberg Faculty Research Fund. I am grateful as well to my colleagues and my dean, John Sexton, for forging an academic culture of learning at the School of Law so hospitable to scholarly work.

Work on this project was aided by the excellent research assistance of Yuval Merin; and my secretary, Lynn Gilbert, ably assisted me in gathering the research materials used in writing this book and preparing the manuscript for publication.

I am grateful as well for the love and support of my sister and friend, Diane Rita Richards, and for the sustaining and creative love of Donald Levy that has graced my life for now well over twenty years. I dedicate this book, with love, to him.

INTRODUCTION

We need now, more than ever, to understand the case for gay rights among the basic human rights that free people enjoy. If gay rights are requirements of such more basic human rights, failure to recognize such rights bespeaks a fundamental injustice in our politics that must be intolerable to reasonable people of good will. In American law, the argument for gay rights arises against a shared background of cumulative historical experience of successful struggles for human rights in various domains—religious tolerance, racial equality, and, most recently, gender equality, all of which now importantly appeal to constitutionally guaranteed principles of the U.S. Constitution, as importantly amended by the Reconstruction Amendments.[1] Serious arguments for gay rights in the United States, which themselves only enjoyed some measure of freedom from censorship after World War II, naturally appealed to these earlier struggles. Indeed, they were clearly empowered by their growing successes: the resistance at Stonewall, for example, drew its larger significance from comparable forms of resistance by African Americans and women.[2] To the extent African Americans and women were successful in recasting the judicial interpretation of basic constitutional principles in terms closer to their vision of basic human rights, gay and lesbian scholars and activists, includ-

1. I make the historical case for this argument at length in David A. J. Richards, *Women, Gays, and the Constitution: The Grounds for Feminism and Gay Rights in Culture and Law* (Chicago: University of Chicago Press, 1998).
2. For relevant historical background, see ibid.; Martin Duberman, *Stonewall* (New York: Plume, 1994).

ing myself, supposed that we might reasonably build on their successes.

A relatively new human rights movement, like gay rights, must select with care among the strands of more long-standing human rights struggles that it takes as guides or models. Considerations of principle and strategy must inform its deliberative choices. Short-term strategic considerations, undertaken with the hope of fitting one's case to an established precedent, sometimes exact too high a price when they cause the centrally legitimate claims for gay rights to be distorted and, worse, when they cause the deeper understanding of the struggles with which gay rights are allied to be sundered. Such bargains betray the ethical potential of the gay rights struggle to liberate gays and lesbians from a range of stultifying stereotypes of gender and sexuality (reflecting uncritical homophobia) that blight their lives. Detaching the gay rights movement from the larger fabric of the human rights movement incurs an unacceptable cost in interpretive understanding of the larger fabric of principles common to all these struggles for human rights.

In this work, I develop, defend, and explore the implications of an identity-based view of the case for gay rights in three stages that critically address three analogies to related struggles for human rights: race (chapter 1), gender (chapter 2), and religious toleration (chapter 3). Each of these analogies can be interpreted in various ways; I criticize some and defend others. For example, one interpretation of the force of the racial analogy has been artificially to compel attention to issues of immutability and salience, as if sexual orientation could only be constitutionally protected from invidious discrimination if it, like race, were an immutable and conspicuous fact of nature; I argue that this view both distorts the case for gay rights and gets decidedly wrong the constitutional evil we condemn as racism. An interpretation of the gender analogy has been a comparably misplaced emphasis on issues of immutability and salience; I argue that this construal of the analogy not only imposes extraneous and irrelevant requirements on the case for gay rights but gets quite wrong the nature and extent of the constitutional evil we condemn as sexism. My alternative analysis identifies the important role that antisexist principles play in the understanding of the case for gay rights, critically examining the unjust force gender stereotypes have traditionally played in the condemnation of homosexuality. On my view, anti-sexist principles, properly understood, liberate all persons from unjust gender stereotypes—male and female, heterosexual and homosexual—and the case for gay rights thus advances general understanding of the proper scope of the constitutional principles that today legitimately condemn sexism as well as racism.

Finally, I explore the case for gay rights in terms of the argument for religious toleration associated with the First Amendment of the U.S. Constitution. I argue that this is the most compelling model for the case for gay rights, namely, as a protection of conscientious ethical claims to gay or lesbian identity on terms of equal respect against the long-standing tradition that condemned homosexuals to unspeakability. My analysis will examine two features that make the analogy, in my judgment, compelling. First, the identity-based case for gay rights normatively depends on the rights of the person of the American tradition of religious toleration. Second, such arguments for gay rights turn as well on a constitutionally compelled skepticism about the sectarian grounds uncritically assumed to rationalize abridgment of such rights. I then examine how this analysis clarifies and supports three legitimate identity-based claims for gay rights: the unconstitutionality of anti-gay/lesbian initiatives, the exclusion of gays and lesbians from the military, and the refusal to recognize same-sex marriage (chapter 3).

I do state, defend, and explore an interpretation of the analogies among race, gender, religion, and sexual preference in terms of the normative conception of *moral slavery*. This interpretation is not only free of the difficulties of other interpretations of these analogies, but, I argue, it powerfully illuminates the common grounds of constitutional principle that condemn extreme religious intolerance, racism, sexism, and homophobia. Moral slavery condemns a structural injustice marked by two interlinked features: first, its abridgment of the basic human rights of a class of persons, and second, the rationalization of such abridgment on inadequate grounds reflecting a history of unjust treatment (involving the dehumanization of the group). My proposal aims to inform and guide contemporary debates over the treatment of persons of color, women, gays, and lesbians in terms of an alternative account of the suspectness of such categories. I thus criticize the common view that suspect classifications turn either on the immutability or salience of a trait or on the alleged powerlessness of a group. Rather, on the alternative view I propose and defend, such classifications are suspect because they illegitimately assume as their basis the culturally constructed stereotypes and prejudices that make up moral slavery. Laws grounded on moral slavery not only lack any acceptable basis in the constitutionally required public reasons for all law of justice and the common good, but work unreason by illegitimately rationalizing its structural injustice. The structure of this account of suspect classification analysis is the condemnation of a basis for law that reflects the degradation of a cultural tradition (moral slavery) with which a person reasonably identifies in terms of their conscientious sense of personal and moral identity. Such unjust devaluation of identity is, I argue, what unites on grounds of principle the interlinked grounds for the suspectness of religion, race, gender, and sexual preference.

My account of suspect classification analysis links this analysis to a structural injustice inflicting indignities on our legitimate moral freedom, which is undermined by the uncritical enforcement of traditions of moral slavery in the domains of religion, race, gender, and sexual preference. Analogous to the comparable struggles against the injustices of anti-Semitism, racism, and sexism, the case for gay rights emerges from the struggle to understand, recognize, and demand one's basic human rights of self-invention of one's personal and ethical life (that is, of free moral personality) against the enforcement of the often interlinked stereotypes (religion, race, gender, and sexual preference) that abridged such rights. Such a struggle against structural injustice is, on the account I offer, best understood as a struggle for self-respecting identity against the unjust terms of the devalued identity uncritically imposed by the dominant culture.

The fruitfulness of this identity-based approach to gay rights is shown in the way it clarifies both the terms of this struggle and the nature and depth of the opposition to it (chapter 4). The power of the religious analogy is its focus on the conscientious character of claims of gay and lesbian identity as both a moral *choice* and a *demand;* the analogy also advances understanding of the nature and depth of the opposition, upholding, as it does, a long-standing sectarian tradition of unspeakability about issues of gender equality now elsewhere conspicuously in doubt. In order to maintain the terms of the traditional dehumanization of homosexuals (in particular, their unspeakability) and the larger assumptions of gender inequality in intimate life that such dehumanization uncritically supports, the traditional culture wages an aggressive attack on identity-based claims of gay rights to equal respect.

This analysis of the case for gay rights (expressing a structural injustice common to extreme religious intolerance, racism, sexism, and homophobia) also advances general understanding of the two mechanisms by which such injustice is entrenched: its privatization and stereotypical sexualization. These mechanisms enforce on homosexuals (as they have on religious minorities, people of color, and women) rigidly defined, hierarchical terms of identity, thereby unjustly reducing human complexity to the simplistic terms of a dehumanizing stereotype of abject servility and silence. Resistance to such imposed hierarchy clarifies and explains the legitimate grounds of contemporary expressions of gay and lesbian identity in the experience of an empowering *choice* and an ethical *demand* of responsibility for self.

ONE

THE RACIAL ANALOGY

The struggle for racial justice plays a central role in American interpretive understanding of the Reconstruction Amendments both as their background in the antebellum abolitionist movement and in the successful African American struggle, after their ratification, to rectify the crudely racist interpretation they had irresponsibly been given by the judiciary.[1] The success of that later struggle culminated in the U.S. Supreme Court's unanimous decision in *Brown v. Board of Education*[2] and the national consensus that now accepts the legitimacy of that opinion as a reasonable fixed point in contemporary discussions of judicially enforceable constitutional principles. Contemporary constitutional theories are importantly defined and valued in terms of the account they give of the legitimacy of *Brown* and its progeny.

In analogizing the civil rights movement to gay rights, some constitutional criticisms focus on the political powerlessness of African Americans, supposing judicial intervention to be appropriate to the extent it rectifies such powerlessness, suitably interpreted.[3] Others associate the constitutional defect with the basis

1. I discuss both these matters at length in David A. J. Richards, *Conscience and the Constitution: History, Theory, and Law of the Reconstruction Amendments* (Princeton: Princeton University Press, 1993); see also David A. J. Richards, *Women, Gays, and the Constitution: The Grounds for Feminism and Gay Rights in Culture and Law* (Chicago: University of Chicago Press, 1998).

2. 347 U.S. 483 (1954) (segregation by race in public schools held unconstitutional).

3. See, for example, Bruce Ackerman, "Beyond *Carolene Products*," *Harvard Law Review* 98 (1985): 713; John Hart Ely, *Democracy and Distrust: A Theory of Judicial Review* (Cambridge: Harvard University Press, 1980).

of the disadvantage (namely, an immutable and salient personal characteristic).[4] Presumably, any plausible elaboration of the principle of *Brown*, as understood by such theories, would require plausible analogies to be made to either the political powerlessness of African Americans or to personal characteristics that, like race, are immutable and conspicuously salient.

The theory of political powerlessness might, on the basis of at least one interpretation,[5] raise much more serious questions about the analogy of gender to race than of race to sexual orientation in view of the majority political power of women versus the minority status of gays and lesbians; but, on the interpretation of political power in terms of relative wealth and media access, the analogy might disfavor judicial protection of gays and lesbians as well.[6]

The theory of immutability and salience (a solid analogy between race and gender) raises the sharpest critical questions about the analogy of principle between race and sexual orientation.[7] The pressure of this theory of the analogy motivated much of the interest of some gay activists in three studies that were conducted in the early 1990s, one in neuroanatomy and two in behavioral genetics, that claimed there were significant links between sexual orientation and biology.[8] On this view of the causal story of homosexual sexual orientation, the alleged biology of sexual orientation conveniently serves as a proxy for the immutability of race and thus a ground for pursuing the constitutional analogy of race and sexual orientation as a basis for a larger reasonable constitutional concern about discrimination.

If this, however, were the alleged short-term strategic price that

4. See, for example, Michael J. Perry, "Modern Equal Protection: A Conceptualization and Appraisal," *Columbia Law Review* 79 (1979): 1023.

5. See Ely, *Democracy and Distrust;* but cf. Ackerman, "Beyond *Carolene Products.*"

6. For Justice Scalia's appeal to this ground for skepticism about the judicial protection of gays and lesbians, see his dissent in *Romer v. Evans,* 116 S. Ct. 1620, 1637 (1996).

7. See Perry, "Modern Equal Protection," 1066–67.

8. See Simon LeVay, "A Difference in Hypothalamic Structure between Heterosexual and Homosexual Men," *Science,* Aug. 30, 1991, pp. 1034–37; J. Michael Bailey and Richard C. Pillard, "A Genetic Study of Male Sexual Orientation," *Archives of Genetic Psychiatry* 48 (1991): 1089; Dean H. Hamer et al., "A Linkage between DNA Markers on the X Chromosome and Male Sexual Orientation," *Science,* July 16, 1993, pp. 321–27.

must be paid to secure protection for gay rights, it is, in my view, a price not worth paying. The reasonable pursuit of scientific research on sexual orientation within ethical parameters about the nature and uses of such research is not the basis of my objection.[9] Rather, it is unreasonable to say that any of these studies have actually *found* a biological cause of homosexuality; none of them makes any such claim, nor are even their limited findings free from scientific doubt.[10] There is reasonable evidence that sexual orientation is for many a largely settled and irreversible erotic preference long before the age of responsibility.[11] But this fact, if it is fact, may more often be true of gay men than lesbians[12] and does not require a biological explanation. Language acquisition may be a useful analogy here: it is certainly made possible by our biological heritage, but also clearly turns on early social experience, after which it remains a fixed and fundamental orientation of our attitude to the world and an immutably profound feature of our humanity.[13]

9. See, for an illuminating and balanced recent study of this issue, Timothy F. Murphy, *Gay Science: The Ethics of Sexual Orientation Research* (New York: Columbia University Press, 1997).

10. For a review of the criticisms which these studies have received, see Janet Halley, "Sexual Orientation and the Politics of Biology: A Critique of the Argument from Immutability," *Stanford Law Review* 46 (1994): 529–46.

11. On irreversibility, see Wainwright Churchill, *Homosexual Behavior among Males* (New York: Hawthorn, 1967), 283–91; Michael Ruse, *Homosexuality* (Oxford: Basil Blackwell, 1988), 59–62. On the early age of its formation, see John Money and Anke A. Ehrhardt, *Man & Woman, Boy & Girl* (Baltimore: Johns Hopkins University Press, 1972), 153–201; C. A. Tripp, *The Homosexual Matrix* (New York: McGraw-Hill, 1975), 251; Donald J. West, *Homosexuality* (Chicago: Aldine, 1968), 266. One study hypothesizes that gender identity and sexual object choice coincide with the development of language, between the age of 18 to 24 months. John Money, J. G. Hampson, and J. L. Hampson, "An Evidence of Some Basic Sexual Concepts: The Evidence of Human Hermaphroditism," *Bulletin of Johns Hopkins Hospital* 97 (1955): 301, 308–10; cf. Alan P. Bell, Martin S. Weinberg, and Sue K. Hammersmith, *Sexual Preference* (New York: Simon & Schuster, 1978). For a recent, judicious review of the scientific literature, see Richard Green, *Sexual Science and the Law* (Cambridge: Harvard University Press, 1992), 62–86; on irreversibility of orientation, see Murphy, *Gay Science*, 185, 190.

12. See Murphy, *Sexual Science*, 184.

13. For development of this analogy, see John Money, *Gay, Straight, and In-Between: The Sexology of Erotic Orientation* (New York: Oxford University Press, 1988), 11–12, 54, 71, 74, 76, 80, 129–30.

In any event, sexual orientation, even it were biologically explicable, is not a fact like race or gender but a complex system of psychological propensities (thoughts, fantasies, desires, vulnerabilities, deeply rooted in our imaginative lives as persons). As such, it may be ethically interpreted and developed by subjects in quite different ways and acted on in correspondingly very different ways, and sometimes not acted on at all. Indeed, for these very reasons, nothing in the alleged immutability of sexual orientation (were it a fact and even a biologically explicable fact) makes it socially transparent in the way that race and gender are usually conspicuous, as the very real debates about outing in the gay and lesbian community make quite clear.[14]

The "biological story" (as a way of invoking the racial analogy in support of gay rights) is objectionable for what it omits and what it distorts within the valid normative case for gay rights. It omits what motivates the rights-based case for the emancipation of gay and lesbian people, namely, a normative analysis of the burdens placed on an ethically responsible choice of one's identity as, significantly, that of a gay or lesbian person. From this perspective, the possible concealment or repression or failure to explore one's sexual preference, as gay or lesbian, is an abhorrent condition of political respect if sexual preference is integral to the authenticity of moral personality and the prejudice against it as unreasonable as racism and sexism. The sacrifice of moral authenticity is not a demand any person could reasonably be asked to make in exchange for freedom from irrational prejudice.

The real threat of the biological story lies in how it distorts the case for gay rights. The biological story malignly reduces to crude physical terms what is essentially a principled argument for the just and ethical emancipation of the moral powers of conscience of gay and lesbian persons in terms that subvert its emancipatory potential. Biological reductionism rationalized the unjust cultural subjugation of African Americans and women as a separate species[15] and has historically wreaked comparable havoc on early ad-

14. See, for example, Larry Gross, *Contested Closets: The Politics and Ethics of Outing* (Minneapolis: University of Minnesota Press, 1993).
15. See Stephen J. Gould, *The Mismeasure of Man* (New York: W. W. Norton, 1981); Carol Tavris, *The Mismeasure of Woman* (New York: Simon & Schuster, 1992).

vocates of gay and lesbian rights by confirming, rather than challenging, the cultural stereotypes of an inferiority rooted in nature (for example, gay men as a congenitally abnormal male who is a female "third sex").[16] Otto Weininger, for example, on this basis combined advocacy of gay rights with grotesque misogyny, racism, and anti-Semitism.[17] What is needed is not the repetition of the terms of our subjugation, but an empowering critical perspective on the cultural terms of our degradation (including its continuities with evils like racism, sexism, and anti-Semitism) and on our corresponding political, ethical, and intellectual responsibilities to exercise our active moral powers of criticism and reconstruction of that culture on terms of justice. Lesbians and gays need responsibly to insist on and to demand our personal and moral identities as lesbian and gay persons and to resist those objectifying stereotypes that have stripped us of our powers of free moral personality.

In fact, such an emphasis on legitimate claims to ethical identity, against the background of a cultural orthodoxy that represses such claims, suggests an alternative way of thinking about the larger fabric of constitutional principles that condemns, as suspect, related evils like racism and sexism. We may have as much reason to question constitutional theories of suspectness, appealing to powerlessness or immutability and salience, in the areas of race or gender as we do in the area of sexual orientation. Maintaining the integrity of the case for gay rights, by resisting the biological model, may have as much to teach us about gay rights as it does about related injustices.

A plausible general theory of suspect classification analysis must unify, on grounds of principle, the claims to such analysis by African Americans, women, and lesbians and gays. "Political powerlessness," as a justification, cannot do so,[18] and further, it fails to

16. For discussion of this development and its malign consequences, see Richards, *Women, Gays, and the Constitution*, 305–6, 313–14, 317, 322–23, 332–36, 369.

17. Otto Weininger, *Sex and Character* (London: William Heinemann, 1907). See, for discussion, Richards, *Women, Gays, and the Constitution*, 332–36, 433, 461, 465.

18. For variant interpretations of political powerlessness, as the controlling idea in understanding suspect classification analysis, see Ackerman, "Beyond *Carolene Products*"; Ely, *Democracy and Distrust*.

capture the plane of ethical discourse of suspect classification analysis as it has been developed in authoritative case law.

An analysis based on political powerlessness wrongly suggests that the gains in political solidarity of groups subjected to deep racial, sexist, or religious prejudice (in virtue of resistance to such prejudice) disentitle them from constitutional protection,[19] as if the often meager political gains of blacks, women, and gays and lesbians (when measured against their claims of justice) are the measure of constitutional justice.[20] This analysis preposterously denies constitutional protection to women because they are a statistical majority of voters.[21] The "political weakness" approach also proves too much: it extends protection to any political group, though subject to no history of rights-denying prejudice, solely because it has not been as politically successful as it might have been (e.g., dentists).[22] Such models of suspect classification analysis suppress the underlying substantive rights-based normative judgments in terms of which equal protection should be and has been interpreted. They neither explanatorily fit the case law nor afford a sound normative model with which to criticize the case law.

Suspect classification analysis focuses on the political expression of irrational prejudices of a certain sort: namely, those rooted in a history and culture of unjust exclusion of a certain group from participation in the political community required by their basic rights of conscience, speech, association, and work. The funda-

19. Ackerman likewise makes this erroneous suggestion. Ackerman, "Beyond *Carolene Products*," 718, 740–46.

20. Racial classifications, for example, remain as suspect as they have ever been irrespective of the political advances of African Americans. See, e.g., *Palmore v. Sidoti,* 466 U.S. 429, 434 (1984) (awarding custody of child on grounds of race of adoptive father held unconstitutional).

21. The Supreme Court has expressly regarded gender as a suspect classification irrespective of the status of women as a political majority. See, e.g., *Frontiero v. Richardson,* 411 U.S. 677, 686 n. 17 (1973); cf. *Craig v. Boren,* 429 U.S. 190, 204 (1976) (holding that gender classification is not substantially related to traffic laws). But cf. Ely, *Democracy and Distrust,* 164–70 (asserting that women should be denied constitutional protection because they constitute a majority of voters and are noninsular).

22. The Supreme Court has declined to regard the mere fact of the greater political success of one interest group over another as relevant to according closer scrutiny to legislation favorable to one group over another. See, e.g., *United States R. R. Retirement Bd. v. Fritz,* 449 U.S. 166, 174–76 (1980); cf. *Williamson v. Lee Optical,* 348 U.S. 483, 488 (1965).

mental wrong of racism and sexism has been the intolerant exclusion of blacks and women from the rights of public culture, exiling them to cultural marginality in supposedly morally inferior realms and stigmatizing identity on such grounds. Homosexuals are likewise victimized, and its rectification entitles sexual orientation to be recognized as a suspect classification.

Analysis of this sort suggests why immutability and salience do not coherently explain even the historical paradigm of suspect classification of race, and therefore cannot normatively define the terms of principle reasonably applicable to other claims to suspect classification analysis. The principle of *Brown v. Board of Education* itself cannot reasonably be understood in terms of the abstract ethical ideal that state benefits and burdens should never turn on an immutable and salient characteristic. There is no such ethical ideal.[23] It is not a reasonable objection that a distribution of goods may be owed persons on the basis of an immutable and salient characteristic if justice requires or allows such a characteristic to be given such weight. Disabled persons are born with disabilities that often cannot be changed; nonetheless, resources are appropriately accorded them because of their disabilities to afford them some fair approximation to the opportunities of nondisabled persons.

The example is not an isolated one; its principle pervades the justice of rewards and fair distribution more generally. For example, we reward certain athletic achievements very highly and do not finely calibrate the components of our rewards attributable to acts of self-disciplined will from those based on natural endowments. Achievement itself suffices to elicit reward even though some significant part of it turns on immutable physical endowments that some have and others lack. Or, we allocate scarce places in institutions of higher learning on the basis of an immutable factor such as geographic distribution, an educational policy we properly regard as sensible and not unfair. The point can be reasonably generalized to include that part of the theory of distributive justice concerned with both maintaining an economic and social minimum and some structure of differential rewards to elicit better per-

23. For a similar analysis, see Ronald Dworkin, *Law's Empire* (Cambridge: Harvard University Press, 1986), 381–99.

formance for the public good. The idea of a just minimum turns on certain facts about levels of subsistence, not on acts of will; we would not regard such a minimum as any the less justly due if the human sciences showed us that some significant component of it turned on immutable factors.

Differential rewards perform the role of incentives to elicit performance required by modern industrial market economies; science may show us that immutable factors such as genetic endowment play some significant role in such performance. Nonetheless, we would not regard it as unjust to reward such performance so long as the incentives worked out with the consequences specified by the theory of distributive justice. Our conclusion, from a wide range of diverse examples, must be that immutability and salience do not identify an ethical ideal that could serve as a reasonable basis for suspect classification analysis.

Race is a suspect classification, not on such grounds (which would include much that we regard as just), but because it expresses a background structural injustice of a certain sort that sustains a rights-denying culture of irrational political prejudice. Persons are not regarded as victimized by this prejudice because they are physically unable to change or mask the trait defining the class, but because the prejudice itself assigns intrinsically unreasonable weight to and burdens on identifications that define one's moral personality.

Race in America is culturally defined by the "one-drop" rule under which quite small proportions of black genes in one's overall genetic makeup are sufficient for a person to be regarded as black, including persons who are for all visibly salient purposes nonblack. Persons who are "blacks" by this definition could pass as white; most, including some historically important African American leaders, chose not to do so.[24] Choosing to pass as white would cut them off from intimately personal relationships to family and community that nurture and sustain self-respect and personal integrity (56–57); the price of avoiding racial prejudice is an unreasonable sacrifice of basic resources of personal and ethical identity that they will not accept. In effect, one avoids injustice by silencing

24. See generally F. James Davis, *Who Is Black? One Nation's Definition* (University Park: Pennsylvania State University Press, 1991), 7, 56–57, 77–78, 178–79.

one's moral powers to protest injustice, degrading moral integrity into silent complicity with evil. The same terms of cultural degradation apply to all victims of racism whether visibly black or not. The demand of supine acceptance unjustly devalues one's identity. Racial prejudice is an invidious political evil because it is directed against significant aspects of a person's cultural and moral identity on irrationalist grounds of subjugation arising from that identity. The point is not that its irrationalist object is some brute fact that cannot be changed, but that it is directed at important aspects of moral personality, in particular, "the way people think, feel, and believe, not how they look"—the identifications that make them "members of the black ethnic community" (179).

Racial prejudice shares common features with certain forms of religious intolerance. In particular, racism and anti-Semitism share a common irrationalist fear: *invisible blackness* or the *secret Jew,* that is, persons who can pass as white or Christian but who are allegedly tainted by some fundamental incapacity fully to identify themselves as authentically a member of the majoritarian race or religion (55–56, 145). Such incapacity is ascribed to persons on the basis of "perceived attitudes and social participation rather than on . . . appearance or lineage" (145). On this basis, any dissent from the dominant racist or anti-Semitic orthodoxy, let alone any sympathetic association with the stigmatized minority, is interpreted as evidence of membership in the defective minority, which thus chills morally independent criticism of racial or religious intolerance and leads a stigmatized minority to accept the legitimacy of subordination.[25] The structural resemblance of racism to a form of religious intolerance is an important feature of its American historical background and is fundamental to a sound interpretation of the suspectness of race under American constitutional law.

The interpretive status of race, as the model of a suspect classification under the American constitutional law of the Equal Protection Clause, arose against the background of the interdependent

---

25. For exploration of this phenomenon, in the form of Jewish anti-Semitism, see, for example, Sander L. Gilman, *Jewish Self-Hatred: Anti-Semitism and the Hidden Language of the Jews* (Baltimore: Johns Hopkins University Press, 1986); Michael Lerner, *The Socialism of Fools: Anti-Semitism on the Left* (Oakland, Calif.: Tikkun Books, 1992).

institutions of American slavery and racism and the persistence of racism; it was further supported by its judicial legitimation in cases like *Plessy v. Ferguson*[26] and *Pace v. Alabama*,[27] which were decided long after the formal abolition of slavery.

Yet racist institutions such as slavery and its legacy of American apartheid[28] evolved from a constitutionally illegitimate religious intolerance against the culture of African Americans held in slavery. In other words, racist prejudice originated as an instance of religious discrimination. This discrimination later developed, in ideological support of the institutions of American slavery, into a systematically unjust cultural intolerance of African Americans as an ethnic group.

This intolerance was interpretively expressed by their degradation from the status of bearers of human rights such as the basic rights of conscience, speech, intimate association, and work.[29] In turn, race is constitutionally suspect when and to the extent the law or public policy expressed and incorporated racial prejudice.[30] The evil of such prejudice lies in its systematic degradation of identifications at the heart of free moral personality, including powers to protest injustice in the name and voice of one's human rights.

African American self-understanding of American racism was deepened and energized by the scholarship and activism of W. E. B. Du Bois in exactly these terms. His historical studies challenged the dominant, often racist orthodoxy of the age,[31] and

26. 163 U.S. 537 (1896) (state segregation by race held constitutional).

27. 106 U.S. 583 (1863) (stronger penalties for interracial, as opposed to intraracial, sexual relations not racially discriminatory).

28. For a recent important study of the persistence of this injustice, see Douglas S. Massey and Nancy A. Denton, *American Apartheid: Segregation and the Making of the Underclass* (Cambridge: Harvard University Press, 1993).

29. I develop this argument at greater length in David A. J. Richards, *Conscience and the Constitution: History, Theory, and Law of the Reconstruction Amendments* (Princeton: Princeton University Press, 1993), 80–89, 150–70; see also, in general, Richards, *Women, Gays, and the Constitution*.

30. For further development of this argument, see Richards, *Conscience and the Constitution*, 170–77.

31. See W. E. B. Du Bois, *The Suppression of the African Slave-Trade*, in *W. E. B. Du Bois*, ed. Nathan Huggins (1896; New York: Library of America, 1986), 3–356; *Black Reconstruction in America, 1860–1880* (1935; New York: Atheneum, 1969).

his 1903 *The Souls of Black Folk*[32] offered a pathbreaking interpretive study of African American culture and the struggle for ethical self-consciousness under circumstances of racial oppression[33]—

> a world which yields him [a black person] no true self-consciousness, but only lets him see himself through the revelation of the other world. It is a peculiar sensation, this double-consciousness, this sense of always looking at one's self through the eyes of others, of measuring one's soul by the tape of a world that looks on in amused contempt and pity. One ever feels his two-ness,—an American, a Negro; two souls, two thoughts, two unreconciled strivings, two warring ideals in one dark body, whose dogged strength alone keeps it from being torn asunder.[34]

The struggle for justice was thus a struggle for self-respecting identity on terms of justice that would transform both:

> The history of the American Negro is the history of this strife,— this longing to attain self-conscious manhood, to merge his double self into a better and truer self. In this merging he wishes neither of the older selves to be lost. He would not Africanize America, for America has too much to teach the world and Africa. He would not bleach his Negro soul in a flood of white Americanism, for he knows that Negro blood has a message for the world. He simply wishes to make it possible for a man to be both a Negro and an American, without being cursed and spit upon by his fellows, without having the doors of Opportunity closed roughly in his face.[35]

I describe Du Bois's theory in terms of a normative struggle for redefining identity as a way of making the best sense of his remarkable insights both against the retrospective background of the tradition of abolitionist dissent he both reflects and elaborates

32. See W. E. B. Du Bois, *The Souls of Black Folk,* in *W. E. B. Du Bois,* ed. Nathan Huggins (1903; New York: Library of America, 1986), 359–586.

33. See, in general, David Levering Lewis, *W. E .B. Du Bois: Biography of a Race, 1868–1919* (New York: Henry Holt, 1993); Eric J. Sundquist, *To Wake the Nations: Race in the Making of American Literature* (Cambridge: Harvard University Press, Belknap Press, 1993), 457–625. For a more critical, less rights-based reading of Du Bois's theory and practice, see Adolph L. Reed, Jr., *W. E. B. Du Bois and American Political Thought: Fabianism and the Color Line* (New York: Oxford University Press, 1997).

34. See Du Bois, *The Souls of Black Folk,* 364–65.

35. Ibid., 365.

and the prospective development of this struggle in the movements for civil liberties that include African Americans, women, and, most recently, gays and lesbians.[36] Du Bois is a towering figure in the history of both the theory and practice of these movements because he speaks so powerfully from within the experience of the ethical struggle for voice and reasonable discourse, as claims of basic human rights, against a cultural tradition that both promised and betrayed basic human rights.

The extraordinary importance of African American dissent to American constitutionalism comes not only from its demands that these basic rights be extended on fair terms to all persons, but from its analysis of the ways in which a structural injustice of subordination (denying a class of persons their very status as bearers of human rights) can be unjustly rationalized in terms of a question-begging entrenchment of such injustice.

I call this injustice *moral slavery*. The most illuminating way to come to terms with the ethical enormity and character of this structural injustice, and the role of claims for identity in protesting it, is to start with the inalienable human right which, more than any other, models both the significance and weight of what an inalienable human right is: the right to conscience.

The normative value placed on conscience, as an inalienable human right, was seminally articulated by John Locke and Pierre Bayle, who argued that toleration was a constitutive principle of justice in politics.[37] Constraints of principle must be placed on the state's power to enforce sectarian religious views, they argued, because the enforcement of such views on society at large entrenched irrationalist intolerance as the measure of legitimate convictions in matters of conscience. Such intolerance caused a limiting of both the standards of debate and the speakers to the sectarian measure that supported dominant political and moral authority. The rights-based evil of such intolerance was the inadequate grounds on

36. See, for further exploration of this retrospective and prospective background, Richards, *Conscience and the Constitution;* Richards, *Women, Gays, and the Constitution.*

37. For full discussion of the terms and scope of their argument and its implications for American constitutionalism, see David A. J. Richards, *Toleration and the Constitution* (New York: Oxford University Press, 1986), 85–281.

which it abridged the inalienable right to conscience, which I identify as the free exercise of the moral powers of rationality and reasonableness in terms of which persons define personal and ethical meaning in living. While the abridgment of this human right, like others, may be justified on compelling secular grounds of protecting public goods reasonably acknowledged as such by all persons (irrespective of other philosophical or evaluative disagreements), the self-entrenchment of a sectarian view was not one of them.[38]

The "argument for toleration," as I call it, was a judgment of and response to such abuses of political epistemology (political enforcement at large of a sectarian view). By the late seventeenth century (when Locke and Bayle wrote), there was good reason to believe that politically entrenched views of religious and moral truth (resting on the Bible and associated interpretive practices) assumed essentially contestable interpretations of a complex historical interaction between pagan, Jewish, and Christian cultures in the early Christian era.[39]

The Renaissance rediscovery of pagan culture and learning (ancient Greece and Rome) reopened the question of how the Christian synthesis of pagan philosophical and Jewish ethical and religious culture was to be understood. Among other things, the development of critical historiography and techniques of textual interpretation had undeniable implications for reasonable Bible interpretation.[40] The Protestant Reformation both assumed and further encouraged these new modes of inquiry, and encouraged as well the appeal to experiment and experience, methodologies associated with the rise of modern science. These new approaches to thought and inquiry had made possible the recognition that there was a gap between the politically enforceable conceptions of religious and moral truth and the kinds of reasonable inquiries that the new approaches made available. The argument for toleration arose from the recognition of this disjunction between the reigning political epistemology and the new epistemic methodologies.

38. Ibid., 244–47.
39. Ibid., 25–27, 84–98, 105, 125.
40. Ibid., 125–26.

The legitimation of religious persecution by both Catholics and Protestants (drawing authority from Augustine, among others) had rendered a politically entrenched view of religious and moral truth the measure of permissible ethics and religion, including the epistemic standards of inquiry and debate about religious and moral truth. The crux of the problem was that unjustly entrenched political conceptions of truth had made themselves the measure both of the standards of reasonable inquiry and of who could count as a reasonable inquirer after truth. But in light of the new modes of inquiry now available, such political entrenchment of religious truth was often seen to rest not only on the degradation of reasonable standards of inquiry, but on the self-fulfilling degradation of the capacity of persons to conduct such inquiries.

In order to rectify these evils, the argument for toleration forbade, as a matter of principle, the enforcement by the state of any such conception of religious truth. The scope of legitimate political concern must appeal to general ends such as life and basic rights and liberties (e.g., the right to conscience). The pursuit of such goods was consistent with the full range of ends free people might rationally and reasonably pursue.

A prominent feature of the argument for toleration was its claim that religious persecution corrupted conscience itself. (Locke and Bayle, for example, forged the argument for toleration as an internal criticism of their own identity as Christians, identifying the abridgment of the right to conscience as corrupting what they took to be the ethical core of true Christianity and calling for the reconstruction of Christian identity on terms of justice.) Such corruption, which is a kind of self-induced blindness to the evils one inflicts, is a consequence of the political enforcement at large of a conception of religious truth that immunizes itself from independent criticism in terms of reasonable standards of thought and deliberation. In effect, the conception of religious truth, though perhaps having once been importantly shaped by more ultimate considerations of reason, ceases to be held or to be understood and defended *on the basis of reason.*

A tradition that loses a sense of its reasonable foundations will stagnate and depend increasingly for allegiance on question-begging appeals to orthodox conceptions of truth and the violent repression of any dissent from such conceptions as a kind of disloyal moral treason. The politics of loyalty rapidly degenerates, as it did in the antebellum South's repression of any criticism of slavery, into a politics that takes pride in widely held community values solely because they are community values. Standards of discussion and inquiry become increasingly parochial and insular; they serve only a polemical role in the defense of the existing community values and are indeed increasingly hostile to any more impartial reasonable assessment in light of such independent standards.[41]

Such politics tends to forms of irrationalism in order to protect its now essentially polemical project. Opposing views relevant to reasonable public argument are suppressed, facts distorted or misstated, values disconnected from ethical reasoning, indeed deliberation in politics denigrated in favor of violence against dissent and the aesthetic glorification of violence. Paradoxically, the more the tradition becomes seriously vulnerable to independent reasonable criticism (indeed, increasingly in rational need of such criticism), the more it is likely to generate forms of political irrationalism (including scapegoating of outcast dissenters) in order to secure allegiance. This *paradox of intolerance* (the internal need for criticism generating repression of dissent) works its irrationalist havoc through its war on the inalienable right to conscience, in particular, constructing a group of scapegoats by means of the unjust denial to them of this central human right.

The history of religious persecution amply illustrates these truths, and as the American antebellum abolitionist advocates of the argument for toleration clearly saw,[42] no aspect of that history more clearly so than Christian anti-Semitism. The politics of such anti-Semitism illustrates the paradox of intolerance, which explains the force of the example for abolitionists, who applied this analysis to their own historical circumstance.

The development of the worst ravages of medieval anti-

41. See John Hope Franklin, *The Militant South, 1800–1861* (Cambridge: Harvard University Press, Belknap Press, 1956); cf. W. J. Cash, *The Mind of the South* (New York: Vintage Books, 1941).
42. See Richards, *Conscience and the Constitution*, 59–63, 67–69.

Semitism (totally baseless beliefs about ritual crucifixions and cannibalism of Christians by Jews) was associated with growing internal doubts about the reasonableness of certain Catholic religious
beliefs and practices (e.g., transubstantiation) and the resolution
of such doubts by the forms of irrationalist politics associated with
anti-Semitism (centering on fantasies of ritual eating of human
flesh that expressed the underlying worries about transubstantiation).[43] Precisely when the dominant religious tradition gave rise
to the most reasonable internal doubts, these doubts were dis-
placed from reasonable discussion and debate into blatant political
persecution of one of the more conspicuous, vulnerable, and innocent groups of dissenters. The long history of Christian Europe's
restrictions on Jews (including access to influential occupations,
intercourse with Christians, living quarters, and the like) was rationalized by Augustine, among others, in the quite explicit terms
of slavery: "The Jew is the slave of the Christian."[44] (This parallel
did not escape the abolitionists.)

The argument for toleration was developed and elaborated as
an internal criticism of cultural traditions so corrupted by construction of cultural identity on terms of injustice that the tradition
no longer served reasonable ethical values. The American abolitionist elaboration of the argument, to condemn both American
slavery and racism,[45] was an internal criticism of their own identities as both Christians (in the pattern of Locke and Bayle) and as
Americans, calling for a reconstruction of Christian and American
identity on terms of justice. In particular, abolitionist moral and
constitutional thought condemned the corruption of American
constitutional guarantees of universal human rights by the structural injustice of slavery and racism.[46] American slavery and racism, like anti-Semitism, reflected the structural injustice of the
abridgment of the basic human rights of a group of persons on
speciously circular grounds of alleged incapacity to be bearers of
human rights that, in fact, assumed their dehumanization.

43. Ibid., 68–69.
44. Cited in Gavin I. Langmuir, *History, Religion, and Anti-Semitism* (Berkeley and
Los Angeles: University of California Press, 1990), 294.
45. See, for further discussion, Richards, *Conscience and the Constitution*, 73–89.
46. On abolitionist constitutional theory, see ibid., 89–107.

For the abolitionists, slavery and discrimination were forms of religious, social, economic, and political persecution motivated by a politically entrenched conception of black incapacity. That conception enforced its own vision of truth against both the standards of reasonable inquiry and the reasonable capacities of both blacks and whites that might challenge the conception. A conception of political unity, subject to rational review as to its basis and merits, had unreasonably resolved its doubts, consistent with the paradox of intolerance, in the irrationalist racist certitudes of group solidarity on the basis of unjust group subjugation. This structural injustice subjugated a group of persons on inadequate, specious grounds.

African Americans were the scapegoats of Southern self-doubt in the same way European Jews had been victims of Christian self-doubt. Frederick Douglass, the leading black abolitionist, stated the abolitionist analysis with a classical clarity:

> Ignorance and depravity, and the inability to rise from degradation to civilization and respectability, are the most usual allegations against the oppressed. The evils most fostered by slavery and oppression are precisely those which slaveholders and oppressors would transfer from their system to the inherent character of their victims. Thus the very crimes of slavery become slavery's best defence. By making the enslaved a character fit only for slavery, they excuse themselves for refusing to make the slave a freeman.[47]

In effect, whites projected their own sins or doubts onto blacks to rationalize racial subordination. Blacks were thus seen as sexually immoral, lazy, violent, and dishonest—qualities likely to be found in slave masters (who were sexually immoral in that they had often had sex outside marriage with slave women who could not say no; lazy in that they enjoyed the fruits of others' labor; violent in their harsh treatment, including torture of people (even children) held in slavery; and dishonest in that they lied about all these matters, denying that much of it occurred).

In his classic account of African American double conscious-

---

47. Frederick Douglass, "The Claims of the Negro Ethnologically Considered," in *The Life and Writings of Frederick Douglass*, ed. Philip S. Foner (New York: International Publishers, 1975), 2:295.

ness in *The Souls of Black Folk,* Du Bois calls for a reconstruction of African American identity on terms of justice that would address injustices in both the construction of black ethnic and American identity. Douglass addresses both; he insists, as Martin Luther King was also later to claim,[48] on holding Americans to their constitutional promises of guarantees of the universal human rights of all persons,[49] but he also addresses, like other ex-slaves like Sojourner Truth and Harriet Jacobs,[50] the unjust terms of the construction of African American identity. As Du Bois clearly saw, the questions could not be separated: the injustice of American racism (including its rights-denying construction of African American identity as subhuman) was made possible by the construction of American identity as, contradictorily, both rights-based and, in light of structural injustices like slavery and racism, rights-denying. African American claims for identity on terms of justice thus moved along both parameters, and no aspect of their struggle more profoundly addressed this problem than their demand to speak and be heard in the ethically transformative exercise of their free moral powers of conscience in protest of the terms of their subjugation.

The force of such rights-based claims for identity is well illustrated by the ultimately successful African American struggle, under the leadership of the legal redress committee of the NAACP (in which Charles Houston and Thurgood Marshall played central roles), to secure the judicial repudiation of *Plessy* and *Pace*.[51] Black Americans in the South and elsewhere asserted and were finally accorded some measure of national protection by the Supreme

48. For a good general study, see Taylor Branch, *Parting the Waters: Martin Luther King and the Civil Rights Movement, 1954–1963* (London: Papermac, 1990).

49. On the various forms of abolitionist constitutional theory, see Richards, *Conscience and the Constitution,* 89–107.

50. See, for further discussion, Richards, *Women, Gays, and the Constitution,* 115–24.

51. See Mark V. Tushnet, *The NAACP's Legal Strategy against Segregated Education, 1925–1950* (Chapel Hill: University of North Carolina Press, 1967); ibid., *Making Civil Rights Law: Thurgood Marshall and the Supreme Court, 1956–1961* (New York: Oxford University Press, 1994); Genna Rae McNeil, *Groundwork: Charles Hamilton Houston and the Struggle for Civil Rights* (Philadelphia: University of Pennsylvania Press, 1983); Jack Greenberg, *Crusaders in the Courts: How a Dedicated Band of Lawyers Fought for the Civil Rights Revolution* (New York: BasicBooks, 1994).

Court (reversing early decisions to the contrary) in the exercise of their First Amendment rights of protest, criticism, and advocacy.[52] On this basis, Martin Luther King brilliantly used and elaborated the right of conscience and free speech to protest American racism very much in the spirit of William Lloyd Garrison's strategy of nonviolence a hundred years before;[53] he thus appealed, as he did in his classic "Letter from Birmingham City Jail," for the need for "nonviolent direct action . . . to create such a [moral] crisis and establish such creative tension that a community that has constantly refused to negotiate is forced to confront the issue."[54] Like Garrisonian radical abolitionists in the antebellum period, King demanded his basic human rights of conscience and speech to engage in reasonable public discourse about basic issues of justice, including criticism of the racist orthodoxy "that degrades human personality" and is therefore "unjust."[55]

No aspect of that criticism was more profound than its attack on the eighteenth-century foundations of American racism as it had been legitimated in *Plessy* and *Pace*.

The comparative science of human nature, developed by Montesquieu and David Hume in the eighteenth century, viewed human nature as more or less constant, yet subject to modification from the environment, history, institutional development, and the like. Both had discussed race differences from this perspective; Montesquieu's position was one of ironic skepticism.[56]

Hume, however, departed from the model of a uniform human nature to suggest significant, constitutionally based race differences inferred from comparative cultural achievements.[57] The Hu-

---

52. See *Gitlow v. New York*, 268 U.S. 652 (1925) (First Amendment held applicable to states under Fourteenth Amendment). See, in general, Harry Kalven, Jr., *The Negro and the First Amendment* (Chicago: University of Chicago Press, 1965).

53. For further discussion, see Richards, *Conscience and the Constitution*, chap. 3.

54. Martin Luther King, "Letter from Birmingham City Jail," in *A Testament of Hope: The Essential Writings of Martin Luther King, Jr.*, ed. James Melvin Washington (1963; New York: Harper & Row, 1986), 291.

55. Ibid., 293.

56. For further discussion, see Richards, *Conscience and the Constitution*, 74.

57. See David Hume, "Of National Characters," in David Hume, *Essays Moral Political and Literary* (Indianapolis: LibertyClassics, 1987), 208 n. 10.

mean suggestion of separate races had an antitheological significance; it was thus condemned, notably by James Beattie,[58] as one
aspect of a larger repudiation of a Christian ethics of equality
based on the Biblical idea of one divine creation of humans.
Hume's suggestion was developed in the nineteenth century into
polygenetic theories of human origins by the American ethnolo-
gists and others,[59] who thought of their theories as part of the
battle of progressive science against reactionary religion.

In the nineteenth century, this artificially drawn contrast hard-
ened into one between certain approaches to the human sciences
and nearly anything else. These approaches, very much under the
influence of models of explanation drawn from the physical sciences, assumed that good explanations in the human sciences must
be crudely reductive to some physical measure, like brain capacity
or cephalic indices.

The role of culture was completely overlooked. Indeed, there
was little attention to, let alone understanding of, culture as an
independent explanatory variable, and thus no concern with the
interpretive dimension of human personality in general and of the
exercise of our moral powers in particular. To the extent culture
was attended to at all, cultural transmission was thought of in Lamarckian terms[60] (even Du Bois may have accepted such a view[61]).
The efforts and resulting achievements of one generation were, as
it were, wired into the physical natures of the offspring of that
generation. As a result, any cultural advantage that one people
might have had was not only peculiarly its own (not necessarily
transmissible to other peoples) but a matter of rational pride for

58. See James Beattie, *An Essay on the Nature and Immutability of Truth* (New York:
Garland Publishing, Inc., 1983), 479–84. See also James Beattie, *Elements of Moral
Science* (Delmar, N.Y.: Scholars' Facsimiles & Reprints, 1976), 183–223.

59. See William Stanton, *The Leopard's Spots: Scientific Attitudes toward Race in
America, 1815–1859* (Chicago: University of Chicago Press, 1960); George M. Fred-
rickson, *The Black Image in the White Mind: The Debate on Afro-American Character and
Destiny, 1817–1914* (Middletown, Conn.: Wesleyan University Press, 1971); Thomas
F. Gossett, *Race: The History of an Idea in America* (New York: Schocken Books, 1965).

60. On the Lamarckian view, cultural advances by a people were hard-wired automatically into heredity. See George W. Stocking, Jr., *Race, Culture, and Evolution: Essays in the History of Anthropology* (New York: The Free Press, 1968), 47–48, 124,
234–69.

61. See Reed, *W. E. B. Du Bois and American Political Thought*, 39, 58.

all those born into such a people. The cultural advances in question were never accidents of time and circumstances, but products of the achieving will with each generation playing its part in further acts of progressive will building on the achievements of past generation.

These views failed to appreciate what culture is, let alone its explanatory weight in the human sciences. They confused culture with acts of will, failing to understand the nature of cultural formation and transmission, the role of contingency and good luck in cultural progress, and the complete impropriety of taking credit for such advances just by virtue of being born into such a culture. This whole way of thinking naturally created ethical space for explanations in terms of superior and inferior races as a proxy for the comparison between the remarkable scientific advances in Western culture in the nineteenth century in contrast to the putative lack of comparable advances nearly everywhere else.[62] If the least such progress appeared to be in African cultures, such peoples must be inferior; and if Egyptian culture clearly had been for some long period advanced and had an important impact on progressive cultures like that of ancient Greece, then Egyptians could not be black.[63]

Assumptions of these sorts explain why the Supreme Court in *Plessy* could be so ethically blind, in the same way pro-slavery thinkers had been blind, to the ignoble contempt that its legitimation of the further cultural degradation of blacks inflicted on black Americans.[64] For the *Plessy* Court, race was not a neutral, morally arbitrary matter, but a kind of moral fact, or fact endowed with intrinsic moral meaning: it was a physical fact connected with other physical facts of rational incapacity for which blacks, being from a nonprogressive culture, *must* be ethically responsible. In contrast, white Americans, taking rational ethical pride in their willed success in sustaining a progressive culture, should take the same pride in their race, and might reasonably protect their achievements from those of another race who were culpably nonprogres-

---

62. Ibid., 234–69.

63. See, for example, Stanton, *The Leopard's Spots*, 50.

64. On the roots of *Plessy* in the dominant racist social science of the nineteenth century, see Charles A. Lofgren, *The Plessy Case* (New York: Oxford University Press, 1987).

sive by nature. Race, a physical fact supposed to be causally connected to other physical facts, had been transformed into a trait
of character. The highly moralistic mind of nineteenth-century
America, once having bought the idea of such transformation, had
no problem protecting people of good moral character from those
who were culpably of unworthy character.

Abolitionist thought had taken the moral insularity of pro-
slavery defenses as an example of the corruption of conscience so
common in the history of religious persecution;[65] modern racism
both in America and Europe comparably exemplified one of human nature's more artfully self-deceiving evasions of the moral responsibilities of liberal political culture—illustrated, in *Plessy*, by
the way in which the culture's respect for science had been manip-
ulated to serve racist ends. Fundamental public criticism of this
view of the human sciences must, by its nature as a form of public
reason bearing on constitutional values, reshape constitutional argument.

The pivotal figure in such criticism was a German Jew and immigrant to the United States, Franz Boas, who fundamentally
criticized the racial explanations characteristic of both European
and American physical anthropology in the late nineteenth century.[66] Boas argued that comparative anthropological study did not
sustain the explanatory weight placed on race in the human sciences. In fact, there was more significant variability within races
than there was between races.[67] Indeed, many of the human features, supposed to be unchangeably physical (like the cephalic in-
dex), were responsive to cultural change; Boas had thus shown that

65. See, for fuller discussion, Richards, *Conscience and the Constitution,* 80–89.
66. See Franz Boas, *The Mind of Primitive Man,* rev. ed. (1911; Westport, Conn.:
Greenwood Press, 1983); George W. Stocking, Jr., ed., *A Franz Boas Reader: The Shaping of American Anthropology, 1883–1911* (Chicago: University of Chicago Press, 1974).
For commentary, see Stocking, *Race, Culture, and Evolution;* Carl N. Degler, *In Search
of Human Nature: The Decline and Revival of Darwinism in American Social Thought*
(New York: Oxford University Press, 1991), 61–83. For a useful recent comparative
study of such developments in the United States and Britain, see Elazar Barkan, *The
Retreat of Scientific Racism: Changing Concepts of Race in Britain and the United States
between the World Wars* (Cambridge: Cambridge University Press, 1992).
67. See Franz Boas, "Race," in Edwin R. A. Seligman, ed., *Encyclopaedia of the
Social Sciences* (New York: Macmillan, 1937), 7:25–36; Boas, *The Mind of Primitive
Man,* 45–59, 179. For commentary, see Stocking, *Race, Culture, and Evolution,* 192–94.

the physical traits of recent immigrants to the United States had changed in response to acculturation.[68] The crucial factor, heretofore missing from the human sciences, was culture; Boas made this point to Du Bois on a visit to Atlanta University, a visit that "had an impact of lasting importance"[69] for Du Bois's interest in black culture and its sources. Cultural formation and transmission could not be understood in terms of the reductive physical models that had heretofore dominated scientific and popular thinking. In particular, Lamarckian explanation—having been discredited in favor of random genetic mutation—was not the modality of cultural transmission, which was not physical at all but irreducibly cultural. One generation born into a progressive culture could take no more credit for an accident of birth than a generation could be reasonably blamed for birth into a less progressive culture. In fact, cultures advance often through accident and good luck and through cultural diffusion of technologies from other cultures. Such diffusion has been an important fact in the history of all human cultures at some point in their histories. No people has been through all points in its history the vehicle of the cultural progress of humankind, nor can any people reasonably suppose itself the unique vehicle of all such progress in the future.[70]

Boas's general contributions to the human sciences were powerfully elaborated in the area of race by his students Otto Klineberg and Ruth Benedict.[71] They argued that the explanatory role of race in the human sciences was, if anything, even less important than the judicious Boas might have been willing to grant.[72] (Boas's student, Margaret Mead, suggested much the same might be true to some significant extent of gender.[73])

68. See Franz Boas, "Changes in Immigrant Body Form," in *A Franz Boas Reader*, 202–14; Boas, *The Mind of Primitive Man*, 94–96. For commentary, see Stocking, *Race, Culture, and Evolution*, 175–80.

69. See Lewis, *W. E. B. Du Bois*, 352; see also ibid., 414, 462.

70. See Boas, *The Mind of Primitive Man*. For commentary, see Stocking, *Race, Culture, and Evolution*.

71. See Otto Klineberg, *Race Differences* (New York: Harper & Brothers, 1935); Ruth Benedict, *Race: Science and Politics* (New York: The Viking Press, 1945).

72. See, for example, Franz Boas, "Human Faculty as Determined by Race," in *A Franz Boas Reader*, 231, 234, 242; Boas, *The Mind of Primitive Man*, 230–31.

73. See Degler, *In Search of Human Nature*, 73, 133–37.

But the most important study of the American race problem was not by an American but by the Swedish social scientist, Gunnar Myrdal. His monumental *An American Dilemma*[74] brought the new approach to culture powerfully to bear on the plight of American blacks who, from the perspective of the human sciences, now were increasingly well understood as victims of a historically entrenched cultural construction of racism. In effect, the advances in morally independent critical standards of thought and analysis in the human sciences had enabled social scientists to make the same sort of argument that abolitionist theorists of race, like Lydia Maria Child[75] and Frederick Douglass (as we earlier saw), had made earlier largely on ethical grounds, namely, that American racism expressed structural injustice (moral slavery) condemned by basic constitutional principles of equal respect for human rights.

Previously, the human sciences had been claimed on the side of race differences against regressive religion and ethics; now, however, developments in the human sciences had cleared away as so much rationalizing self-deception the false dichotomy between science and ethics and revealed the ethically regressive uses to which even science may be put by politically entrenched epistemologies concerned to preserve the politics of race. Such political epistemologies, a modernist expression of essentially sectarian conceptions of religious and moral truth, cannot legitimately be the basis of political enforcement on society at large. Rather, legitimate political power must be based on impartial standards of reasonable discussion and debate not hostage to entrenched political orthodoxies. An old ethical point—that of the argument for toleration already used by the abolitionists against slavery and racism—was articulated yet again, now used in the service of an articulate argument of public reason against the force that American racism had been permitted to enjoy in the mistaken interpretation of equal protection in cases like *Plessy*.

This point of public reason was much highlighted in the American public mind by the comparable kind of racism that had flour-

74. See Gunnar Myrdal, *An American Dilemma: The Negro Problem and Modern Democracy*, 2 vols. (1944; New York: Pantheon Books, 1972). For commentary, see David W. Southern, *Gunnar Myrdal and Black–White Relations: The Use and Abuse of an American Dilemma, 1944–1969* (Baton Rouge: Louisiana State University Press, 1987).

75. See Richards, *Conscience and the Constitution*, 82–85.

ished in Europe in the relevantly same period in the form of modern anti-Semitism. As I have elsewhere argued,[76] during this period both American racism and European anti-Semitism evolved into particularly virulent political pathologies under the impact of the respective emancipations of American blacks from slavery and European Jews from various civil disabilities keyed to their religious background. In both cases, the respective emancipations were not carried through by consistent enforcement of guarantees of basic rights (in the United States, in despite of clear constitutional guarantees to that effect).

The characteristic nineteenth-century struggles for national identity led, in consequence, to rather stark examples of the paradox of intolerance in which the exclusion of race-defined cultural minorities from the political community of equal rights became itself the irrationalist basis of national unity. Strikingly similar racist theorists evolved in Europe to sustain anti-Semitism (Houston Chamberlain[77]) and in America to sustain a comparable racism against the supposedly non-Aryan (Madison Grant[78]). American constitutional institutions were, as a consequence, misinterpreted, but nonetheless increasingly were the vehicle of organized black protest and dissent, including the forms of protest we have already mentioned. Certainly, American institutions did not collapse on the scale of the German declension into atavistic totalitarianism and the genocide of five million European Jews.[79] In both cases, however, the underlying irrationalist racist dynamic was strikingly similar: emancipation, inadequate protection of basic rights, a devastating and humiliating defeat that took the excluded minority as an irrationalist scapegoat.

Boas's important criticism of the role of race in the human sciences had, of course, been motivated as much by his own experience of European anti-Semitism as by American racism; Boas as much forged his own self-respecting identity as a Jew against anti-

---

76. Ibid., 156–60.

77. See Houston Stewart Chamberlain, *The Foundations of the Nineteenth Century*, trans. John Lees, 2 vols. (London: John Lane, 1911).

78. See Madison Grant, *The Passing of the Great Race: or The Racial Basis of European History* (New York: Charles Scribner's Sons, 1919).

79. See Raul Hilberg, *The Destruction of the European Jews* (New York: Holmes & Meier, 1985), 3:1201–20.

Semitism as Frederick Douglass or Du Bois defined theirs as African Americans against American racism. The subsequent elaboration of his arguments by Klineberg, Benedict, and Myrdal had further raised the standards of public reason to expose both the intellectual and ethical fallacies of racism both in America and Europe.

World War II itself, not unlike the Civil War, played an important role in stimulating the development of much more enlightened public attitudes on racial questions than had prevailed theretofore. Not only did the distinguished military service of African Americans in both wars call for recognition of full citizenship; the allied victory in World War II raised corresponding questions about the state of American constitutionalism prior to the war not unlike those raised by the Reconstruction Amendments about antebellum American constitutionalism. The United States successfully fought that war in Europe against a nation that, like the American South in the Civil War, defined its world historic mission in self-consciously racist terms. The political ravages of such racism— both in the unspeakable moral horrors of the Holocaust and in the brutalities World War II inflicted on so many others—naturally called for a moral interpretation of that war, again like the Civil War, in terms of the defense of the political culture of universal human rights against its racist antagonists. In the wake of World War II and its central role in the allied victory and in the European reconstruction, the United States took up a prominent position on the world stage as an advocate of universal human rights. America was thus naturally pressed critically to examine not only at home but abroad as well practices like state-sponsored racial segregation in light of the best interpretation of American ideals of human rights in contemporary circumstances.[80]

World War II played, as it were, a role in American moral and political thought of a kind of Third American Revolution (the Civil War being the second such revolution[81]). American ideals of revolutionary constitutionalism were tested against the aggression

---

80. See Mary L. Dudziak, "Desegregation as a Cold War Imperative," *Stanford Law Review* 41 (1988): 41; Fredrickson, *The Black Image in the White Mind*, 330.
81. I develop this thought at length in Richards, *Conscience and the Constitution*.

on human rights of a nation, Nazi Germany, that attacked every-thing the American constitutional tradition valued in the idea and constitutional institutions of respect for universal human rights.[82] The self-conscious American defense of human rights against the totalitarian ambitions of Nazi Germany required Americans, after the war, to ask if their own constitutionalism was indeed adequate to their ambitions.

In fact, the painful truth was what Du Bois and Boas and others had long argued, namely, that America had betrayed the revolu-tionary constitutionalism of its Reconstruction Amendments in ways and with consequences strikingly similar to the ways in which Germany had betrayed the promise of universal emancipation. Americans did not, however, have to reconstruct their constitu-tionalism in order to do justice to this sense of grievous mistake. Unlike the question that faced the nation in the wake of the Civil War, the problem was not one of a basic flaw in the very design of American constitutionalism. Rather, the issue was corrigible inter-pretive mistake. The judiciary had failed to understand and give effect to the moral ambitions of the Reconstruction Amendments themselves, namely, that the American political community should be a moral community committed to abstract values of human rights available on fair terms of public reason to all persons, not a community based on race.

The focus for such testing of American interpretive practice was, naturally, *Plessy v. Ferguson*, in which the Supreme Court had accepted the exclusion of black Americans from the American community of equal rights. However, the intellectual and ethical foundations of *Plessy*, to the extent it ever had such foundations, had collapsed under the weight of the criticism we have already discussed at some length. The idea of natural race differences had been thoroughly discredited as itself the product of a long Ameri-can history of the unjust cultural construction of racism in the same way that European anti-Semitism had been discredited. The Supreme Court, which in 1896 in *Plessy* could rationalize itself as merely following nature or history, faced in the early 1950s a

---

82. See, in general, Hannah Arendt, *The Origins of Totalitarianism* (New York: Harcourt Brace Jovanovich, 1973).

wholly different space for moral choice, which Boasian cultural studies and African American activism had opened up.

Thurgood Marshall in his argument to the Supreme Court for the NAACP morally dramatized this choice in terms of the blue-eyed innocent African American child indistinguishable in all reasonable respects from other children playing with them and living near them except for the role the Supreme Court would play in legitimating a constructed difference (segregated education) which enforced, in fact, an irrationalist prejudice backed by a long history of subjugation.[83] The Supreme Court was compelled to face, on behalf of American culture more generally, a stark moral choice *either* to give effect to a culture of dehumanization *or* to refuse any longer to be complicitous with such rights-denying evil. It could not evade its moral responsibility. In effect, Marshall, as an African American, stood before the Court in the full voice of his moral personality as a free person and asked the Court to accept its responsibility for either degrading him as subhuman or to refuse any longer to degrade any person.

State-sponsored racial segregation, once uncritically accepted as a reasonable expression of natural race differences, now was construed as itself an unjust construction of an irrationalist dehumanization that excluded citizens from their equal rights as members of the political community, and, as such, unconstitutional. In 1954 in *Brown v. Board of Education* the Supreme Court articulated this deliberative interpretive judgment for the nation by unanimously striking down state-sponsored racial segregation as a violation of the Equal Protection Clause of the Fourteenth Amendment.

The constitutionality of state antimiscegenation laws was struck down by a unanimous Supreme Court in its 1967 decision in *Loving v. Virginia*.[84] Repeating, as it had in *Brown,* that the dominant interpretive judgments of the Reconstruction Congress could not be interpretively dispositive in contemporary circumstances, the Court rejected the equal application theory of *Pace v. Alabama.* The

83. See Anthony G. Amsterdam, "Thurgood Marshall's Image of the Blue-Eyed Child in *Brown,*" *New York University Law Review* 68 (1993): 226.

84. 388 U.S. 1 (1967); cf. *McLaughlin v. Florida*, 379 U.S. 184 (1964).

Equal Protection Clause condemned all state-sponsored sources of invidious racial discrimination and, the Court held, antimiscegenation laws were one such source. Indeed, the only basis for such laws was the constitutionally forbidden aim of white supremacy.

Antimiscegenation laws had come to bear this interpretation as a consequence of the Court's endorsement of the cultural theory of the rights-denying construction of racism first suggested by Lydia Maria Child in 1833[85] and importantly elaborated by Ida Wells-Barnett in 1892.[86] Child had examined and condemned both American slavery and racism in light of the argument for toleration: basic human rights of the person were abridged on wholly inadequate sectarian grounds that Child, like other radical abolitionists, expressly analogized to religious persecution. Antimiscegenation laws violated the basic human right of intimate association on such inadequate grounds, thus dehumanizing a whole class of persons as sub-human animals unworthy of the forms of equal respect accorded rights-bearing persons.

Ida Wells-Barnett elaborated the theory of the rights-denying sexual dehumanization of African Americans under slavery made clear earlier by Harriet Jacobs;[87] she analyzed Southern racism after emancipation in these terms sustained by antimiscegenation laws and related laws and practices, including lynching. The point of such laws and practices was, Wells showed, not only to condemn all interracial marriages (the focus of Child's analysis), but to assault the legitimacy of all sexual relations (marital and otherwise) between white women and black men. Illicit relations between white men and black women were, in contrast, if not legal, certainly socially acceptable. The asymmetry was rationalized in terms of a sectarian sexual and romantic idealized mythology of white women and a corresponding devaluation (indeed, dehumanization) of black women and men as sexually animalistic. Illicit sexual relations of white men with black women were consistent with this political epistemology, and thus were tolerable; both licit

85. For citations and commentary, see Richards, *Conscience and the Constitution*, 80–89.

86. For citations and commentary, see Richards, *Women, Gays, and the Constitution*, 182–90.

87. For citations and commentary, see ibid., 117–24.

and illicit consensual relations of black men with white women were not, and thus were ideologically transformed into violent rapes requiring lynching.

W. E. B. Du Bois, a life-long feminist like Frederick Douglass, condemned in related terms the role the idealized image of women (as either virgin or prostitute) played in sustaining not only racism, but a sexism that unjustly treated all women:

> The world wants healthy babies and intelligent workers. Today we refuse to allow the combination and force thousands of intelligent workers to go childless at a horrible expenditure of moral force, or we damn them if they break our idiotic conventions. Only at the sacrifice of intelligence and the chance to do their best work can the majority of modern women bear children. This is the damnation of women.
>
> All womanhood is hampered today because the world on which it is emerging is a world that tries to worship both virgins and mothers and in the end despises motherhood and despoils virgins.
>
> The future woman must have a life work and economic independence. She must have knowledge. She must have the right of motherhood at her discretion. The present mincing horror at free womanhood must pass if we are ever to be rid of the bestiality of free manhood; not by guarding the weak in weakness do we gain strength, but by making weakness free and strong.
>
> The world must choose the free women or the white wraith of the prostitute. Today it wavers between the prostitute and the nun.[88]

American racism, on this analysis, reflected a culturally constructed and sustained racialized sexual mythology of gender (white virgin versus black prostitute); and antimiscegenation laws were unconstitutional because of their role in sustaining this sectarian ideology. Both Jacobs and Wells-Barnett had analyzed this injustice from the perspective of black women who had experienced its indignities at first hand.

88. See W. E. B. Du Bois, "The Damnation of Women" (1920), in *W. E. B. Du Bois*, 952–53. On the specifically racist use of such an unjust idealization, see ibid., 958: "one thing I shall never forgive, neither in this world nor the world to come: its wanton and continued and persistent insulting of the black womanhood which it sought and seeks to prostitute to its lust."

James Baldwin, one of the greatest American writers of his generation and a black homosexual, brought the same experienced sense of indignity to bear on his later explorations of American sexual racism.[89] When he traveled in the South, Baldwin wrote "about my unbelieving shock when I realized that I was being groped by one of the most powerful men in one of the states I visited."[90] He wrote searingly of his indignation from his experience as a black man, and what he learned of the way racism fulfilled men's "enormous need to debase other men":

> To be a slave means that one's manhood is engaged in a dubious battle indeed, and this stony fact is not altered by whatever devotion some masters and some slaves may have arrived at in relation to each other. In the case of American slavery, the black man's right to his women, as well as to his children, was simply taken from him and whatever bastards the white man begat on the bodies of black women took their condition from the condition of their mothers: blacks were not the only stallions on the slave-breeding farms! And one of the many results of this loveless, money-making conspiracy was that, in giving the masters every conceivable sexual and commercial license, it also emasculated them of any human responsibility—to their women, to their children, to their wives, to themselves. The results of this blasphemy resound in this country, on every private and public level, until this hour. When the man grabbed my cock, I didn't think of him as a faggot, which, indeed, if having a wife and children, house, cars, and a respectable and powerful standing in that community, mean anything, he wasn't: I watched his eyes, thinking with great sorrow, *The unexamined life is not worth living.*[91]

Baldwin made clear the general role that sexual dehumanization played in American racism: the mythological reduction of both black women and men to their sexuality on terms that fundamentally denied their moral personalities and their human rights to respect for conscience, speech, work, and, of course, intimate life, including their right to love on terms of respect (a right, for

89. See, in general, David Leeming, *James Baldwin* (New York: Knopf, 1994).
90. See James Baldwin, *No Name in the Street* (New York: Dell, 1972), 61.
91. Ibid., 62–63.

Baldwin, owed all persons, heterosexual or homosexual, male or female, white or nonwhite).[92] Obviously, African American rights-based protest of the terms of their subordination led, on grounds of principle, to protest of related forms of the structural injustice of moral slavery, as the antisexist arguments of Jacobs, Wells-Barnett, and Du Bois and the antihomophobic arguments of Baldwin make quite clear. To challenge the unjust terms of the structural injustice of American racism was, as Du Bois made clear, to demand one's ethnic and American identity be recognized and acknowledged in a new way. The moral empowerment of making claims to one's basic human rights in one domain generalizes, on grounds of rights-based principle, to empowering claims to revise the terms of all identities marred by such structural injustice. Such protest, based on the self-respecting sense of one's humanity as a bearer of human rights, calls for often fundamental criticism of the cultural forms that have sustained such injustice—not only political protest but the creation of new cultural forms that make imaginative space for moral and human protest affirming a self-respecting sense of the creative and critical powers expressive of one's sense of one's human rights.[93] Under the pressure of such criticism, as we have seen, a matter that had been supposed to be a fundamentally important physical difference comes reasonably to be regarded as a profoundly unjust construction of difference in service of an indefensible conception of national identity. If there is nothing in the traditional American importance attached to race but culture, then we have ethically responsible choices to make about addressing and rectifying the history and culture that have sustained such choices. The African American struggle is a rights-based narrative of choices made to identify and protest injustice, exposing to the American public mind its ugly nescience and complacency in the face of fundamental injustice rationalized as in the nature of

---

92. For Baldwin's frankest first-person treatment of these issues, see James Baldwin, "Here Be Dragons," in James Baldwin, *The Price of the Ticket: Collected Nonfiction, 1948–1985* (New York: St. Martin's, 1985), 677–90; for a much more elliptical, self-hating treatment, see James Baldwin, "The Male Prison," in ibid., 101–5.

93. See, for example, George Hutchinson, *The Harlem Renaissance in Black and White* (Cambridge: Harvard University Press, 1995).

things. Nothing in this dynamic of self-respecting claims to an identity based on justice corresponds to the terms of immutability and salience in which much constitutional theory addresses this matter. Indeed, it gets it quite perversely wrong, repeating the way of regarding the problem (as a physical fact) that it should protest. The protest is not to giving weight to immutable and salient facts as such, but to the imposition of a cultural identity of dehumanizing self-contempt resting, as we have seen, on structural injustice.

I have suggested that the abridgment of the inalienable right to conscience should normatively frame our understanding of such injustice; self-respecting claims on the basis of this right address the dehumanizing evil both by affirming what the evil denies and making possible reasonable debate and discourse about the irrationalist basis on which the evil has been sustained. The perspective opens up a new way of understanding not only, as we have seen, the structural injustice of racism but the way in which we should interpret that analogy in the understanding of sexism and homophobia.

Two

THE GENDER ANALOGY

The struggle for a strong antiracist constitutional principle had implicit within it a criticism of the racialized ideal of gender roles in persistent patterns of American racism. The constitutional repudiation of antimiscegenation laws clearly reflected this criticism. Since the purpose of state-sponsored segregation was to discourage even the possibility of such intimate relations, the unconstitutionality of segregation reflected this critical theme as well.

Some of the most important exponents of this criticism had been black women, like Harriet Jacobs and Ida Wells-Barnett, who spoke from within their own moral experience about the indignity this dehumanizing stereotype of black sexuality inflicted on them. The criticism was, in its nature, an assault upon the normative conception of women in suffrage feminism that placed white women on a romantically idealized pedestal of wife and mother allegedly inconsistent with the rights and responsibilities of men.[1] For this reason, Ida Wells-Barnett was at loggerheads with the leading suffrage feminist advocate of this conception, Frances Willard, over Willard's refusal to acknowledge the ugly facts of consensual inter-racial sex underlying the lynching of black men in the South.[2] Activist antiracist black women, like Wells-Barnett and others, were for good reasons skeptical of a feminism rooted in such an ideology, and would continue to be so

---

1. For fuller discussion of this normative conception, see David A. J. Richards, *Women, Gays, and the Constitution: The Grounds for Feminism and Gay Rights in Culture and Law* (Chicago: University of Chicago Press, 1998), chap. 4.

2. For fuller discussion, see ibid., 182–90.

for a long period.[3] Only a feminism, itself skeptical of this ideology, would have the promise of both advancing antiracist and antisexist principles in an acceptable way and thus engage the moral convictions of black as well as white women.

Second Wave feminism arose on such a basis,[4] and, in the wake of the earlier described successes of the NAACP in securing judicial recognition rendering racial classifications constitutionally highly suspect, gradually persuaded the Supreme Court to regard gender classifications as similarly suspect.[5] Indeed, a recent case, *United States v. Virginia,*[6] suggests that the Supreme Court may be shifting the standard of review accorded gender to a level of scrutiny much closer to that of race. In striking down the exclusion of women from the Virginia Military Institute, the Court invoked the standard of whether the justification for exclusion was "exceedingly persuasive,"[7] was quite skeptical of the weight accorded putative gender differences as a rationale for the exclusion,[8] and expressly invoked an important racial case, *Sweatt v. Painter,*[9] as a relevant analogy for the unconstitutionality of separate-but-equal in the realm of gender.[10] Consistent also with its views on the unconstitutionality

3. See, for a good general study, Paula Giddings, *When and Where I Enter . . . : The Impact of Black Women on Race and Sex in America* (New York: William Morrow, 1984). See also bell hooks, *Ain't I a Woman: Black Women and Feminism* (Boston: South End Press, 1981); ibid., *Feminist Theory: From Margin to Center* (Boston: South End Press, 1984).

4. See, for elaboration of this point, Richards, *Women, Gays, and the Constitution,* chap. 5.

5. See, for example, *Reed v. Reed,* 404 U.S. 71 (1971) (mandatory preference for men over women in the appointment of the administrator of a decedent's estate held unconstitutional); *Frontiero v. Richardson,* 411 U.S. 677 (1973) (federal law permitting male members of armed forces an automatic dependency allowance, but requiring servicewomen to prove that their husbands were dependent, held unconstitutional); *Craig v. Boren,* 429 U.S. 190 (1976) (gender distinction between men and women in drinking age—men at 21, women at 18—held unconstitutional). But cf. *Michael M. v. Superior Court,* 450 U.S. 464 (1981) (statutory rape law, holding only men liable for intercourse with female under 18, held constitutional); *Rostker v. Goldberg,* 453 U.S. 57 (1981) (Congressional limitation of registration for draft to men held constitutional).

6. 116 S. Ct. 2264 (1996).

7. Id. at 2274.

8. Id. at 2276, 2280.

9. 339 U.S. 629 (1950) (establishment of separate law school for blacks held unconstitutional).

10. *United States v. Virginia,* 116 S. Ct. at 2285, 2286.

of antimiscegenation laws, the Court has also struck down laws imposing criminal penalties on the right of reproductive autonomy, which are often not unreasonably thought of as unjust enforcement of traditional views of gender and sexuality.[11] The Supreme Court declined, however, to extend this principle to consensual adult homosexual relations in *Bowers v. Hardwick.*[12] How are we to understand the constitutional analogy thus developed between race and gender in various domains? How should we interpret the analogy in the understanding of the case for gay rights? In the previous chapter, I stated and criticized constitutional theories of this matter that emphasize either powerlessness or the immutability and salience of the basis for discrimination. We need a new start, one that affords not only a better theory of the constitutional analogy between race and gender but uses the analogy to illuminate the case for gay rights. I begin with the analogy between race and gender, and then turn to the use of the analogy in making the case for gay rights.

THE ANALOGY BETWEEN RACE AND GENDER

The constitutional analogy between race and gender must be understood as the elaboration of an interpretive development whose roots lie in abolitionist feminism. Abolitionist feminism was a movement of radical antebellum abolitionists who constructed, on what they called the same platform of human rights, common principles to condemn racism and sexism (namely, the normative theory of moral slavery).[13] The principles of that movement were compromised, in increasingly racist and sexist directions, during the struggles of suffrage feminism.[14] Second Wave feminism, building

11. See *Griswold v. Connecticut,* 381 U.S. 479 (1965) (criminalization of use of contraceptives held unconstitutional); *Roe v. Wade,* 410 U.S. 113 (1973) (criminalization of abortion services held unconstitutional). The Supreme Court reaffirmed the central principle of *Roe* in 1992 in *Planned Parenthood of Southeastern Pennsylvania v. Casey,* 505 U.S. 833 (1992).

12. 478 U.S. 186 (1986).

13. For elaboration of this background, see Richards, *Women, Gays, and the Constitution,* chap. 3.

14. For elaboration of this background, see ibid., chap. 4.

on the insights of abolitionist feminism, arose in the wake of the most profound public criticism and action against American racism since antebellum radical abolitionism, and based its antisexist principles on the same platform of human rights as the antiracist principles that increasingly informed both American public opinion and the constitutional interpretation of the Reconstruction Amendments. The development of the principled elaboration of the analogy between race and gender required both a practice and theory of a certain kind of struggle appealing to basic inalienable human rights and calling for a closer scrutiny of traditional grounds for abridgment of such rights in light of the kinds of independent standards of public reason that the argument for toleration requires.

Thus the antiracist and antisexist struggles used and sponsored increasingly muscular rights of conscience, speech, intimate life, and work; both struggles subjected traditional grounds for the abridgment of such rights to a more searching and reasonable public examination. In both cases, such rights empowered traditionally subjugated groups to come to understand and to demand their basic rights of moral personality and to engage increasingly in the reasonable public discourse and debate in their own voice that such rights make possible. Two prominent strands in the development and articulation of Second Wave feminism illustrate this approach: the seminal argument of Betty Friedan and the development of antisexist principles by women within the antiracist civil rights movement. Although rooted in different backgrounds and experiences, both strands exemplify, consistent with Du Bois's theory of double consciousness, an overlapping reasonable consensus on the importance of rights-based claims to identity as the common grounds of antiracist and antisexist principles.

Betty Friedan's 1963 *The Feminine Mystique*[15] struck a responsive chord among American women, more of whom now worked outside the home than before,[16] when she critically addressed both

---

15. See Betty Friedan, *The Feminine Mystique* (1963; London: Penguin, 1982).

16. For the changes in the 1940s, see William H. Chafe, *The Paradox of Change: American Women in the 20th Century* (New York: Oxford University Press, 1991), 166–72; for the 1950s, see ibid., 188–92.

the idealized conception of gender roles and the force it had over women's lives.[17] Citing abolitionist feminist dissatisfaction with the claims of domesticity as the occasion for distinctively feminist claims,[18] Friedan argued that American women in the post–World War II period experienced a comparable crisis of identity but over contemporary gender roles so impoverished that they "had no name for the problem troubling them" (10). Friedan spoke from her own personal experience of an advanced education that went unused in domestic life (26, 62–63)[19] and of the unjust epistemological power over women's consciousness and lives of the normative conception of gender roles that pathologized any feminist dissent (37, 107, 139, 169–70).[20]

A woman's problematic sense of herself, Friedan argued, was not to be dismissed or trivialized as merely psychologically personal and deviant as perceived through the prism of this normative conception when its political force was so demonstrably unjust. Otherwise, injustice would be the measure of the awakening sense of justice that alone might protest it. Friedan's criticisms of the justice of this normative conception, the feminine mystique, questioned not only its substance—its making of femininity an end in itself (38, 40–41), or making sex a women's exclusive career (228)—but its sectarian religious force (38, 44, 111, 173) that permitted no reasonable doubts to be raised (44) and fictionalized facts (53). Indeed, using the very terms of the paradox of intolerance, Friedan

17. On the importance of Friedan's book, see Chafe, *The Paradox of Change*, 195; Jo Freeman, *The Politics of Women's Liberation: A Case Study of an Emerging Social Movement and Its Relation to the Policy Process* (New York: Longman, 1975), 27, 53; Judith Hole and Ellen Levine, *Rebirth of Feminism* (New York: Quadrangle, 1971), 17, 82; Nancy E. McGlen and Karen O'Connor, *Women's Rights: The Struggle for Equality in the Nineteenth and Twentieth Centuries* (New York: Praeger, 1983), 29; Carl N. Degler, *At Odds: Women and the Family in America from the Revolution to the Present* (New York: Oxford University Press, 1980), 443.

18. For discussion of Stanton's dissatisfaction as the motivation for her role in calling the Seneca Falls Convention, see Friedan, *The Feminine Mystique*, 81–82.

19. On her background as well in labor activism, see Daniel Horowitz, *Betty Friedan and the Making of "The Feminine Mystique"* (Amherst: University of Massachusetts Press, 1998).

20. For discussion of Lundberg and Farnham's *Modern Women: The Lost Sex*, a work that took this view, see Richards, *Women, Gays, and the Constitution*, 197–98.

pointed to an ideology whose polemical force became most insistent when it was most reasonably open to doubt. She called this:

> the basic paradox of the feminine mystique: that it emerged to glorify women's role as housewife at the very moment when the barriers to her full participation in society were lowered, at the very moment when science and education and her own ingenuity made it possible for a woman to be both wife and mother and to take an active part in the world outside the home. The glorification of "woman's role," then, seems to be in proportion to society's reluctance to treat women as complete human beings; for the less real function that role has, the more it is decorated with meaningless details to conceal its emptiness (210).

The general terms of the analysis are, of course, familiar from our earlier examination of the elaboration of the argument for toleration to develop the theory of moral slavery and the critical applications of that theory to American slavery and racism (chapter 1). What was so striking and original in Friedan's analysis was the way she plausibly applied it both to popular American culture and the uncritical social scientists who supported its cult of women's domesticity in the mid-twentieth century.[21] Friedan self-consciously saw herself quite rightly as in a similar position to leading advocates of abolitionist feminism like Theodore Parker and Elizabeth Stanton; just as Parker and Stanton argued critically against the dominant views on gender in the antebellum period (as enforcing women's moral slavery), Friedan targeted her critique on traditional American gender roles, largely immunized from serious rights-based analysis by suffrage feminism (which had thus reinforced women's unjust subordination).[22] All the terms of the abolitionist feminist analysis of moral slavery were in place in Friedan's critique. The force of the sectarian ideology of gender roles depended on the abridgment of basic human rights to critical mind and speech (59, 282–83), associated rights to critical education

---

21. For social background, see Glenna Matthews, *"Just a Housewife": The Rise and Fall of Domesticity in America* (New York: Oxford University Press, 1987).

22. See, in general, Betty Friedan, *The Feminine Mystique*, 72–90; on critical versus uncritical uses of social science, see ibid., 149; on Parker, see ibid., 76; on Stanton, ibid., 81–82; on securing the suffrage and the death of feminism, ibid., 88.

(155, 158, 211, 223), fair terms for rights to intimate life (148–49), and the right to creative work (289–91). The result was the cultural dehumanization of women (244, 251, 264–68) in terms of an objectified sexuality (72, 228, 233) or biology (275). Women's struggle was thus one for personal identity (67–68, 289–91) on terms responsive to a morally independent basis to live a life from convictions of conscience, the voice within (29, 207, 331).

Friedan importantly made reference early in her book (16) to Simone de Beauvoir's pathbreaking *The Second Sex*, which had prominently explored analogies among anti-Semitism, racism, and sexism.[23] The terms of Friedan's analysis were drawn from a tradition, certainly familiar to her, that had recently applied all the terms of analysis used by her to the criticism of American racism; she acknowledged as much when she criticized the application of separate-but-equal to women's education (which had been struck down by the Supreme Court in 1954 as applied to the education of African Americans) on the ground that such "sex-directed education segregated recent generations of able American women as surely as separate-but-equal education segregated able American Negroes from the opportunity to realize their full abilities in the mainstream of American life" (158, 211). Friedan used the analogy to address a constitutional culture on whom "[t]he black civil rights movement had a very profound effect."[24] Gunnar Myrdal himself, at the conclusion of his masterwork, noted that the status of women had been "the nearest and most natural analogy"[25] for those justifying slavery and racism and might be subject to similar rights-based criticism, as indeed the abolitionist feminists had earlier urged. Friedan's argument assumed the analogy, including the very terms of a personal struggle for moral identity and self-consciousness, that Du Bois had brought to the black struggle for a stronger antiracist constitutional principle of equal protection.

Friedan also assumed and used a critical analysis of stronger

23. See Simone de Beauvoir, *The Second Sex*, trans. H. M. Parshley (first published in English in 1953) (New York: Vintage, 1974), xvi, xx, xxi, 131, 144 (citing Sartre and Myrdal), 335.

24. See Freeman, *The Politics of Women's Liberation*, 27.

25. See Gunnar Myrdal, "A Parallel to the Negro Problem," in *An American Dilemma*, appendix 5 (New York: Harper & Row, 1944), 2:1073.

antiracist principles that the Supreme Court had accepted, namely, the Boasian cultural science that had reframed issues from the pseudo-science of race to an unjust culture of racist subjugation. That principle was plausibly applied not only to race but, as Myrdal suggested, to gender as well. Franz Boas had laid the foundations, but his students Margaret Mead and Ruth Benedict had elaborated the point.[26] Indeed, such skepticism may first have been suggested about gender differences by those skeptical of the dominant suffrage feminist ideology of basic differences and then extended to race differences.[27] The greater and earlier political success of the racial case may be due to historical accident (an organized black movement that employed the argument, a divided woman's movement many of whom espoused physical differences), not to the underlying issues of principle.[28] Friedan acknowledged Mead for having made a form of the argument, but then criticized her for not carrying it far enough.[29] Clearly, the recent success of the argument in the racial area made it much easier to deploy a form of the argument, as a matter of principle, in the criticism of the unjust cultural construction of gender. If *The Feminine Mystique* was about anything, it was about that.

The dimensions of the analogy of principle became explicit in the moral experience of the black and white women who participated in the civil rights movement of the 1960s, as Sara Evans has made clear in her now classic study of this period.[30] Drawing an explicit analogy to the transformative experience of the Grimke sisters as pathbreaking abolitionist feminists (24–26, 57, 101, 120), Evans described a struggle of black and white women to end racial discrimination that led women to develop a heightened consciousness of their own oppression. In the 1950s, the civil rights movement had grown in both confidence and sense of vision. Black

26. See Rosalind Rosenberg, *Beyond Separate Spheres: Intellectual Roots of Modern Feminism* (New Haven: Yale University Press, 1982), 162–69, 177, 213–32.

27. For Jane Addams on physical differences as the ground for women's superiority, see ibid., 41; on skepticism about this ideology, see ibid., 111, 176–77, 236; on race differences, see ibid., 108, 195, 245.

28. See ibid., 245.

29. See Friedan, *The Feminine Mystique*, 129–31.

30. See Sara Evans, *Personal Politics: The Roots of Women's Liberation in the Civil Rights Movement and the New Left* (New York: Vintage, 1980).

women played major roles in this effort, from the actions of Rosa Parks and Jo Ann Robinson in starting the Montgomery bus boycott in 1955 to Ella Baker's role in the 1960 founding of the Student Non-Violent Coordinating Committee (SNCC).[31] As the civil rights movement became a central topic in American news media, Americans became sensitized to the existence of profound constitutional injustices (including racial segregation and antimiscegenation laws) that had been rationalized on grounds that denied whole classes of persons any decent respect for their basic human rights. Like their abolitionist feminist ancestors, many women who became active in this movement only came to a realization of the comparable injustices to which they were subjected when they experienced sexism from their own male colleagues in the movement.

One group of women who realized the link between race and sex discrimination were young Southern activists who took part in SNCC's direct-action civil rights struggle. Both black and white, these women found their moral voice in the protests, including sit-ins, of the civil rights movement; as one white woman later testified, "To this day I am amazed. I just did it."[32] For the white women, in particular, such activism constituted a moral revolt, similar in moral force to that of the Grimke sisters, against the idealized conception of white women of Southern racism: "[i]n the 1830's and again in the 1960s the first voices to link racial and sexual oppression were those of Southern white women" (25).

These women, responsive to a Protestant sense of radical personal conscience and ethical responsibility, took as their model black women like Ella Baker whose life realized in practice Anna Cooper's transformative model of "[w]omen in stepping from the pedestal of statue-like inactivity in the domestic shrine, and daring to think and move and speak."[33] In so doing, these white women spiritually exiled themselves from their own mothers in as radical a way as Angelina and Sarah Grimke's physical exile from the South, an experience, like the Grimkes, "exceptionally lonely, for

31. See Chafe, *The Paradox of Change*, 197.
32. See ibid., 38.
33. See Anna Julia Cooper, *A Voice from the South*, ed. Mary Helen Washington (1892; New York: Oxford University Press, 1988), 121–22.

it shattered once-supportive ties with family and friends" (43). Falling back upon personal resources they did not know they had, "they developed a sense of self that enabled them to recognize the enemy within as well—the image of the 'southern lady' " (43). In contrast to northern students who came and left the South, "southern white students were in an important sense fighting for their own identities" (45).

These white dissenting women were struggling with and against the idealized conception of white women's sphere that, as we have seen, enforced the correlative dehumanization of black men and women as sexually animalistic. No action more outraged this ideology than the idea of consensual sexual relations between white women and black men. Not only antimiscegenation laws but the whole structure of Southern apartheid were rationalized as measures directed against this ultimate mythological evil. The participation of white women in interracial co-operation protesting these and other such laws represented for many of their Southern white parents "a breakdown in the social order" (44); one such father, when his daughter announced "she wanted to leave school to work in a small-town black community, accused her of being a whore and chased her out of the house in a drunken rage, shouting that she was disowned" (44). Within a movement of antiracist struggle led by Southern black men and women, such young white women had "to forge a new sense of themselves, to redefine the meaning of being a woman quite apart from the flawed image they had inherited" (57); their struggle was the one Du Bois had earlier defined as the antiracist struggle for a new kind of identity and self-consciousness. They self-critically recognized that the struggle for racial equality called for fundamental changes in gender roles, including what they now recognized and condemned as a conspicuously sectarian religiously based moral "defense of white women's sexual purity in a racist society [that] held them separate from and innocent of the 'real world' of politics" (58).

One important catalyst for the development of a rights-based feminism, on the model of abolitionist feminism, was the pervasive attitude of male supremacy these women encountered *within* SNCC. Their self-critical development and support of antiracist principles had required them to question and reject traditional gender roles, regarding "the term 'southern lady' . . . [as] an obscene epithet" (57). They thus asserted their own human rights to conscience, speech, intimate life, and work against a sectarian racist orthodoxy that had traditionally abridged these rights. Yet within SNCC, these hard-fought personal rights were again put at hazard: rights of conscience and speech were subordinated in decision making, rights of intimate life compromised by expectations that women would automatically acquiesce when men asked them to sleep with them, rights of work by limiting them to the sphere of housework (83–101). More and more of these young women talked with one another about their common experiences. Initially, the hope was that simply pointing out the problem in an anonymous memorandum would bring change (233–35). Stokely Carmichael's infamous rebuttal ("The only position for women in SNCC is prone.") (87) led them to conclude that they must be as assertive in defense of their own rights as they had been—together with men—in the struggle for racial equality.

Increasingly, their moral experience in this rights-based struggle led them to link the two causes directly. In a summation of their thinking addressed to women in the peace and freedom movement, Casey Hayden and Mary King declared in the fall of 1965 that women, like blacks, "seem to be caught up in a common-law caste system that operates, sometime subtly, forcing them to work around or outside hierarchical structures of power which may exclude them. Women seem to be placed in the same position of assumed subordination in personal situations too. It is a caste system which, at its worst, uses and exploits women" (235). The identity-transforming struggle for a morally independent exercise of basic rights, which had led them "to think radically about the personal worth and abilities of people whose role in society had gone unchallenged before," required the same analysis and criticism of "the racial caste system" and "the sexual caste system" (236). Failure to extend the criticism of racial caste to sexual caste reflected, Hayden and White argued, the depth of the injustice of the sexual caste system and the dimensions of the problem of remedy. In particular, they pleaded for open discussion of these issues among women, creating "a community of support for each other so we can deal with ourselves and others with integrity and can therefore keep working" (237) thus identifying the centrality to rights-based feminism of the praxis of consciousness raising (203–4, 214–5). As the development of the Black Power movement made it increasingly difficult at this time for white and black women to cooperate across racial lines, the white women veterans of the civil rights struggle took such sentiments into the student movement, the antiwar movement, and the like, becoming in the process the cutting edge of Second Wave feminism as itself a civil rights movement (156–232).

The emerging feminism of these women overlapped significantly with that of Betty Friedan and others. Both took inspiration from the successes of the civil rights movement and targeted feminist discourse toward a rights-based criticism of the normative gender roles that had largely been immunized from such criticism. Rather than idealizing these gender roles as the source of a higher morality, on the model of a Catharine Beecher or Frances Willard,[34] the roles themselves (including their idealization) were now critically examined in the light of morally independent values of human rights. A new emphasis was placed on both the appeal to basic human rights (conscience, free speech, association, and work), and on the lack of the kind of compelling secular public justification constitutionally required before such rights might be abridged. Indeed, books like Kate Millett's 1969 *Sexual Politics*[35] and Shulamith Firestone's 1970 *Dialectic of Sex*[36] initiated the serious American study of the cultural depth and polemical power of the traditional sectarian ideology of gender, its fundamental rights-denying injustice, and the extent of imaginative (even utopian) theory and practice of change that might be required to dislodge and subvert this ideology and make space available for women to understand and claim their human rights, as persons, on fair terms.

This fundamental criticism of gender roles (already an ingredient of the stronger antiracist principle that many black and white women now defended) made normative space available for the

---

34. See, for explorations of their views, Richards, *Women, Gays, and the Constitution*, 72–78, 144–55.

35. See Kate Millett, *Sexual Politics* (New York: Avon, 1969).

36. See Shulamith Firestone, *The Dialectic of Sex: The Case for Feminist Revolution* (1970; London: Woman's Press, 1988).

reasonable aspiration of black and white women to find common ground.[37] The very terms of rights-based feminism required white women to raise questions about racialized ideals of gender[38] and suggested as well that the integrity of both the stronger antiracism and antisexism appealed to common principles of nondiscrimination that should be pursued together.

While not all Second Wave feminists emerged directly from the activism of the civil rights movement (Friedan and other important leaders were never in SNCC, for example[39]), they did interpret the achievements of the civil rights movement as a normatively relevant model of how to proceed to secure change. Virtually every legislative act, judicial decree, and executive order that applied to race could, in their view, apply to gender as well.

For example, one of the great legislative achievements of the civil rights movement was the Civil Rights Act of 1964. When the act was debated in Congress, new language was introduced to Title VII to prohibit discrimination in employment on grounds of sex as well as race. Although a conservative opponent of the bill had proposed these additional grounds as a ludicrous attempt to cripple support for the legislation (and liberal supporters opposed it for that reason),[40] the leading feminist in the House, Martha Griffiths of Michigan, held off from sponsoring the addition because she knew that the conservative's addition would bring one hundred votes with him. Determined leadership by the congresswomen supporting the addition and vigorous lobbying by its supporters, including the National Women's Party, used the logic of the connection between race and sex to persuade a majority to support the new language.[41]

The civil rights movement also supplied a model of how to proceed organizationally to implement the changes that the new leg-

<hr />

37. On this development, see, in general, Paula Giddings, *When and Where I Enter*.

38. See, for example, Ruth Frankenberg, *The Social Construction of Whiteness: White Women, Race Matters* (Minneapolis: University of Minnesota Press, 1993).

39. For a recent exploration, however, of Friedan's background in labor activism, see Daniel Horowitz, *Betty Friedan and the Making of "The Feminine Mystique"* (Amherst: University of Massachusetts Press, 1998).

40. See Hole and Levine, *Rebirth of Feminism*, 30–31.

41. See Freeman, *The Politics of Women's Liberation*, 53–54; McGlen and O'Connor, *Women's Rights*, 175–76.

islation required. In response to the failure of implementation of the ban on sex discrimination in employment, women in the various states who had served on the various state commissions on the status of women joined with activists like Betty Friedan to form in 1966 the National Organization for Women (NOW), an organization in the civil rights mode that vowed to use lobbying, litigation, and other political means to force the Equal Employment Opportunities Commission to make women's issues as central to its mandate as racial issues. Friedan was elected its first president.[42] Groups like NOW and others[43] took responsibility not only for securing compliance with progress in women's rights already achieved, but initiating new struggles to secure further victories for gender equality. Second Wave feminism embraced a range of issues and concerns, from abortion rights to equal pay to the Equal Rights Amendment (ERA) itself.[44]

The important place of the ERA on the Second Wave feminist agenda shows how far it had departed from its predecessors. What had once been a marginal position among feminists now became mainstream. Title VII of the Civil Rights Act led to numerous court rulings invalidating state laws protective of women. Many groups, formerly opposed to the ERA because of their support for these laws, had changed their minds.[45] The ERA was sent to the states in 1972, where, after a spirited right-wing opposition, it failed in 1982.[46] But the level of support it now enjoyed both among feminists and the nation at large (the Congress and thirty-five states had ratified it[47]) suggests the crucial importance in the appeal of contemporary rights-based feminist theory and practice of arguments about the unjust cultural construction of gender and the need to alter such arrangements accordingly. The appeal to differences, which had been accepted as axiomatic and the basis

---

42. See Hole and Levine, *Rebirth of Feminism,* 81–95.

43. Ibid., 95–107.

44. See Chafe, *The Paradox of Change,* 201.

45. See Freeman, *The Politics of Women's Liberation,* 212.

46. See, on this political struggle, Donald G. Mathews and Jane Sherron De Hart, *Sex, Gender, and the Politics of ERA: A State and the Nation* (New York: Oxford University Press, 1990); Jane J. Mansbridge, *Why We Lost the ERA* (Chicago: University of Chicago Press, 1986).

47. See Mansbridge, *Why We Lost the ERA,* 1.

for a higher morality of women by Frances Willard and Jane Addams,[48] was now the basis for rights-based criticism (the differences, being unjustly culturally constructed, could be criticized and changed in light of justice).

In all of this, the civil rights movement was the impetus both for the new forms of substantive argument women now made and for women organizing themselves into a rights movement. It was also indispensable in preparing the constitutional mind of the nation for greater concern for related issues of constitutional justice, and indeed urging the judiciary interpretively to recognize such claims. As we have seen, the Supreme Court both responded to and encouraged such claims of a significant analogy between race and gender.

The claim of a rights-based analogy between racism and sexism was in the similar method of structural injustice inflicted in both cases, namely, "that others have controlled the power to define one's existence,"[49] or as I have termed it earlier, "moral slavery." This structural injustice is marked by two features: first, abridgment of basic human rights to a group of persons; and second, the unjust rationalization of such abridgment on the inadequate grounds of dehumanizing stereotypes that reflect a history and culture of such abridgment. I call this injustice moral slavery because a category of persons, subject to this injustice, has been culturally dehumanized (as nonbearers of human rights) to rationalize their servile status and roles; its moral condemnation is, properly understood, the abstract normative judgment of the Thirteenth Amendment of the United States Constitution.[50] From the perspective of the constitutional condemnation of such structural injustice, race and gender should be equally suspect as grounds for state action or inaction. Women and African Americans share a common history of rights-denying moral degradation that contin-

48. See Rosenberg, *Beyond Separate Spheres*, 41.

49. See William H. Chafe, *Women and Equality: Changing Patterns in American Culture* (New York: Oxford University Press, 1977), 77; on the similar methods of repression, see ibid., 58–59, 75–76.

50. See, for extensive defense of this claim, Richards, *Women, Gays, and the Constitution*.

ued with the complicitous support of law long after their formal emancipation and enfranchisement and unjustly persists today.

The guarantee of equal protection in the Fourteenth Amendment was ratified in 1868, but was held inapplicable to women until 1971[51] and was interpreted until 1954[52] to allow racial segregation. In both cases, the Supreme Court and the constitutional culture it reflects and shapes acted as powerful agents in the transmission and reinforcement of moral slavery in the domains of gender and race. The betrayal of basic rights expressly guaranteed is even less morally excusable or justifiable when such betrayal reinforces, through the rationalizing power of the paradox of intolerance, the political force of sexism and racism as forms of moral slavery. Racial apartheid in the United States was an instrument of racial subjugation of blacks, isolating them from their basic rights of fair access on equal terms to public culture on specious racist grounds; as such, it gave powerful political legitimacy to the illegitimate force of racism in American public and private life, and thus to a continuing unjust cultural pattern of moral slavery in the domain of race that persists in various illegitimate forms today.[53]

The wholesale failure even to acknowledge the evils of the subjugation of women lent constitutional support to the illegitimate force of sexism in American public and private life, and thus to moral slavery in the domain of gender; gender segregation in separate spheres was, as in the case of race, a pivotal institutional mechanism of such degradation; and a still largely unchallenged sexist political epistemology of gender roles, operative in still powerful sectarian religious and moral traditions, undercuts the resources of public reason by which such mechanisms might be subjected to criticism and reform. Such silencing of the morally independent critical voice of reason rendered unjustly entrenched patterns of gender hierarchy largely unquestioned and unquestionable.

From the perspective of the theory of moral slavery, the constitutional injury of racism and sexism placed a cultural burden of

---

51. See *Reed v. Reed,* 404 U.S. 71 (1971).

52. See *Brown v. Board of Education,* 347 U.S. 483 (1954).

53. See, for example, Douglas S. Massey and Nancy A. Denton, *American Apartheid: Segregation and the Making of the Underclass* (Cambridge: Harvard University Press, 1993).

contempt on identifications important to moral personality. Du Bois made this point in characterizing the struggle of African Americans as two souls in one body: the one an African, the other an American identity, and the struggle to reconstruct both identities on terms of the rights-based justice of American revolutionary constitutionalism. Friedan also defined women's struggle on similar grounds as "a problem of identity,"[54] the struggle to reconstruct American culture on terms of justice that would reconcile the identity of oneself as a woman and as a rights-bearing person and equal citizen. In both cases, the struggle for constitutional justice would by its nature reconstruct both personal identity and public (including constitutional) culture. The personal and the political would become inextricably intertwined questions of both personal and moral-constitutional identity.

This perspective clarifies the justice of the remarkable interpretive development in American public law in the twentieth century that, on the basis of a radical abolitionist interpretation of the argument for toleration, subjected the cultural construction of racism and later of sexism to increasingly demanding skeptical constitutional principles as suspect (antisubordination argument).[55] Arguments of toleration and antisubordination are, on this analysis, not contradictory and, properly understood, not even in tension. It is, on this view, a self-defeating mistake so to interpret antisubordination argument in terms that render it hostile to protection of basic human rights (like the rights of conscience and speech); such defective antisubordination analysis often worsens the injustice it claims to rectify.[56]

Antisubordination is, on the alternative analysis I offer, a structurally more profound form of cultural intolerance along the two dimensions of the argument for toleration: identification of certain basic rights of the moral person and the requirement of a compelling form of reasonably public justification for the abridgment of

54. See Friedan, *The Feminine Mystique*, 68.
55. For further defense of this claim, see, in general, Richards, *Women, Gays, and the Constitution*.
56. For a criticism along these lines of Catharine MacKinnon's identification of pornography as a central feminist issue in the subordination of women, see ibid., 242–43.

such basic rights. In particular, moral slavery identifies a structural injustice marked by both its abridgment of such basic rights to a certain class of persons and the unjust enforcement at large of irrationalist stereotypical views whose illegitimate force has traditionally degraded the class of persons from their status as full bearers of human rights. European anti-Semitism (with its associated ideology of Jews as the slaves of Christians) is a case study that, in my approach, classically exemplifies a form of structural injustice along these two dimensions: it is certainly a species of religious intolerance but, in its European forms, a form of unjust subordination as well.

Suspect classification analysis, on this view, skeptically condemns the expression through law of the structural injustices underlying such unjust subordination (reflected in the cultural stereotypes of race and gender that express such unjust subordination). Equal protection requires that political power must be reasonably justifiable in terms of equal respect for human rights and the pursuit of public purposes of justice and the common good.[57] Suspect classification analysis enforces this principle by rendering constitutionally suspect grounds for laws that not only lack such public reasons, but war against public reason by illegitimately rationalizing, on inadequate grounds, structural injustice. Laws whose irrationalist bases thus war on public reason lack constitutional legitimacy and are, for this reason, subjected to demanding tests of constitutional skepticism. The unconstitutionality of state-sponsored racial segregation and antimiscegenation laws show the force of this constitutional skepticism in the area of race, and the judicial developments in the sphere of gender reflect a comparable skepticism (both in protecting basic rights, including aspects of the right to reproductive autonomy, and in subjecting gender classifications to a constitutional scrutiny increasingly close to that accorded race). All these interpretive developments by the judiciary are systematically clarified and organized by the insights afforded by the theory and practice of rights-dissent of the terms of one's

---

57. For the classic statement of equal protection as a form of public reasonableness, see Joseph Tussman and Jacobus tenBroek, "The Equal Protection of the Laws," *California Law Review* 37 (1949): 341; cf. Jacobus tenBroek, *Equal under Law* (New York: Collier, 1969).

moral slavery. On the view I take, such judicial developments have appropriately elaborated and defended basic liberal arguments of principles in ways that are interpretively sound.[58]

In particular, the recent interpretive heightening of the standard of review for gender closer to that for race is supported by the theory of moral slavery. Much of the Court's work, heightening the level of scrutiny for gender, is well explained by the theory of moral slavery, the terms of which, including various analogies between the abridgment of the rights of blacks and women, were quite self-consciously invoked in Justice Brennan's important opinion in *Frontiero v. Richardson.*[59] Further, Justice Brennan's skepticism about the enforcement of gender stereotypes (including statistics that reflect the unjust cultural force of such stereotypes) through public law in *Craig v. Boren*[60] also is well explained by this theory.

On the view taken by the theory of moral slavery, the proper interpretation of gender, as a suspect classification, must be contextually sensitive to the rights-denying cultural background of appeals to gender in the illegitimate service of the moral slavery of women as nonbearers of human rights. In particular, such illegitimate appeals to gender have been culturally grounded in unjust moral paternalism; a public and private culture, unjustly based on the exclusion of women from rights of conscience, speech, association, and work, illegitimately dehumanized its victims in terms of a nature in love with and only capable of their servile dependency, and on that basis paternalistically moralized their dependency.

---

58. To this extent, my argument disagrees with the court-skeptical view that such judicial activism has not effected significant social change with respect to racism and sexism. For such a view, see Gerald N. Rosenberg, *The Hollow Hope: Can Courts Bring About Social Change?* (Chicago: University of Chicago Press, 1991).

59. 411 U.S. 677 (1973) (federal law permitting male, but not female, members of armed forces an automatic dependency allowance for their spouses held unconstitutional) (8–1 opinion). See, for further discussion, Richards, *Women, Gays, and the Constitution,* 257–58.

60. 429 U.S. 190 (1976) (gender distinction between men and women in drinking age—men at 21, women at 18—held unconstitutional). Justice Brennan, writing for the Court, accepted the legitimacy of the state's ostensible purpose for the statute, traffic safety, but found its means-end reasoning defective, in particular, the role statistical evidence played in rationalizing the use of gender as a legislative classification. For further discussion, see Richards, *Women, Gays, and the Constitution,* 258–60.

Accordingly, the constitutional scrutiny of both express and implied gender-based classifications must be skeptical of those gender distinctions that unjustly ascribe to women stereotypes of dependency, passivity, or lack of autonomous judgmental and other capacities linked to the traditional cultural forms that illegitimately rationalized their subjugation. In particular, those stereotypes must be suspect that enforce a sexist political epistemology of servile gender roles resulting from deprivation of rights of conscience, speech, association, and work—a conception of women's natural sphere defined by, for, and in terms of the sexual and other interests of men untested in terms of public reasons expressive of the dignity of women's free moral powers of conscience, speech, association and work, and reasonably acceptable to them in such terms. In the abolitionist feminist terms of analysis,[61] indulging such gender stereotypes through law distorts public understanding and acknowledgment of the principles of ethical responsibility incumbent on all persons, as such, and, for this reason, flouts constitutional principles of equal citizenship. On this normative view, it should be irrelevant to the constitutional analysis of the suspectness of gender distinctions of such sorts that they reflect gender-linked statistical probabilities. Otherwise, the fact of the longstanding enforcement of an unjust sexist orthodoxy, to which its victims have accommodated themselves as best they can, would undercut the legitimacy of constitutional scrutiny where it is, in fact, exigently needed on grounds of justice.

The antiracist and antisexist practice of abolitionist feminism was as integral to these interpretive developments as was their theory. Rights-based arguments against moral slavery, whether by African Americans or women, took the form of originating claims of basic human rights in one's own voice that, skeptical as they were of traditionally dominant orthodoxies of race or gender (the mythologizing pedestal being common to both), morally transformed personal identity in the way the civil rights movement transformed both racial and gender identity; Second Wave feminism as a civil rights movement, if anything, reinforced this momentum. To give voice to one's human rights of moral independence, against the

---

61. For further discussion, see Richards, *Women, Gays, and the Constitution,* chap. 3.

background of a subjugating tradition of moral slavery, is to forge a new personal and moral-constitutional identity on the platform of human rights. This new identity demands, on grounds of principle, not only one's basic rights of moral personality but a private and public culture that no longer gives expression to an unjust tradition of dehumanization and marginalization.

The practice of such protest of the terms of one's moral slavery both expresses and elaborates not only new forms of identity but of consciousness and the dissident associations that sustain such consciousness. Consciousness in turn gives rise to the need for new forms of critical theory. Personally, morally, and politically transformative arguments of human rights require a complementary and mutually reinforcing theory and practice. Such protest of the terms of one's moral slavery must be examined closely as the background to the increasingly suspect character of gender under American public law. Two features of such protest are especially important in this connection: first, its challenge to the conventional terms of the public/private distinction; second, its worries about the weight placed on gender stereotypes in the distribution of rights and responsibilities.

With respect to the public/private distinction, the condemnation of moral slavery in the Thirteenth Amendment extends as broadly as the underlying rights-denying evil, including the traditions pivotal in the subjection of women. Moral slavery was as much an injury to private as it was to public life; indeed, the attempt to privatize injustice was one of its most insidious and morally corrupting evils (one's slave or one's wife as most intimately oneself).[62] Our constitutional concern under the Thirteenth Amendment should thus extend to both public and private dimensions both of racism[63] and of sexism.[64] This concern in-

---

62. Ibid., 253, 347–48, 367–68.

63. See *Jones v. Alfred H. Mayer Co.*, 392 U.S. 409 (1968) (under the Thirteenth Amendment, Congress has power to forbid racial discrimination in both public and private sales and rentals of property); *Sullivan v. Little Hunting Park, Inc.*, 396 U.S. 229 (1969) (congressional power under Thirteenth Amendment reaches racial discrimination in leasing by residents' association); *Runyon v. McCrary*, 427 U.S. 160 (1976) (congressional power under Thirteenth Amendment extends to racial discrimination by private, nonsectarian schools).

64. For a different argument to the same effect, see Emily Calhoun, "The Thirteenth and Fourteenth Amendments: Constitutional Authority for Federal Legislation

cludes the uncritical privatization of interspousal violence and resistance, which obfuscates rights-based normative issues of constitutional dimensions.[65]

The ever-increasing level of constitutional skepticism about the
enforcement of gender stereotypes through law may be reasonably
understood and evaluated against the background of increasing
skepticism about the ways in which unjust cultural traditions of
gender roles had been and were enforced through law. The very
exclusion of women from the traditional understanding of basic
human rights (of conscience, speech, intimate association, and
work) appealed to an unjustly gendered conception of the person
that provided the uncritical benchmark for questions of equality;
the abolitionist feminist criticism of this exclusion crucially demanded that the background ideal of moral personality must not
assume such unjust culturally constructed differences, but the demands of moral personality reasonably accessible to all. The objection of this rights-based feminism to the trajectory of suffrage
feminism was precisely along these lines, namely, the temperance
and purity movements unjustly assumed gender differences that
failed to subject their claims to an appropriately reasonable standpoint on the demands of moral personality (to which all persons
are subject), thus enforcing not only sexism but racism and ethno-
centrism as well.[66]

Even the abolitionist feminists, however, appealed to those aspects of women's moral experience that, in their view, better stated
and enforced the appropriately demanding normative standpoint

---

against Private Sex Discrimination," *Minnesota Law Review* 61 (1977): 355–58. For
the background of such arguments, see Note, "The 'New' Thirteenth Amendment: A
Preliminary Analysis," *Harvard Law Review* 82 (1969): 1294; Note, "Jones v. Mayer:
The Thirteenth Amendment and the Federal Anti-Discrimination Laws," *Columbia
Law Review* 69 (1969): 1019. For a classic background historical study arguing for
the pivotal role of the Thirteenth Amendment in the structure of the Reconstruction
Amendments, see Jacobus tenBroek, "Thirteenth Amendment to the Constitution of
the United States: Consummation to Abolition and Key to the Fourteenth Amend-
ment," *California Law Review* 39 (1951): 171.

66. For an important exploration of this issue along these lines, see Jane Maslow
Cohen, "Regimes of Private Tyranny: What Do They Mean to Morality and for the
Criminal Law?" *University of Pittsburgh Law Review* 57 (1996): 757.

66. See, for further discussion, Richards, *Women, Gays, and the Constitution*,
chaps. 3–5.

of universal justice on issues of race and gender (for example, the appeal to white women's experience as wives and mothers to yield moral insight into the indignities inflicted on the intimate lives of African American men and women).[67] Such ideas of women's distinctive moral experience are often metaphors or tropes calling for interpretation, and lend themselves to quite inconsistent interpretations.[68] Abolitionist feminism suggests an interpretation that enhances appropriate respect for universal human rights.

Perhaps, as some contemporary feminists have argued,[69] some such arguments (exploring women's moral experience to enlarge public understanding of the critical demands of universal human rights) may be appropriate in our circumstances as well; arguments among contemporary feminists continue to debate for these reasons whether equality or difference feminism better advances justice.[70] Certainly, any reasonable concern for rights-based justice to women, in the related areas of family life and employment opportunities, must not assess such matters in terms of a superficially formal or neutral standard that, in fact, imposes an uncritical masculine standard either of family responsibilities or of competitive success in work that reflects injustice in the conception of the fair distribution of basic rights and opportunities of intimate life and of work.[71] Indeed, insistence on standards of formal equality may, in the area of race as much as gender, perpetuate and not deconstruct structural injustice when, for example, they are used to condemn programs (like affirmative action) that reasonably remedy such injustice or to rationalize standards of review that fail appro-

---

67. Ibid., 82–85, 282.

68. For example, the idea of protecting the home, which was used by temperance women to advocate constitutional entrenchment of Prohibition, was later used by women to urge constitutional repeal of Prohibition. For recent illuminating discussion of this paradoxical ideological point, see Kenneth D. Rose, *American Women and the Repeal of Prohibition* (New York: New York University Press, 1996), 63–89.

69. For an argument along these lines, see Sara Ruddick, *Maternal Thinking: Towards a Politics of Peace* (Boston: Beacon Press, 1989).

70. For some sense of the range of views among contemporary feminists on the merits of equality versus difference feminism in contemporary circumstances, see Marianne Hirsch and Evelyn Fox Keller, *Conflicts in Feminism* (New York: Routledge, 1990).

71. See, for an incisive general argument to this effect, Susan Moller Okin, *Justice, Gender, and the Family* (New York: Basic Books, 1989).

priately to identify and condemn racist and sexist motives as unacceptable grounds for state action.[72] Nothing in rights-based liberalism, as I understand and defend it in this work, weds it to either the advocacy of formal equality or, as my earlier argument about the Thirteenth Amendment shows, the defense of conventional views of the public/private distinction in interpreting the scope of constitutional principles that condemn prejudices rooted in moral slavery; rather, such liberalism, in my judgment, best explains why formal equality or the public/private distinction often fail to do justice to these issues.

On the other hand, Second Wave feminism arises from skepticism about the abusive use of uncritical conceptions of gender roles to abridge the basic rights of both women and men. We need to be both interpretively charitable and yet appropriately critical of the force of such women-centered arguments in the history of American feminism. Such interpretations of women's roles were not only empowering of voice but often rooted in strategic political judgments based on some real concerns (for example, interspousal violence linked to alcohol abuse). Yet such an insular politics, however historically understandable, also often ideologically obfuscated basic issues of human rights in service of reinforcing uncritical conceptions of gender roles that legitimated sexism as well as racism along various dimensions.[73] In light of this historical experience and our contemporary interpretive concerns for articulating and elaborating common antiracist and antisexist constitutional principles properly contextualized in our circumstances, we must, at least as a matter of constitutional law, set a high standard of skepticism for the enforcement through law of conventional gender roles particularly when such roles are alleged uncritically to reflect the appropriate normative weight to be accorded natural facts like pregnancy or mothering.

The tradition of moral slavery, which abolitionist feminism identified and criticized, rationalized its subjugation of women in

---

72. See, for a fuller defense of this claim, including criticism of judicial opinions to the contrary, Richards, *Conscience and the Constitution*, 170–77; Richards, *Women, Gays, and the Constitution*, 285–87.

73. For fuller discussion of this point, see Richards, *Women, Gays, and the Constitution*, chap. 4.

terms of the unjust interpretation accorded pregnancy. The ground for the abridgment of basic rights of conscience, speech, association, and work was the reduction of women solely to this biological possibility as a kind of fate; such consignment did not even acknowledge their basic equal rights of moral personality, in terms of which they might rationally and reasonably decide (against a background of equal justice and fair opportunity in public and private life) what weight, if any, this biological possibility, among manifold other such possibilities, should and would play in their conception of a good and ethical life. Against this background, any interpretation given pregnancy, as a basis for the differential treatment, must be skeptically scrutinized to insure that it does not unjustly impose an uncritical conception of gender roles that enforces, rather than contests the traditional moral slavery of women.[74]

It is in light of these concerns that we may reasonably understand and evaluate the judicial elaboration of antisexist principles to condemn public legitimation of the way traditional gender roles defined domesticity, including entitlements to caretaking women as such. A number of these cases involved benefits keyed to the understanding of domesticity in terms of a gendered dichotomy between ideal worker and caretaking spouse: a statutory preference for males to be administrators of decedents' estates;[75] a policy that servicemen, but not servicewomen, had the automatic right to

74. For an opinion that failed to observe the appropriate level of skeptical scrutiny about these issues, see *Michael M. v. Superior Court*, 450 U.S. 464 (1981). But see Frances Olsen, "Statutory Rape: A Feminist Critique of Rights Analysis," *Texas Law Review* 63 (1984): 387. For related opinions that also fail to observe the appropriate level of scrutiny, see *Geduldig v. Aiello*, 417 U.S. 484 (1974) (exclusion of pregnancy from California's disability insurance system held constitutional); *General Electric Co. v. Gilbert*, 429 U.S. 125 (1976) (holding that Title VII of the Civil Rights Act of 1964 did not bar exclusions of pregnancies from private disability plans); but see *Nashville Gas Co. v. Satty*, 434 U.S. 136 (1977) (*Gilbert* distinguished in case where pregnant employees were not only required to take pregnancy leaves and denied sick pay while on leave, but also lost all accumulated job seniority when they returned to work). The *Gilbert* holding was overturned by Congress when it amended Title VII in 1978; see 92 Stat. 2076. For a recent decision that gives proper weight to the relevant considerations, see *International Union v. Johnson Controls, Inc.*, 499 U.S. 187 (1991) (violation of Title VII for an employer to preclude women from holding certain jobs because of a fear that those jobs would endanger the health of a fetus).

75. *Reed v. Reed*, 404 U.S. 71 (1971).

claim their spouses as dependents for purposes of eligibility for housing and medical benefits;[76] a policy allowing mothers, but not fathers, to claim survivors' benefits to care for the decedent's children;[77] and policies that automatically awarded survivors' benefits to women but not men.[78] In all these cases, the gender distinctions were struck down as unconstitutional; a program designed to help women marginalized by traditional gender roles would have to be drafted as a program to help caregivers not as a program to help women as such. Moreover in these and other cases, the condemnation extends to gender stereotypy as such whether immediately harmful to women or to men.[79]

These cases reflect a principled interpretation and condemnation of sexism in terms of the unjust construction of gender roles by the enforcement of such roles through law on both women and men. If the mythological idealization of women's roles was the price exacted to obfuscate this injustice, we must address this ideological problem in terms of the common grounds of basic human rights reasonably available to all persons. An insistence on functional categories, in terms of which the rights and responsibilities of both men and women may be understood and evaluated, corresponds to this critical imperative of justice. That men as well as women may benefit from such assessment confirms its justice, in particular, that it addresses the ideological problem posed by the rights-denying structural injustice of sexism.

The injustice is not based in biological sex or biology at all (any more than racism is rooted in biology), but in a cultural tradition that has defined and enforced gender and its significance in ways that have divided men and women from their common humanity by appeal to stereotypes that rationalize structural injustice. Sexism as much distorts the life of women as it does that of men in

---

76. *Frontiero v. Richardson,* 411 U.S. 677 (1973).

77. *Weinberger v. Weisenfeld,* 420 U.S. 636 (1975).

78. *Califano v. Goldfarb,* 430 U.S. 199 (1977); *Wengler v. Druggists Mutual Insurance Co.,* 446 U.S. 142 (1980).

79. For cases that protect women from such harm, see *Reed* (right to administer estates); *Frontiero* (dependency allowances to servicewomen); *Stanton v. Stanton,* 421 U.S. 7 (1975) (child support for education). For cases that protect men, see *Wengler* (widower's right to death benefits); *Craig v. Boren,* 429 U.S. 190 (1976) (age of drinking for men).

THE GENDER ANALOGY 65

the same way, as Du Bois observed, racism as much deforms the image of African Americans as it does the image of white America. It is for this reason, as we have seen, that rights-based constitutional protest of the terms of one's moral slavery transforms not only one's own identity, as an African American or a woman, but the identity of Americans (as white, or as masculine). The theory and practice of such protest includes challenge to the cultural weight of race and gender as ethical dichotomies. Such challenge to the weight of gender reasonably includes critical appeal to principles of justice that affirm the common rights and responsibilities of all. Only principles of this sort correspond critically to addressing the depth of the structural injustice. Understanding the constitutional evil of sexism in this way not only illuminates authoritative case law, but also suggests the role that the analogy of gender might play in addressing constitutional issues relating to sexual orientation.

THE ANALOGY BETWEEN GENDER AND SEXUAL ORIENTATION

Sexism, as a constitutional evil, informs in several related ways a reasonable understanding of the case for gay rights. First, the issues of identity, so important in understanding the suspectness of gender, illuminate issues of identity of the case for gay rights. Second, the grounds for skepticism about state purposes, developed in areas of gender (both protecting basic rights and in constitutional suspicion about traditional grounds for abridging such rights), apply, as a matter of principle, to related areas in the case of sexual orientation. Indeed, several of the familiar ways in which the constitutional evils of racism and sexism were constructed (namely, the distortion of the public/private distinction, segregation, antimiscegenation) reasonably inform understanding of the constitutional evil of homophobia. In these important respects, the analogy of gender crucially sets the stage for making the full case for gay rights in the next chapter.

As we have seen, sexism has achieved the status it has, as a constitutional evil, because of the unjust burdens thus placed on pivotal identifications of moral personality, in particular, those associated with gender identity. Gender identity has been accorded this constitutional status because rights-based protest to the structural injustice of sexism was aimed at the terms unjustly imposed on such identity. The terms of such injustice included imposing on gender a script that not only excluded women as such from the status of bearers of basic human rights of conscience, speech, association, and work, but did so on grounds of depersonalizing stereotypes that, in a vicious circle, reflected such dehumanization. The consequence of such injustice was to impose a natural hierarchy keyed to gender on human consciousness and life and to make of any deviation from such hierarchy, literally, an unnatural and inhuman act.[80]

The rights-based protest of the terms of such injustice has thus, crucially, attacked such naturalization of injustice. Indeed, such protest, made on the grounds of the basic human rights the injustice structurally denied, demanded exactly the scope of self-defining personal and ethical choice of identity, on rational and reasonable terms, that self-originating claims based on human rights call for. Sexism is the profound constitutional evil that it is now acknowledged to be because it submerged and silenced the freedom and reason of a deliberative autonomous choice of a good and ethical life of half the human race. Gender identity is so pivotal a feature of this constitutional development because its very terms (as a form of identity) makes the appropriate normative space for raising the questions that addressing the evil of sexism requires of us. Persons afflicted by this injustice must be guaranteed a respect for their basic human rights that allows them not only to contest the traditional naturalization of such injustice, but the normative resources to acknowledge the range of rational and reasonable choice of gender identity, as an identity, available to them, as a free and equal rational persons endowed with basic human rights.

The operative point is not that gender, any more than race, is immutable and salient, for, as we have seen (chapter 1), many

---

80. See, for example, Horace Bushnell, *Women Suffrage: The Reform against Nature* (New York: Charles Scribner and Co., 1869).

other things about us are both and yet raise no comparable issues of structural injustice. The point is that gender, like race, is freighted with an impersonal script whose cultural power draws its force from a naturalization of injustice, denying any space for coming to understand and claim the basic human rights that rationally and reasonably contest the naturalized terms of such injustice.

This script accords gender a totalizing force in the shape of human lives, marked by a gender-based dichotomy in the choices and opportunities that define the personal and ethical meaning and value of human lives. The burdens thus placed on gender identity (namely, insistence on rigid conformity to the impersonal script) raise such profound issues of structural injustice, like the comparable burdens placed on racial identity, because the cultural imposition of the impersonal script derives its totalizing force from the abridgment of the basic human rights of conscience, speech, intimate life, and work that might rationally and reasonably contest the script. In particular, the abridgment of conscience, as in the area of race, takes on such importance in understanding the unjust political force of sexism because denial of the free exercise of the rational and reasonable powers of conscience to a class of persons makes possible the enforcement of a tightly scripted conception of gender against either the persons or the kinds of arguments that might rationally and reasonably contest it. Literally, thoughts, feelings, arguments, and critical debate—the resources of a life lived from an internal sense of rationally and reasonably tested personal and ethical conviction—are rendered unthinkable.

It is against this background of structural injustice, once we have come to acknowledge and address it as an intolerable constitutional evil, that the terms of gender identity become so important an object of constitutional concern. Gender identity takes on the significance that it now constitutionally has for us because rectifying this injustice crucially calls both for extending basic human rights of conscience, speech, intimate life, and work to persons that reasonably contest the gender orthodoxy, and for skeptical assessment of the enforcement through law of the gender orthodoxy itself (imposing, as it does, rigid burdens on gender identity). For these reasons, all the terms of the gender orthodoxy must become contestable and contested, making space, in particular, for the free

exercise of rational and reasonable conviction about how and on
what terms gender should and will play a role in the shape of a
good and ethical life in light of choices and opportunities fairly
available to all consistent with equal respect for basic human rights
of conscience, speech, intimate life, and work. The interpretation
of one's gender identity thus becomes possible and thinkable not
as an externally imposed natural script or fact of nature to be con-
formed to, but as an intensely personal matter calling for the responsible exercise of one's moral powers of freedom and reason,
consistent with respect for human rights, both in reflecting on
one's desires, needs, and talents and in critically independent assessment of and revision of the cultural terms of gender as a force
in the shape of one's life.

One's gender identity becomes, for this reason, so profoundly
personal a matter because the issues, traditionally governed by the
impersonal script, now are so exquisitely and intimately personal,
indeed, for many of us, at what we self-identify as the core of our
sense of ourselves as an ethically responsible person and agent.
The issues of gender identity now open to deliberative choice
and debate—conscience, speech, intimate life, and work—are the
questions raised and addressed when we think of ourselves, as all
persons do, as responsible for finding personal and ethical meaning
in living and thus, over all, in life itself.

There is, of course, no necessary conceptual linkage between
gender identity and sexual orientation; one may have a secure
sense of one's identity as a man or as a woman and also as either
heterosexual or homosexual. The relationship, if any, between
gender identity and sexual orientation and practice has differed
and differs among human cultures; in ancient Greece, one's identity as a man was consistent with both heterosexuality and homosexuality; indeed, ancient Greek culture not only tolerated, but
idealized pederastic male homosexual relations as important elements in Greek pedagogy and artistic and political culture (only
passivity in same-sex relations was inconsistent with adult male
gender identity).[81] The relationship between gender identity and

---

81. Important studies include William Armstrong Percy III, *Pederasty and Pedagogy
in Archaic Greece* (Urbana: University of Illinois Press, 1996); Kenneth J. Dover, *Greek*

sexual orientation is thus historically contingent. But such historical contingencies (as in the areas of race and gender) are sometimes culturally profound, indeed constitutive of patterns of structural injustice that we now, on grounds of constitutional principle, condemn. If our cultural linkage of acceptable gender identity and sexual orientation implicates such injustice (for example, sexism), it should be equally questioned and condemned.

In the contemporary American culture that is of concern to us, the unjust cultural construction and enforcement of an impersonal script of gender orthodoxy has historically been and continues to be freighted, on sexist grounds, with a rigid script of heterosexuality. The script has importantly been coded in the terms of gender: being gay has thus been coded and indeed stigmatized as improperly (or unthinkably or unnaturally) a woman—and a fallen woman (a prostitute)⁸² at that—and being a lesbian coded as (unnaturally) a man.⁸³ Such coding raises fundamental issues of justice for homosexuals as well as heterosexuals because its enforcement through law, as compulsory heterosexuality, is an important structural feature of the unjust imposition of the gender orthodoxy itself.⁸⁴

I earlier argued that authoritative American case law now interprets the constitutional evil of sexism in terms of the unjust enforcement of gender stereotypes on both men and women and defended that view as a principled interpretation of the structural

Popular Morality in the Time of Plato and Aristotle (Oxford: Basil Blackwell, 1974); Kenneth J. Dover, *Greek Homosexuality* (London: Duckworth, 1978); Kenneth J. Dover, "Greek Homosexuality and Initiation," in *The Greeks and Their Legacy* (Oxford: Blackwell, 1988), 115–34; Peter Green, "Sex and Classical Literature," in *Classical Bearings: Interpreting Ancient History and Culture* (New York: Thames and Hudson, 1989), 130–50; Eva Cantarella, *Bisexuality in the Ancient World,* trans. Cormac O'Cuilleanain (New Haven: Yale University Press, 1992); David M. Halperin, *One Hundred Years of Homosexuality: and Other Essays on Greek Love* (New York: Routledge, 1990); David M. Halperin, John J. Winkler, and Froma I. Zeitlin, eds., *Before Sexuality: The Construction of Erotic Experience in the Ancient Greek World* (Princeton: Princeton University Press, 1990).

82. On the coding of male homosexuality as prostitution, see Richards, *Women, Gays, and the Constitution,* 295–97, 300, 310, 329, 370, 433, 443, 447, 461.

83. For the general historical background of this gender stereotyping of gays and lesbians, see ibid., 289–97.

84. For an important statement of this position, see Adrienne Rich, "Compulsory Heterosexuality and Lesbian Existence," in Catharine R. Stimpson and Ethel Spector Person, *Women: Sex and Sexuality* (Chicago: University of Chicago Press, 1980), 62–91.

injustice of sexism. That interpretation reasonably extends, as a matter of principle, to all forms of the enforcement of gender stereotypes that unjustly entrench the structure injustice of an indefensible gender orthodoxy. One of the ways in which the gender orthodoxy erases questioning of its injustice is by rendering unthinkable and thus unspeakable claims that sexual and intimate relations might be conducted free of the hierarchy in these matters demanded by the gender orthodoxy.

Modernist scapegoating of homosexuals, in terms of the gender orthodoxy, historically arose in the early modern period (as a reaction to growing political acceptance of universal principles of human rights) as one way, among others, of domesticating claims for gender equality in terms that could normatively resist rights-based arguments that pressed for equality of basic human rights between men and women,[85] including equal rights and opportunities in both private and public life. The way ideologically to achieve such a truncated public understanding of gender equality and of human rights was to render unthinkable serious debate about the structural injustice we call sexism, including its ideologically driven interpretation of the public/private distinction as a male/female distinction.

The most important ideological mechanism for such truncation was the development of an idealized stereotype of women's higher moral nature, as wife and mother, a stereotype that usefully rationalized the inapplicability to the assessment of gender roles of basic values of human rights.[86] The modernist scapegoating of homosexuals further reinforced the stereotype by rendering unthinkable the kinds of relations between men or between women or between men and women that would challenge the stereotype both of rigid gender hierarchy and the public/private ideology that supports it. If the values of sexual intimacy could be realized in same-sex relations, such relations need no longer be structured by the inequality of genders required by the idealizing stereotype of the nature of

85. See Richards, *Women, Gays, and the Constitution*, 294–97. For an important recent study of this development, see Randolph Trumbach, *Sex and the Gender Revolution* (Chicago: University of Chicago Press, 1998), vol. 1.

86. See, for elaboration of this ideological development and its malign political consequences, Richards, *Women, Gays, and the Constitution*, chap. 4.

gender, nor need the relations between men and women either in or outside private life be rigidly defined as essentially romantic and sexual (as the stereotype required). Neither public nor private life could any longer be reasonably confined to the rigid terms of the gender stereotype, which must now itself be impartially assessed in terms of requirements of equal rights and opportunities. The condemnation of homosexuality (on the basis of its deviation from gender stereotypes) expresses and enforces sexism not only on homosexuals but on heterosexuals as well, removing from reasonable public discourse serious discussion of conducting public and private life on terms of gender equality. The most principled understanding of the evil of sexism accordingly requires that we interpret the scope of injustice as not only inflicted on men as well as women but on heterosexuals as well of homosexuals.

For this reason, in a culture like ours that thus codes homosexuality in terms of unjust gender stereotypes, the experience of one's identity as a homosexual will raise issues of one's gender identity as well. On the analysis of the constitutional evil of sexism I have proposed, rights-based protest of the stigmatized terms of one's identity, as gay or lesbian, may plausibly be structured as well in terms of a rights-based protest of the unjust cultural terms of one's gender identity, viz., as a protest of a form or manifestation of sexism. If such protest is of sexism, the personal and ethical issues of identity will be at least as profound as those of our now conventional understanding of issues of race or gender. Certainly, abridgment of the rights of conscience, speech, intimate life, and work has been as complete in the case of homosexuals as it has historically been for African Americans and heterosexual women, and the grounds for such abridgment depend on dehumanizing stereotypes analogous to those that supported racism and sexism. If so, the issues of identity, for gays and lesbians, work at a level at least as profound as those for racial minorities or heterosexual women.

The struggle for justice here, as elsewhere, must engage personal and ethical resources of thought, feeling, reason, and conviction in the self-defining reconstruction of identity against an impersonal script of naturalized injustice that has reduced the moral complexity of homosexual passion, love, and life to the crude and objectifying measure of a sexist fantasy (see chapter 4). The protest of such injustice must extend as broadly and deeply as the injustice itself, critically addressing the yet unexplored issues of sexism that still popularly sustain such structural injustice. The object of such protest is here, as elsewhere, not the immutability and salience of the basis for the injustice, but the unjust imposition of an impersonal script of gender and sexuality on grounds that naturalize injustice.

The case for gay rights is properly understood, like Du Bois on antiracism and Friedan on antisexism, as a rights-based struggle for personal and ethical identity on terms of justice against objectifying sexist stereotypes rationalized as natural. To make claims in this spirit is not to reflect an identity which is somehow naturally given, but, quite the opposite, to protest the cultural stereotype of naturally given differences that, in a vicious circle, rationalize injustice. Making such protests on such grounds is to forge an identity, as a responsible moral agent, through the deliberative free exercise of one's moral powers of rationality and reasonableness.

The analogy of sexism thus clarifies, indeed explains the identity-based focus of the case for gay rights. But the case for gay rights is incomplete without further examination of the inadequate grounds traditionally supposed to rationalize abridgment of such rights. I will explore such grounds further in the next chapter, and have already suggested reasons for thinking that such grounds include sexism. The analogy of sexism affords yet further illumination both in terms of its case for protection of basic rights and its skepticism about traditional grounds for abridgment of such rights. I focus here on two such issues: the right to intimate life, and the construction of the structural injustice of sexism.

In 1965 the Supreme Court in *Griswold v. Connecticut*[87] constitutionalized the argument for a basic human right to contraception that had been persistently and eloquently advocated by Margaret Sanger for well over forty years (a decision which Sanger lived to see).[88] The Court extended the right to cover abortion services in

---

87. 381 U.S. 479 (1965).
88. See Ellen Chesler, *Woman of Valor: Margaret Sanger and the Birth Control Movement in America* (New York: Anchor, 1992), 11, 230, 376, 467.

1973 in *Roe v. Wade*[89] (reaffirming its central principle in 1992[90]), and denied its application in 1986 to consensual homosexual sex acts in *Bowers v. Hardwick;*[91] a related form of analysis was used, albeit inconclusively, in cases involving the right to die.[92] Three of these cases (contraception, abortion, homosexuality) can be understood on the grounds of a basic right to intimate personal life, one of them (death) involving another basic right (an aspect of the right to life or meaningful life).[93] I focus here on the first three cases.

Sanger's argument for the right to contraception was very much rooted in rights-based feminism.[94] Sanger's opponents certainly made that point very clear. When her then husband, Bill Sanger, was convicted of obscenity for distributing one of his wife's publications, the judge emphasized that the dispute was over woman's role:

> Your crime is not only a violation of the laws of man, but of the law of God as well, in your scheme to prevent motherhood. Too many persons have the idea that it is wrong to have children. Some women are so selfish that they do not want to be bothered with them. If some persons would go around and urge Christian women to bear children, instead of wasting their time on woman suffrage, this city and society would be better off.[95]

Sanger's argument had two prongs, both of which were implicit in the Supreme Court's decisions in *Griswold* and later cases: first, a basic human right to intimate life and the role of the right to

---

89. 410 U.S. 113 (1973).
90. See *Planned Parenthood of Southeastern Pennsylvania v. Casey*, 505 U.S. 833 (1992).
91. 478 U.S. 186 (1986).
92. See *Cruzan v. Director, Missouri Dept. of Health*, 496 U.S. 261 (1990). Justice Rehnquist, writing for a 5–4 majority, accepts that a right to die exists and applies to the case but denies that the state has imposed an unreasonable restriction on the right on the facts of the case. But see *Vacco v. Quill*, 117 S. Ct. 2293 (1997) (unanimously upholding prohibition on physician assisted suicide).
93. For further discussion, see David A. J. Richards, *Sex, Drugs, Death, and the Law: An Essay on Human Rights and Overcriminalization* (Totowa, N.J.: Rowman and Littlefield, 1982), 215–70.
94. For elaboration of this point, see Richards, *Women, Gays, and the Constitution*, 178–81.
95. Chesler, *Woman of Valor*, 127.

contraception as an instance of that right; and second, the assessment of whether laws abridging such a fundamental right met the heavy burden of secular justification that was required.

The fundamental human right to intimate life was, as Lydia Maria Child, Stephen Andrews, and Victoria Woodhull had earlier made clear,[96] as basic an inalienable right of moral personality (respect for which is central to the argument for toleration) as the right to conscience. Like the right to conscience, it protects intimately personal moral resources (thoughts and beliefs, intellect, emotions, self-image and self-identity) and the way of life that expresses and sustains them in facing and meeting rationally and reasonably the challenge of a life worth living—one touched by enduring personal and ethical value. The right to intimate life protects these moral resources as they bear on the role of loving and being loved in the tender and caring exfoliation of moral personality, morally finding one's self, as a person, in love for and the love of another moral self.

The human right of intimate life was not only an inalienable human right in the argument for toleration, but a right interpretively implicit in the historical traditions of American rights-based constitutionalism. In both of the two great revolutionary moments that framed the trajectory of American constitutionalism (the American Revolution and the Civil War), the right to intimate life was one of the basic human rights the abridgment of which rendered political power illegitimate and gave rise to the Lockean right to revolution.[97]

At the time of the American Revolution, the background literature on human rights, known to and assumed by the American revolutionaries and founding constitutionalists, included what the influential Scottish philosopher Francis Hutcheson called "the natural right each one to enter into the matrimonial relation with any one who consents."[98] Indeed, John Witherspoon, whose lec-

---

96. For citations and discussion, see Richards, *Women, Gays, and the Constitution*, chap. 4.

97. See, on American revolutionary constitutionalism as framed by these events, David A. J. Richards, *Foundations of American Constitutionalism* (New York: Oxford University Press, 1989); Richards, *Conscience and the Constitution*.

98. See Francis Hutcheson, *A System of Moral Philosophy* (1755; New York: Augustus M. Kelley, 1968), 299.

tures Madison heard at Princeton, followed Hutcheson in listing even more abstractly as a basic human and natural right a "right to associate, if he so incline, with any person or persons, whom he can persuade (not force)—under this is contained the right to marriage."[99] Accordingly, leading statesmen at the state conventions ratifying the Constitution, both those for and against adoption, assumed that the Constitution could not interfere in the domestic sphere. Alexander Hamilton of New York denied that federal constitutional law did or could "penetrate the recesses of domestic life, and control, in all respects, the private conduct of individuals."[100] And Patrick Henry of Virginia spoke of the core of our rights to liberty as the sphere where a person "enjoys the fruits of his labor, under his own fig-tree, with his wife and children around him, in peace and security."[101] The arguments of reserved rights both of leading proponents (Hamilton) and opponents (Henry) of adoption of the Constitution thus converged on the private sphere of domestic married life.

At the time of the Civil War, the understanding of marriage as a basic human right took on a new depth and urgency because of the antebellum abolitionist rights-based attack on the peculiar nature of American slavery; such slavery failed to recognize the marriage or family rights of slaves,[102] and indeed inflicted on the black family the moral horror of breaking them up by selling family members separately.[103] One in six slave marriages thus were ended by force or sale.[104] No aspect of American slavery more dramatized its radical evil for abolitionists and Americans more generally than its brutal deprivation of intimate personal life, including undermining the moral authority of parents over children.

---

99. See John Witherspoon, *Lectures of Moral Philosophy*, ed. Jack Scott (East Brunswick, N.J.: Associated University Presses, 1982), 123. For further development of this point, see Richards, *Toleration and the Constitution*, 232–33.

100. See Jonathan Elliot, *The Debates in the Several State Conventions on the Adoption of the Federal Constitution* (Washington, D.C.: Printed for the Editor, 1836), 2:269.

101. Ibid., 3:54.

102. See Kenneth M. Stampp, *The Peculiar Institution* (New York: Vintage, 1956), 198, 340–49; Eugene D. Genovese, *Roll, Jordan, Roll: The World the Slaves Made* (New York: Vintage Books, 1974), 32, 52–53, 125, 451–58.

103. See Stampp, *The Peculiar Institution*, 199–207, 333, 348–49; Herbert G. Gutman, *The Black Family in Slavery and Freedom, 1750–1925* (New York: Vintage Books, 1976), 146, 318, 349.

104. See Gutman, *The Black Family in Slavery and Freedom*, 318.

Slaves, Weld argued, had "as little control over them [children], as have domestic animals over the disposal of their young."[105] Slavery, thus understood as an attack on intimate personal life,[106] stripped persons of essential attributes of their humanity.

It is against this historical background (as well as background rights-based political theory) that it is interpretively correct to regard the right to intimate life as one of the unenumerated rights protected both by the Ninth Amendment and the Privileges and Immunities Clause of the Fourteenth Amendment, as Justice Harlan may be regarded as arguing in his concurrence in *Griswold*.[107] The Supreme Court quite properly interpreted the Fourteenth Amendment in particular as protecting this basic human right against unjustified state abridgment, and, as Sanger had urged, regarding the right to use contraceptives as an instance of this right. The right to contraception was, for Sanger, so fundamental a human right for women because it would enable women, perhaps for the first time in human history, reliably to decide whether and when their sexual lives will be reproductive. Respect for this right was an aspect of the more basic right of intimate life in two ways. First, it would enable women to exercise control over their intimate relations to men, deciding whether and when such relations will be reproductive. Second, it would secure to women the right to decide whether and when they will form the intimate relationship to a child. Both forms of choice threatened the traditional gender-defined role of women's sexuality as both exclusively and mandatorily procreational and maternally self-sacrificing, and were resisted, as by Bill Sanger's judge, for that reason.

But second, this human right, like other such rights, may only be regulated or limited on terms of public reason not themselves

---

105. See Theodore Weld, *American Slavery as It Is* (1839; New York: Arno Press, 1968), 56.

106. See Ronald G. Walters, *The Antislavery Appeal: American Abolitionism after 1830* (New York: W. W. Norton, 1978), 95–96.

107. Justice Harlan, in fact, grounds his argument on the Due Process Clause of the Fourteenth Amendment, but the argument is more plausibly understood, as a matter of text, history, and political theory, as based on the Privileges and Immunities Clause of the Fourteenth Amendment for reasons I give in chapter 6 of *Conscience and the Constitution*. For further elaboration of this interpretation of *Griswold*, see Richards, *Toleration and the Constitution*, 256–61.

hostage to an entrenched political hierarchy (for example, compulsorily arranged marriages[108]) depending on the abridgment of such rights. For example, from the perspective of the general abolitionist criticism of slavery and racism, the pro-slavery arguments in support of Southern slavery's treatment of family life were transparently inadequate, not remotely affording adequate public justification for the abridgment of such a fundamental right.

These arguments were in their nature essentially racist:

His natural affection is not strong, and consequently he is cruel to his own offspring, and suffers little by separation from them.[109]

Another striking trait of negro character is lasciviousness. Lust is his strongest passion; and hence, rape is an offence of too frequent occurrence. Fidelity to the marriage relation they do not understand and do not expect, neither in their native country nor in a state of bondage.[110]

The blind moral callousness of Southern pro-slavery thought was nowhere more evident than its treatment of what were in fact agonizing, crushing, and demeaning family separations[111]:

He is also liable to be separated from wife or child . . . —but from native character and temperament, the separation is much less severely felt.[112]

With regard to the separation of husbands and wives, parents and children, . . . Negroes are themselves both perverse and comparatively indifferent about this matter.[113]

The irrationalist racist sexualization of black slaves was evident in the frequent justification of slavery in terms of maintaining the

108. See Werner Sollors, *Beyond Ethnicity: Consent and Descent in American Culture* (New York: Oxford University Press, 1986), 112.
109. Thomas R. R. Cobb, *An Inquiry into the Law of Negro Slavery in the United States of America* (1858; New York: Negro Universities Press, 1968), 39.
110. Ibid., 40.
111. See, in general, Gutman, *The Black Family in Slavery and Freedom*.
112. See William Harper, "Memoir on Slavery," in *The Ideology of Slavery: Proslavery Thought in the Antebellum South, 1830–1860,* ed. Drew Gilpin Faust (Baton Rouge: Louisiana State University Press, 1981), 110.
113. See James Henry Hammond, "Letter to an English Abolitionist," in Faust, ed., *The Ideology of Slavery,* 191–92.

higher standards of sexual purity of Southern white women.[114] Viewed through the polemically distorted prism of such thought, the relation of master and slave was itself justified as an intimate relationship like husband and wife that should similarly be immunized from outside interference.[115] In this Orwellian world, where truth is distorted by power, the defense of slavery became the defense of freedom.[116] Arguments of these sorts assumed interpretations of facts and values completely hostage to the polemical defense of entrenched political institutions whose stability required the abridgment of basic rights of blacks and of any whites who ventured reasonable criticism of such institutions.

If the antebellum experience of state abridgments of basic rights informs a reasonable interpretation of the Privileges and Immunities Clause,[117] the protection of intimate personal life must be one among the basic human rights thus worthy of national protection. The remaining question is whether there is any adequate basis for the abridgment of so basic a right, namely, in the case of contraception, the right to decide whether or when one's sexual life will lead to offspring, indeed, to explore one's sexual and emotional life in personal life as an end in itself.

That right can only be justified by a compelling public reason, not on the grounds of reasons that are today sectarian (internal to a moral tradition not based on reasons available and accessible to all). In fact, the only argument that could sustain such laws (namely, the Augustinian[118] and Thomistic[119] view that it is immoral to en-

114. See, for example, Harper, "Memoir on Slavery,"107, 118–19; Hammond, "Letter to an English Abolitionist," 182–84.

115. See, for example, Thomas Roderick Dew, "Abolition of Negro Slavery," in Faust, ed., *The Ideology of Slavery*, 65; Harper, "Memoir on Slavery," 100 (citing Dew).

116. For a good general discussion of such inversions, see Kenneth S. Greenberg, *Masters and Statesman: The Political Culture of American Slavery* (Baltimore: The Johns Hopkins University Press, 1985).

117. For further defense of this position, see Richards, *Conscience and the Constitution*, chap. 6.

118. See Augustine, *The City of God*, trans. Henry Bettenson (Harmondsworth: Penguin, 1972), 577–94.

119. Thomas Aquinas elaborates Augustine's conception of the exclusive legitimacy of procreative sex in a striking way. Of the emission of semen apart from procreation in marriage, he wrote: "[A]fter the sin of homicide whereby a human nature already in existence is destroyed, this type of sin appears to take next place, for by it the generation

gage in nonprocreative sex) is not today a view of sexuality that can reasonably be enforced on people at large. Many people regard sexual love as an end in itself and the control of reproduction as a reasonable way to regulate when and whether they have children consistent with their own personal and larger ethical interests, that of their children, and of an overpopulated society at large. Even the question of having children at all is today a highly personal matter, certainly no longer governed by the perhaps once compelling secular need to have children for necessary work in a largely agrarian society with high rates of infant and adult mortality.[120] From the perspective of women in particular, as Sanger made so clear, the enforcement of an anticontraceptive morality on society at large not only harms women's interests but impersonally demeans them to a purely reproductive function; it deprives them of the rational dignity of deciding as moral agents and persons, perhaps for the first time in human history, whether, when, and on what terms they will have children consistent with their other legitimate aims and ambitions (including the free exercise of all their basic human rights). Political enforcement of such a morality assumes a now conspicuously sectarian conception of gender hierarchy in which women's sexuality is defined by mandatory procreative role and responsibility. That conception, the basis of the unjust construction of gender hierarchy, cannot reasonably be the measure of human rights today.[121]

Similar considerations explain the grounds for doubt about the putative public, nonsectarian justifications for laws criminalizing abortion and homosexual sexuality. Antiabortion laws, grounded in the alleged protection of a neutral good like "life," unreasonably equate the moral weight of a fetus in the early stages of pregnancy with that of a person and equate abortion with murder. Such laws fail to take seriously the weight that should be accorded a woman's

---

of human nature is precluded." Thomas Aquinas, *On the Truth of the Catholic Faith: Summa Contra Gentiles,* trans. Vernon Bourke (New York: Image, 1956), pt. 2, chap. 122(9), p. 146.

120. On how personal this decision now is, see, in general, Elaine Tyler May, *Barren in the Promised Land: Childless Americans and the Pursuit of Happiness* (New York: Basic Books, 1995).

121. For further discussion of the right to privacy and contraception, see Richards, *Toleration and the Constitution,* 256–61.

basic right to reproductive autonomy in making highly personal moral choices of her most intimate bodily and personal life against the background of the lack of reasonable public consensus that fetal life, as such, can be equated with that of a moral person.[122] Society has legitimate interests in giving weight at some point to fetal life as part of making a symbolic statement about the importance of taking the lives of children seriously and caring for them. These interests are analogous to the symbolic interest society may have in preventing cruelty to animals or in securing humane treatment to the irretrievably comatose to advance humane treatment of persons properly understood, but such interests do not constitutionally justify forbidding abortion as such throughout all stages of pregnancy.[123] Rather, they can be accorded their legitimate weight after a reasonable period has been allowed for the proper scope of a woman's exercise of her decision whether to have an abortion.

Once one takes seriously that fetal life is not a reasonable public value sufficient to outweigh the right of reproductive autonomy, the argument for criminalizing abortion is revealed to be not a constitutionally reasonable argument for regarding abortion as homicide, but a proxy for complex background assumptions often no longer reasonably believed in the society at large, namely, a now controversial, powerfully sectarian ideology about proper sexuality and gender roles. The moral arguments for the prohibition of abortion cluster around certain traditional conceptions of the natural processes of sexuality and gender. From this perspective, the prohibitions on abortion encumber what many now reasonably regard as a highly conscientious choice by women regarding their bodies, their sexuality and gender, and the nature and place of pregnancy, birth, and child rearing in their personal and ethical lives.

The traditional condemnation of abortion fails, at a deep ethical level, to take seriously the moral independence of women as free and rational persons, lending the force of law, like comparable anticontraceptive laws, to theological ideas of biological natural-

---

122. Ibid., 261–69; Ronald Dworkin, *Life's Dominion: An Argument about Abortion, Euthanasia, and Individual Freedom* (New York: Knopf, 1993), 3–178.

123. See Richards, *Toleration and the Constitution*, 266–67.

ness and one's fate (defined by gender hierarchy) that degrade the constructive moral powers of women themselves to establish the meaning of their sexual and reproductive life histories. The underlying conception appears to be at one with the sexist idea that women's minds and bodies are not their own but the property of others, namely, men or their masculine God, who may conscript them and their bodies, like cattle on the farm, for the greater good. The abortion choice is thus one of the choices essential to the just moral independence of women, centering their lives in a body image and aspirations expressive of their moral powers. The abortion choice is a just application of the right to intimate life, because the right to the abortion choice protects women from the traditional degradation of their moral powers, reflected in the assumptions underlying antiabortion laws.

Antihomosexuality laws have even less semblance of a public justification (like fetal life) that would be acceptably enforced on society at large and brutally abridge the sexual expression of the companionate loving relationships to which homosexuals, like heterosexuals, have an inalienable human right. That right encompasses the free moral powers through which persons forge enduring personal and ethical value in living a complete life. The decision in *Bowers v. Hardwick* was, for this reason, an interpretively unprincipled failure properly to elaborate the principle of constitutional privacy in an area of populist prejudice where the protection of that right was exigently required.[124]

In the background of the laws at issue in all these cases lies a normative view of gender roles. That is quite clear, as I earlier suggested, in *Griswold*, less obviously so in *Roe* and *Bowers*. On analysis, however, the little weight accorded women's interests and the decisive weight accorded the fetus in antiabortion laws make sense only against the background of the still powerful traditional conception of mandatory procreational, self-sacrificing, caring, and nurturant gender roles for women; it is its symbolic violation of that normative idea that imaginatively transforms abortion into murder. Similarly, the failure of the majority of the Supreme

---

124. For further discussion, see Richards, *Toleration and the Constitution*, 269–80; Richards, *Foundations of American Constitutionalism*, 202–47.

Court in *Bowers* to accord *any* weight whatsoever to the rights to privacy of homosexuals and decisive weight to incoherently anachronistic traditional moralism reflect, as we shall later see, a still powerful ideology of unnatural gender roles that renders homosexuals constitutionally invisible, voiceless, and marginal.

The gender analogy thus helps us to understand why intimate life now enjoys the status of a constitutionally protected right, and further usefully advances understanding of the role the abridgment of such a fundamental right importantly has played in the unjust construction of structural injustices like sexism and racism. Both the antiracist and antisexist struggles have included significant focus on protecting the right to intimate life on fair terms. Antislavery and antiracist argument, as we have seen, thus identified abridgment of the rights to marry and custody of children as components of the dehumanization of African Americans as cattle; and the long struggle against antimiscegenation laws, from Lydia Maria Child to Ida Wells-Barnett,[125] condemned the place of such laws and their enforcement in the unjust construction of a racialized mythology of gender (the sexual purity of white women versus the sexual impurity of black women); such enforcement rationalized, on the one hand, lynchings for what was often, in fact, consensual interracial sex between white women and black men and, on the other hand, de facto tolerance for what were often exploitative, even coercive sexual relations of white men to black women. Comparably, rights-based feminism, as we have seen, regarded unjust abridgment of the right to reproductive autonomy (both anticontraception and antiabortion laws) as constructive elements in the dehumanizing objectification of women in terms of compulsory heterosexuality and mandatory procreational roles. Securing constitutional recognition of women's rights to intimate life was thus not only intrinsically valuable on its own terms (as a basic human right extended on fair terms of principle to women), but instrumentally valuable in rectifying one of the cultural supports of the sexist devaluation of women as nonbearers of human rights.

---

125. For further discussion of Child, see Richards, *Women, Gays, and the Constitution,* 55–56, 115; of Wells-Barnett, see ibid., 185–90.

Both the antiracist and antisexist concerns for the right of intimate life suggest useful analogies for the case for gay rights that
may be brought into play in criticism of not only the legitimacy of
Bowers, but the populist political outrage at the idea of same-sex
marriage.[126] Andrew Koppelman has persuasively explored, in this
connection, the analogy of the antimiscegenation laws.[127] The prohibition of racial intermarriage was to the cultural construction of
racism what the prohibition of same-sex marriage is to sexism and
homophobia: "just as miscegenation was threatening because it
called into question the distinctive and superior status of being
white, homosexuality is threatening because it calls into question
the distinctive and superior status of being male."[128] The condemnation of same-sex intimacies (including same-sex marriage) is,
on this view, a crucial aspect of the cultural construction of the
dehumanization of homosexuals as a kind of fallen woman (for
further discussion, see chapter 3).[129]

Finally, the gender analogy, like the racial analogy, suggests the
general importance of segregation in sustaining long-standing
patterns of structural injustice. The segregation of African Americans and of women effectively constructed servile roles that walled
them off from access to basic rights of conscience, speech, intimate
life, and work, and unjustly rationalized it as "in the nature of
things." The operative analogy, for the case for gay rights, may
be not the servile roles culturally constructed for homosexuals to
occupy, but the absence of any such legitimate role (as an intolerable heresy to any acceptable values in living). Such radical illegitimacy suggests that, while the gender analogy clarifies many important features of the case for gay rights, there is another analogy
that must also be appealed to and elaborated in the full understanding of the normative case for gay rights: namely, the religious analogy.

126. For further discussion of this point, see ibid., 438–53.
127. See Andrew Koppelman, "The Miscegenation Analogy: Sodomy Laws as Sex
Discrimination," *Yale Law Journal* 98 (1988): 145.
128. Ibid., 159–60.
129. On the close ideological relationship between the condemnation of prostitution and homosexuality, see Richards, *Women, Gays, and the Constitution,* 295–97, 300,
310, 329, 370, 433, 443, 447, 461.

THREE

THE RELIGIOUS ANALOGY

The constitutional evil of both racism and sexism can, I have argued, be plausibly understood as an elaboration of the argument for toleration to identify and condemn structural injustice marked by two features: abridgment of basic human rights of conscience, speech, intimate life, and work of a certain class of persons, and rationalization thereof in terms of dehumanizing stereotypes unjustly derived from the culture of such abridgment. Rights-based protest of the terms of such injustice both challenges and transforms identity. The case for gay rights, as we shall see, is also based on such structural injustice, and its protests are similarly identity challenging and transforming.

Another aspect of the case for gay rights draws not only on the account of structural injustice which is, as we have seen, an elaboration of the argument for toleration, but directly on the argument for toleration itself. We can see this quite clearly in the way contemporary arguments for gay rights emerged after World War II in the wake of both the antiracist and antisexist movements earlier discussed. For the first time in American history, such arguments were not met with a brick wall of censorship.

Such censorship was the earlier American response to the pathbreaking arguments for gay rights in the poetry and prose of Walt Whitman, a moral vision that affirmed homosexual love on the ground of an interpretation of rights-based feminism (extending human rights to all irrespective of unjust gender stereotypes).[1] The

---

1. See, for fuller discussion of Whitman from this perspective, David A. J. Richards, *Women, Gays, and the Constitution: The Grounds for Feminism and Gay Rights in Culture and Law* (Chicago: University of Chicago Press, 1998), 297–310.

contrast between the European and American responses to Whitman illustrate the point dramatically. Whitman was reasonably interpreted, for example, in Great Britain by John Addington Symonds, Oscar Wilde, and Edward Carpenter as a visionary prophet of a new view of sexuality in general and of homosexuality in particular, one that called for the articulate development of arguments of gay rights that were, as by Carpenter, importantly linked to arguments of rights-based feminism.[2] At the same time, blatant American censorship through prominent obscenity prosecutions crushed any such correlative development in Whitman's own country.[3]

For example, Emma Goldman, inspired by Whitman, defended a rights-based feminism critical of the sectarian moralism and unjust gender stereotyping of suffrage feminism and, on that basis, affirmed the right to free love of women as well as homosexuals. She was subjected to repressive obscenity prosecutions and ultimately deported in 1919.[4] If any person were capable of forging in America the kind of "comrade-alliances"[5] between homosexuals and women that Carpenter had earlier urged in Britain, it was and would have been Goldman. But, in America, Goldman's views were interpreted as those of an antifeminist (meaning an anti-suffrage feminist) and an anti-American to boot. Carpenter's proposed rights-based alliances between women and homosexuals could hardly be even plausible in America in light of the censorship claims like those of Goldman suffered.

The contemporary movement in the United States for gay rights emerged decades later out of the growing sense of the rights of gays and lesbians fighting for their country in World War II[6] and afterward, in the wake of the antiracist and rights-based feminist movements, when broader protections of constitutional guarantees of conscience and speech were extended to dissent in matters of race and gender as well as sexuality.[7] In particular, for gays

2. Ibid., 311–27.

3. Ibid., 327–37; on the repressive role of such obscenity prosecutions, see ibid., 14, 161, 163, 168, 172, 178–79, 181, 238–44, 298, 316, 329–30, 431.

4. Ibid., 156, 173–78, 181, 238–39, 329–30.

5. Ibid., 324.

6. See, on this point, Allan Berube, *Coming Out under Fire: The History of Gay Men and Women in World War Two* (New York: Free Press, 1990.

7. See, for fuller discussion of this development, Richards, *Women, Gays, and the Constitution*, 238–44, 337–73.

and lesbians, such broader protections of conscience and speech gave rise to the increasingly prominent role in contemporary arguments for gay rights of self-identifying claims to a gay and lesbian identity on terms of justice,[8] which made possible as well the rediscovery and exploration of the common grounds between rights-based feminism and the case for gay rights (for example, in this work among others).[9] The crucial importance of such identity-based claims in the contemporary case for gay rights is best understood as an expression of the inalienable right to conscience; and some contemporary forms of political aggression against gay rights (specifically targeted at such identity-based assertions of basic human rights) must be understood correspondingly as the expression through public law of constitutionally forbidden religious intolerance. Accordingly, I examine here the role the argument for toleration plays in understanding such identity-based claims for gay rights, and also examine anti-lesbian/gay initiatives as well as the exclusions of gays and lesbians from the military and from marriage in light of this perspective.

As we earlier saw (chapter 1), the argument for toleration calls for constraints of principle to be placed on the power of the state to enforce sectarian religious views because the enforcement of such views on society at large entrenched, as the measure of legitimate convictions in matters of conscience, irrationalist intolerance; such intolerance was unjustly rationalized by limiting standards of debate and speakers to the sectarian measure that supported dominant political authority. The rights-based evil of such intolerance was its unjust abridgment of the inalienable right to conscience, the free exercise of the moral powers of rationality and reasonableness in terms of which persons define personal and ethical meaning in living. While this human right, like others, may be abridged on grounds of secular goods reasonably acknowledged as such by all persons (irrespective of other philosophical or evaluative disagreements), a sectarian view is not sufficient.

The argument for toleration underlies and clarifies the place

8. See, on this point, Nan D. Hunter, "Identity, Speech, and Equality," *Virginia Law Review* 79 (1993): 1695.

9. See, for fuller exploration of the development of this theme, Richards, *Women, Gays, and the Constitution*, 288–457.

and weight of the central human rights protected as constitutional rights by the U.S. Constitution, as amended, in particular, the rights of conscience and free speech protected by the First Amendment and the right to intimate life protected by the Ninth and Fourteenth Amendments.[10] The American constitutional tradition of the protection of the right to conscience is a particularly robust one, rooted, as it is, in the guarantees of religious liberty found in the First Amendment, whose clauses protect different aspects of the exercise of the right to conscience. The Free Exercise Clause thus addresses the exercise of settled conscientious convictions, condemning as suspect state burdens placed on the exercise of such convictions unsupported by a compelling secular justification;[11] and its companion Establishment Clause renders suspect state support of sectarian religious views, again unsupported by an independently compelling secular justification, at stages of acquisition or change in conscientious views, for example,

10. See, for an extended statement and defense of this position, David A. J. Richards, *Toleration and the Constitution* (New York: Oxford University Press, 1986).

11. Ibid., 141–46. Free exercise analysis was somewhat narrowly interpreted in *Employment Division of Oregon Department of Human Resources v. Smith*, 494 U.S. 872 (1990) (religiously inspired use of peyote not constitutionally exempt from neutral criminal statute criminalizing such use, and thus state permitted to deny employment benefits to persons dismissed from their jobs because of such use). The case, however, notably acknowledges the continuing authority of leading free exercise cases like *Sherbert v. Verner*, 374 U.S. 398 (1963) (state unemployment benefits, unavailable to Seventh Day Adventist because of failure to work on Sabbath day, unconstitutionally burdens free exercise rights), and *Wisconsin v. Yoder*, 406 U.S. 205 (1972) (state compulsory education law unconstitutionally burdens free exercise rights of Amish parents to remove children from school after eighth grade). In *Church of the Lukumi Babalu Aye, Inc. v. City of Hialeah*, 508 U.S. 520 (1993), the Supreme Court clarified that *Smith* in no way limited the availability of free exercise analysis of a state law that nonneutrally targeted a specific religion (in this case, criminalizing animal sacrifice in Santeria religious rituals). The authority of *Smith* was cast in doubt in light of the Religious Freedom Restoration Act of 1993, S. Rep. 111, 103d Cong., 1st sess. 14 (1993); for commentary, see Douglas Laycock, "Free Exercise and the Religious Freedom Restoration Act," *Fordham Law Review* 62 (1994): 883. The constitutionality of the Religious Freedom Restoration Act of 1993 was recently assessed by the Supreme Court in light of whether, on grounds of section 5 of the Fourteenth Amendment, it constitutionally expands or unconstitutionally contracts the constitutional right judicially defined by the Supreme Court in its free exercise jurisprudence, including *Smith*. For relevant case law on this question, see *South Carolina v. Katzenbach*, 383 U.S. 301 (1956); *Katzenbach v. Morgan*, 384 U.S. 641 (1966); *Oregon v. Mitchell*, 400 U.S. 112 (1970). The Act was held unconstitutional. See *City of Boerne v. P. F. Flores*, 117 S. Ct. 2157 (1997).

contexts of state action that support or encourage the teaching of and/or conversion to such views.[12] The state may not discriminate either against or in favor of sectarian conscience, but must extend equal respect to all forms of conscience.

The constitutional protection of conscientious conviction in this way makes sense against the background of history and political theory which these guarantees reflect. As noted earlier, both Locke and Bayle, who importantly state the argument for toleration as a constitutive principle of legitimate politics, were concerned to protect the free exercise of moral powers of rationality and reasonableness, in terms of which persons define the personal and ethical meaning of their lives, against sectarian impositions on this basic moral freedom; such impositions had, in their views as believing Christians, corrupted the ethical core of Christianity (simple and elevated imperatives of humane mutual respect and charity) by degrading conscience itself to the measure of sectarian theological dogmas.[13] Both Locke and Bayle, consistent with the dominant Protestant theological ethics of their age, limited the scope of protected conscience (excluding Catholics and atheists[14]); but Locke and Bayle were surely wrong in linking ethical independence to theism in general or Protestant theism in particular, as Jefferson and Madison—the central architects of the religion clauses—acknowledged in extending protected conscience to include Catholics and atheists.[15] By the twentieth century, consistent with an even wider understanding of the diverse sources of reasonable ethical conviction, the scope of conscience includes a wide range of religious and irreligious views protected by both the Free Exercise and Establishment Clauses of the First Amendment.[16]

12. See Richards, *Toleration and the Constitution*, 146–62.

13. See, for further argument on this point, ibid., 89–98.

14. Ibid., 95–98.

15. Ibid., 111–13.

16. Under the Free Exercise Clause, the Supreme Court has tended, in the interest of reasonably developing the basic value of equality, to expand the constitutional concept of religion to protect conscience as such from coercion or undue burdens. See, for example, *United States v. Ballard*, 322 U.S. 78 (1944) (forbidding any inquiry into the truth or falsity of beliefs in a mail fraud action against the bizarre "I am" movement of Guy Ballard [alias "Saint Germain, Jesus, George Washington, and Godfre Ray King"]); *Torcaso v. Watkins*, 367 U.S. 488 (1960) (declaring unconstitutional a state requirement that state officials must swear belief in God); and *United States v. Seeger*,

No small part of the background of this contemporary interpretive attitude lies in our experience, as a people, with the role of
often quite religiously heterodox ethical dissent as the motor of
some of the most important and enlightened constitutional reform
movements in our history. I have in mind the abolitionist movement that structured the nation's normative understanding, in
wake of the Civil War, of both the meaning of that conflict and of
the Reconstruction Amendments, and the antiracist and antisexist
movements that have cumulatively transformed our understanding
of how constitutional guarantees (including the Reconstruction
Amendments) should be interpreted.[17] As we have already seen,
such dissent protested the unjust enforcement of the dominant
proslavery or racist or sexist orthodoxy as the sectarian measure of
claims and speakers, because such enforcement repressed the claims
and speakers who would most reasonably challenge the justice of
its views and practices. To subject the dominant orthodoxy to this
kind of fundamental ethical criticism, such dissent often questioned the unjust role of established churches in the support of
such rights-based evils as slavery or racism or sexism; such dissent
was empowered often by conscientious convictions which were, to

---

380 U.S. 163 (1965), and *Welsh v. United States*, 398 U.S. 333 (1970) (congressional
statutory exemption from military service—limited to religiously motivated conscientious objectors to all wars—extended to all who conscientiously object to all wars).
But see *Smith*, 495 U.S. 872 (religiously inspired peyote use not exempt from general
prohibition on such drug use and thus may be properly invoked by state to deny unemployment benefits to persons dismissed from their jobs because of such religiously inspired use). And under the Establishment Clause, the Supreme Court has notably insisted that the public education curriculum may not privilege sectarian religious rituals
and views over others See, for example, *Engel v. Vitale*, 370 U.S. 421 (1962) (use of
state-composed "nondenominational" prayer in public schools held violative of Establishment Clause); *Abington School District v. Schempp*, 374 U.S. 203 (1963) (reading of
selections from Bible and Lord's Prayer in public schools violative of Establishment
Clause); *Wallace v. Jaffree*, 472 U.S. 38 (1985) (state authorization of one-minute period of silence in public schools "for meditation or voluntary prayer" held violative of
Establishment Clause); *Lee v. Weisman*, 504 U.S. 462 (1992) (nondenominational
prayer at high school graduation held violative of Establishment Clause); *Epperson v.
Arkansas*, 393 U.S. 97 (1968) (state statute forbidding teaching of evolution in public
schools violative of Establishment Clause); *Edwards v. Aguillard*, 482 U.S. 578 (1987)
(state statute requiring balanced treatment of creationist and evolution science held
violative of Establishment Clause).

17. See, in general, Richards, *Conscience and the Constitution*; Richards, *Women,
Gays, and the Constitution*.

say the least, highly unorthodox in religious terms and sometimes not conventionally religious at all.[18] The American tradition of religious liberty, because it made space for ethically independent criticism of politically enforceable religious and moral views, opened the public mind of the nation to the ethical voices and views that addressed its gravest injustices, including the role such injustices played in the corruption of basic constitutional principles and ideals.

It is against this background that we must understand and evaluate what must be the most striking feature of the kind of protest involved in the contemporary case for gay rights. It protests a structural injustice of the sort also exemplified by racism and sexism, namely, abridgment of basic human rights of conscience, speech, intimate life, and work, unjustly rationalized in terms of dehumanizing stereotypes. But the traditional cultural status of homosexuals was not a servile social status thus rationalized, but no space at all. Homosexuals, on this view, were outside any conception of moral community at all, an exiled society given expression by the striking normative idea of homosexuality as unspeakable. It was, in Blackstone's words, "a crime not fit to be named; *peccatum illud horribile, inter christianos non nominandum*"[19]—not mentionable, let alone discussed or assessed. Such total silencing of any reasonable discussion rendered homosexuality into a kind of cultural death, naturally thus understood and indeed condemned as a kind of ultimate heresy or treason against essential moral values.[20] The English legal scholar, Tony Honoré, captured this point exactly by his observation about the contemporary status of the homosexual: "It is not primarily a matter of breaking rules but of dissenting attitudes. It resembles political or religious dissent, being an atheist in Catholic Ireland or a dissident in Soviet Russia."[21]

The case for gay rights thus centrally challenges the cultural

18. For specific elaboration and defense of this point, see David A. J. Richards, "Public Reason and Abolitionist Dissent," *Chicago-Kent Law Review* 69 (1994): 787; see also, in general, Richards, *Women, Gays, and the Constitution*.

19. William Blackstone, *Commentaries on the Laws of England 1765–1769*, ed. Thomas A. Green (Chicago: University of Chicago Press, 1979), vol. 4, *215.

20. See, on this point, Richards, *Toleration and the Constitution*, 278–79.

21. See Tony Honoré, *Sex Law* (London: Duckworth, 1978), 89.

terms of the unspeakability of homosexuality, the claim of its exclusion from the scope of religious and nonreligious conscience
that, on grounds of principle, now ostensibly enjoys constitutional
protection. It does so in the two ways familiar from the similar
protests to racism and sexism: it demands basic human rights of
conscience, speech, intimate life, and work; and it challenges, in
terms of its own moral powers of rationality and reasonableness,
the sectarian terms of the moral orthodoxy that have traditionally
condemned homosexuality. We must shortly assess the merits of
both claims, but the important point for present purposes is that
the very making of such claims challenges the terms (unspeakability) of the underlying structural injustice. As such, claims of gay
and lesbian identity—whether irreligiously, nonreligiously, or religiously grounded—are decidedly among the dissident forms of
conscience that should fully enjoy protection under the American
tradition of religious liberty. This is shown as much by the nature
of the claims made as by the character of the political opposition
to them.

The case for gay rights rests, of course, on arguments of justice
that must be assessed by the larger society in such terms (as we
shall shortly see). But their empowering significance to homosexuals is that they offer them, perhaps for the first time in human
history, the responsible personal and ethical choice of a private and
public identity of equal dignity with that of heterosexuals.

Such a choice of identity has two compelling features for the
homosexuals who increasingly make it. First, it integrates one's
authentic sexual passions with a compelling interpretation of the
personal and moral good of homosexual friendship and love
(grounded in the basic human good of love) as the basis of a life
well and ethically lived. Second, it offers and elaborates arguments
of public reason about the injustice and ethical wrong of the condemnation and marginalization of homosexuality as a legitimate
way of life (namely, the unprincipled failure to respect the self-
authenticating right of all persons to the humane and basic good
of love). Such arguments, properly developed, advance understanding of claims of justice to homosexuals and deepen public
understanding of the arguments of principle that explain our con-

demnation of interlinked injustices like racism, sexism, and homophobia. The identity expresses itself in varied personal and political associations of mutual recognition, support, and respect and in demands for equal justice and for a public culture (including institutional forms) adequate to the reasonable elaboration and cultivation of its ethical vision of humane value in public and private life. Both its constructive and critical arguments are, in their nature, ethical arguments of public reason, appealing to the fundamental and broadly shared ethical imperative of treating persons as equals.[22]

The self-understanding, by homosexuals, of gay rights in these terms corresponds to the political opposition to it. Colorado Amendment Two, which the Supreme Court struck down as unconstitutional,[23] expressly made its reactionary point in terms of banning all laws that recognized antidiscrimination claims of gay and lesbian people; its target was specifically the claims to justice that constitute gay and lesbian identity.[24] Its aim was decisively that advocates of gay and lesbian identity should be compelled to abandon their claims to personal and ethical legitimacy and either convert to the true view or return to the silence of their traditional unspeakability. The political opposition to gay rights agrees with the case for gay rights on one thing: gay and lesbian identity is a choice. Whereas, however, the opposition (on sectarian religious grounds) interprets the choice as moral heresy beyond the pale of acceptable views, its advocates construe the choice as an exercise of legitimate moral freedom long overdue.

Both the advocacy and opposition to gay rights suggest the dis-

22. On the pervasiveness of this ideal in Western religious and ethical culture, see Richards, *Toleration and the Constitution*, 69, 71, 78, 93, 123–28, 134, 272–73, 275. For an exploration of the form, content, and force of the critical and constructive aspects of these ethical arguments on behalf of lesbian and gay identity, see ibid., 269–80; Richards, *Sex, Drugs, Death, and the Law* (Totowa, N.J.: Rowman and Littlefield, 1982), 29–83; Richards, "Unnatural Acts and the Constitutional Right to Privacy: A Moral Theory," *Fordham Law Review* 45 (1977): 1281; Richards, "Sexual Autonomy and the Constitutional Right to Privacy: A Case Study in Human Rights and the Unwritten Constitution," *Hastings Law Journal* 30 (1979): 957.

23. *Romer v. Evans*, 116 S. Ct. 1650 (1996).

24. For fuller discussion, see Richards, *Women, Gays, and the Constitution*, chap. 7.

tinctively illuminating power of the religious analogy in understanding the case for gay rights. The constitutional protection of religion never turned on its putative immutable and salient character (people can and do convert, and can and do conceal religious convictions), but on the traditional place of religion in the conscientious reasonable formation of one's moral identity in public and private life and the need for protection, consistent with the inalienable right to conscience, of persons against state impositions of sectarian religious views. In particular, the identifications integral to one's self-respect as a person of conscience are not to be subject to sectarian impositions through public law that unreasonably burden the exercise of one's conscientious convictions (the free exercise principle) or encourage conversions of such convictions to sectarian orthodoxy (the antiestablishment principle).

Claims by lesbian and gay persons today have, for both proponents and opponents, exactly the same ethical and constitutional force. For proponents, they are in their nature claims to a self-respecting personal and moral identity in public and private life through which they may reasonably express and realize their ethical convictions of the moral powers of friendship and love in a good, fulfilled, and responsible life protesting against an unjust and now conspicuously sectarian tradition of moral subjugation. For opponents, the political reaction to such claims, reflected in Colorado Amendment Two, is based on sectarian religious objection to the conscientious claims of justice made by and on behalf of lesbian and gay identity as a form of conscience that is entitled to equal respect under fundamental American constitutional guarantees of freedom of conscience. At bottom, for opponents, the point is that the very fact of lesbian and gay identity, in virtue of its conscientious claims to justice, is as unworthy of respect as a traditionally despised religion like Judaism; the practice of that form of heresy may thus be abridged, and certainly persons may be encouraged to convert from its demands or, at least, be supinely and ashamedly silent.

Of course, to state the opposition to gay rights in this way is constitutionally to condemn it, for nothing can be clearer than that, if imposing burdens on gay identity is analogous to anti-

Semitism, it is forbidden; "[h]eresy trials are foreign to our Constitution."[25] There are two ways to resist this conclusion; neither is defensible. First, gay and lesbian identity may be dismissed as not a conscientious view. Second, even assuming it is a conscientious view, there are adequate secular grounds for it to be disfavored and even condemned.

Several ways to limit the scope of protected conscience (excluding gay identity) may be rejected easily. The constitutional protections for liberty of conscience, grounded on equal respect for conscience, have not been and cannot reasonably be limited to established or traditional churches or the dogmas of such churches; the traditional condemnation of homosexuality by traditional American religions cannot be a ground to exclude it from constitutional protection. The American tradition of liberty of conscience has protected, indeed fostered, the many forms of new forms of conscience that arose uniquely in America,[26] including, as we have seen, the claims of conscience expressed through the abolitionist movement that were so sharply critical of established churches.[27] Claims to gay and lesbian identity stand foursquare in this distinguished tradition of new forms of dissenting conscience, and are, as such, fully entitled to constitutional protection on terms of principle. Correlatively, the American tradition of religious liberty cannot be and has not been limited to theistic forms of conscience as such, but embraces all forms of conscience.[28] Nor has the tradition been limited to protect only the conscientious identities in which one has been born, for its guarantees are no less for recent converts and include robust guarantees of state neutrality in cir-

---

25. *United States v. Ballard,* 322 U.S. 78, 86 (1944) (Douglas, J., writing for the Court).

26. See, in general, Sydney E. Ahlstrom, *A Religious History of the American People* (New Haven: Yale University Press, 1972), especially 491–509 (Shakers, Society of the Public Universal Friend, New Harmony, Oneida Community, Hopedale, Brook Farm, the Mormons), 1019–33 (Science of Health [Christian Science], New Thought, Positive Thinking), 1059–78 (Black Pentecostalism, Father Divine, Sweet Daddy Grace, Nation of Islam, Booker T. Washington, Martin Luther King).

27. For specific elaboration and defense of this point, see Richards, "Public Reason and Abolitionist Dissent"; see also Richards, *Conscience and the Constitution,* 58–107.

28. For further development of this argument, see Richards, *Toleration and the Constitution,* 67–162.

cumstances that would lend the state's sectarian encouragement to conversion to one form of belief as opposed to another.[29] All forms of conscientious conviction, whether old or new, theistic or non-theistic, are thus guaranteed equal respect on terms of a constitutional principle that renders issues of conscience morally independent of factionalized political incentives.

It would trivialize such guarantees, indeed render them nugatory, not to extend them when they are most constitutionally needed, namely, to antimajoritarian claims of conscience that challenge traditional wisdom on nonsectarian grounds of public reason. Otherwise, the mere congruence of sectarian belief among traditional religions (for example, about the alleged unspeakable evil of homosexuality) would be, as it was in antebellum America on the question of slavery,[30] the measure of religious liberty in particular and human and constitutional rights in general. The traditional orthodoxy, to which any form of dissenting conscience takes objection on grounds of public reason, would be permitted to silence as unworthy the newly emancipated voice of such progressive claims of justice. In effect, the culture of degradation that sets the terms of a structural injustice like racism or sexism would, on this view, set the terms of argument on their behalf. It is, however, such claims of justice of dissenting, antimajoritarian conscience that most require, on grounds of principle, constitutional protection against nescient majorities, who would aggressively and uncritically repress such a group on the ground of its daring to make claims to justice critical of the dominant religio-cultural orthodoxy.

The only remaining ground for excluding gay and lesbian identity from the scope of protected conscience must be to dismiss it as not a conscientious view of the requisite sort, presumably because it is concerned with sex. But there are two difficulties with this view.

First, on the assumption that gay and lesbian identity is about sex or sexual life, that fact would, if anything, bring it closer to

29. Ibid., 146–62.

30. For further development of this point, see Richards, "Public Reason and Abolitionist Dissent."

central concerns of the human conscience in general and religions in particular. Religions organize the terms of sexual life and its place in the mysteries of birth, love, and death under the aspect of eternity, supplying rituals that endow the cycle of living with a sense of enduring personal and ethical values before the terrors of loneliness, loss, decline, and death. Moreover, the experience of one's sexuality is, from its inception, a mysterious, even awful force fraught with a sense of ultimate concern with the other, a longing for communion and transcendence in relationship with a beloved though alien other. It is, thus, no accident, in the American rights-based constitutional tradition (see chapter 2), that the right to intimate life is as much a basic human right as the right to conscience; conscience is so personally engaged with the issues of intimate sexual life because both involve the resources of thought, conviction, feeling, and emotion at the heart of the ultimate concerns of moral personality.

The claims of gay and lesbian identity address these traditionally religious ultimate concerns and are no less religious for doing so than more traditional approaches to these questions. Indeed, the significance of gay and lesbian identity, for many contemporary homosexuals (including myself), is that it enables us, as responsible moral persons and agents, to make redemptive personal and ethical sense of the human depth of our experience of sexuality on equal terms with heterosexuals. We need no longer acquiesce in the unjust stereotypes of our sexuality as inhuman or unnatural or even a diabolic possession, but responsibly engage in rights-based protest of such stereotypes, reclaiming our sexuality and our moral powers of love and transcendence on terms of equal justice.

Second, from the perspective of the case for gay rights, homosexuality is, as Walt Whitman seminally suggested,[31] no more or less exclusively about sex than heterosexuality. We have no difficulty, surely, in understanding the place of heterosexuality in nurturing and sustaining the relationships, more than any other, that are touched with enduring personal and ethical value in living, in-

---

31. For citations and commentary, see Richards, *Women, Gays, and the Constitution,* 307, 366, 434.

deed, that are, if anything is, the personal relationships of mutual transparency, respect, and tender care and concern through which we understand what divine love could mean or reasonably be taken to mean. It does not count against the conscientiousness or even the religiosity of such convictions that opposite-sex intimacies are involved, because our traditions—both secular and religious—afford us the moral vocabulary to interpret them as expressions of love (sometimes even as models of divine love) as well as sensual delight. The case for gay rights argues that homosexuals, on grounds of structural injustice, have been denied such moral vocabulary, indeed denied any vocabulary (on the grounds of unspeakability); such repression often sustained and was sustained by unjust stereotypes that crudely sexualized homosexuality in ways structurally similar to the unjust sexualization that supported racism and sexism.[32] The appeal to sexual content (as a ground for excluding gay and lesbian identity from protected conscience) fatally begs the question by arguably indulging such prejudice rather than responsibly facing what must be addressed: whether there is an adequate ground for burdening this form of conscientious conviction. And conscientious conviction it certainly is, as much as any other convictions about the ethical meaning of personal love that are the common sense of our romantic age.

We need, then, to investigate what acceptable secular grounds, if any, exist to burden gay and lesbian identity as conscientious convictions that are, like any other, entitled to equal respect. The question applies not just to the right to conscience, but to the other human rights traditionally denied to gay and lesbian persons, namely, rights to free speech, intimate life, and work. In all these cases, such basic human rights may only be abridged on grounds of compelling secular grounds of public reason. In fact, as we shall see, there are no acceptable secular grounds for such abridgment in any of these areas, which supports the argument that abridgment of these basic rights to homosexuals is rooted in the same structural injustice as racism and sexism (what I there called moral slavery).

32. On this point, see, in general, Elisabeth Young-Bruehl, *The Anatomy of Prejudices* (Cambridge: Harvard University Press, 1996).

To be clear on this point, we need to examine critically the grounds traditionally supposed to rationalize the condemnation of homosexuality. Plato in *The Laws* gave influential expression to the moral condemnation in terms of two arguments: its nonprocreative character, and (in its male homosexual forms) its degradation of the passive male partner to the status of a woman.[33] Neither of these two traditional moral reasons for condemning homosexuality can any longer be legitimately and indeed constitutionally imposed on society at large or any other person or group of persons.

One such moral reason (the condemnation of nonprocreational sex) can, for example, no longer constitutionally justify laws against the sale to and use of contraceptives by married and unmarried heterosexual couples.[34] The mandatory enforcement at large of the procreational model of sexuality is, in circumstances of overpopulation and declining infant and adult mortality, a sectarian ideal lacking adequate secular basis in the general goods that can alone reasonably justify state power; accordingly, contraceptive-using heterosexuals have the constitutional right to decide when and whether their sexual lives shall be pursued to procreate or as an independent expression of mutual love, affection, and companionship.[35]

And the other moral reason for condemning homosexual sex (the degradation of a man to the passive status of a woman) assumes the sexist premise of the degraded nature of women that has been properly rejected as a reasonable basis for laws or policies

33. See Plato, *Laws*, Book 8, 835d–842a, in *The Collected Dialogues of Plato*, ed. Edith Hamilton and Huntington Cairns (New York: Pantheon, 1961), 1401–2. On the moral condemnation of the passive role in homosexuality in both Greek and early Christian moral thought, see Peter Brown, *The Body and Society: Men, Women, and Sexual Renunciation in Early Christianity* (New York: Columbia University Press, 1988), 30, 382–83. But, for evidence of Greco-Roman toleration of long term homosexual relations even between adults, see John Boswell, *Same-Sex Unions in Premodern Europe* (New York: Villard Books, 1994), 53–107. I am grateful to Stephen Morris for conversations on this point. Whether these relationships were regarded as marriages may be a very different matter. For criticism of Boswell's argument along this latter line, see Brent D. Shaw, "A Groom of One's Own?" *The New Republic*, July 18 & 25, 1994, pp. 33–41.

34. See *Griswold v. Connecticut*, 381 U.S. 479 (1965); *Eisenstadt v. Baird*, 405 U.S. 438 (1972).

35. For further discussion, see Richards, *Toleration and the Constitution*, 256–61.

on grounds of suspect classification analysis.[36] If we constitutionally accept, as we increasingly do (chapter 2), the suspectness of gender on a par with that of race, we must in principle condemn, as a basis for law, any use of stereotypes expressive of the unjust enforcement of gender roles through law.[37] As authoritative case law makes clear, that condemnation extends to gender stereotypy as such whether immediately harmful to women or to men.[38]

Nonetheless, although each moral ground for the condemnation of homosexuality has been independently rejected as a reasonable justification for coercive laws enforceable on society at large (applicable to both men and women), they unreasonably retain their force when brought into specific relationship to the claims of homosexual men and women for equal justice under constitutional law.[39] These claims are today in their basic nature arguments of principle made by gay men and lesbians for the same respect for their intimate love life and other basic rights, free of unreasonable procreational and sexist requirements, now rather generously accorded men and women who are heterosexually coupled (including, as we have seen, even the right to abortion against the alleged weight of fetal life). Empirical issues relating to sexuality and gen-

36. See, for example, *Frontiero v. Richardson*, 411 U.S. 677 (1973); *Craig v. Boren*, 429 U.S. 190 (1976). On homophobia as rooted in sexism, see Young-Bruehl, *The Anatomy of Prejudices*, 143, 148–51.

37. The argument applies *a fortiori* to the modernist form of homophobia that, in contrast to the ancient Greek condemnation of the passive partner in male homosexuality, condemns homosexual relations as such as improperly feminine (if gay) or masculine (if lesbian). See discussion of this point in chapter 2.

38. For cases which protect women from such harm, see *Reed v. Reed*, 404 U.S. 71 (1971) (right to administer estates); *Frontiero v. Richardson*, 411 U.S. 677 (1973) (dependency allowances to servicewomen); *Stanton v. Stanton*, 421 U.S. 7 (1975) (child support for education). For cases that protect men, see *Wengler v. Druggists Mutual Ins. Co.*, 446 U.S. 142 (1980) (widower's right to death benefits); *Craig v. Boren*, 429 U.S. 190 (1976) (age of drinking for men).

39. On the continuities among heterosexual and homosexual forms of intimacy in the modern era, see, in general, John D'Emilio and Estelle B. Freedman, *Intimate Matters: A History of Sexuality in America* (New York: Harper & Row, 1988), 239–360; Anthony Giddens, *The Transformation of Intimacy: Sexuality, Love, and Eroticism in Modern Societies* (Cambridge, U.K.: Polity, 1992). See also Barbara Ehrenreich, Elizabeth Hess, and Gloria Jacobs, *Remaking Love: The Feminization of Sex* (New York: Anchor, 1986); Anne Snitow, Christine Stansell, and Sharon Thompson, eds., *Powers of Desire* (New York: Monthly Review Press, 1983); Carole S. Vance, ed., *Pleasure and Danger: Exploring Female Sexuality* (Boston: Routledge & Kegan Paul, 1984).

der are now subjected to more impartial critical assessment than they were previously, and the resulting light of public reason about issues of sexuality and gender should be available to all persons on fair terms. However, both the procreational mandates and the unjust gender stereotypy, constitutionally condemned for the benefit of heterosexual men and women, are ferociously applied to homosexual men and women.[40] It bespeaks the continuing political power of the traditional moral subjugation of homosexuals that such a claim of fair treatment (an argument of basic constitutional principle if any argument is) was contemptuously dismissed by a majority of the Supreme Court of the United States (5–4) in 1986 in *Bowers v. Hardwick*.[41] No skeptical scrutiny whatsoever was accorded state purposes elsewhere acknowledged as illegitimate. Certainly, no such purpose could be offered of the alleged weight of fetal life that has been rejected as a legitimate ground for criminalization of all forms of abortion; any claim of public health could be addressed, as they would be in comparable cases of heterosexual relations involving the basic constitutional right of intimate life, by constitutionally required alternatives less restrictive and more effective than criminalization (including use of prophylactics by those otherwise at threat from transmission of AIDS).[42]

Traditional moral arguments, now clearly reasonably rejected in their application to heterosexuals, were uncritically applied to a group much more exigently in need of constitutional protection on grounds of principle.[43] Reasonable advances in the public under-

---

40. On the unjust gender stereotypy uncritically applied to homosexual men and women, see Susan Moller Okin, "Sexual Orientation and Gender: Dichotomizing Differences," in *Sex, Preference, and Family: Essays on Law and Nature*, ed. David M. Estlund and Martha C. Nussbaum (New York: Oxford University Press, 1997), 44–59.

41. 478 U.S. 186 (1986).

42. The argument applies, in any event, only to those forms of sex by gay men likely to transmit the disease; it does not reasonably apply to lesbians, nor does it apply to all forms of sex (including anal sex) by gay men. So, the argument that sex acts as such can be criminalized on this basis is constitutionally overinclusive inconsistent with the basic right thus abridged. The regulatory point is that even gay men at threat by virtue of their sexual practices can take preventive measures against this threat (by using condoms). For a recent discussion of what further such reasonable preventive measures the gay men at threat might also take, see Gabriel Rotello, *Sexual Ecology: AIDS and the Destiny of Gay Men* (New York: Dutton, 1997).

43. For further criticism, see Richards, *Foundations of American Constitutionalism*, 209–47.

standing of sexuality and gender, now constitutionally available to all heterosexuals, were suspended in favor of an appeal to the sexual mythology of the Middle Ages.[44] It is an indication of the genre of dehumanizing stereotypes at work in *Bowers v. Hardwick*, stripping a class of persons (blacks, women, Jews, homosexuals) of moral personality by reducing them to a mythologized sexuality, that the Court focused so obsessionally on one sex act (sodomy); as Leo Bersani perceptively observed about the public discourse (reflected in *Bowers*), it resonates in images (inherited from the nineteenth century) of homosexuals as sexually obsessed prostitutes.[45] The transparently unprincipled character of *Bowers*[46] in such terms thus suggests a larger problem, which connects such treatment of homosexuals with the now familiar structural injustice underlying racism and sexism.

As we have seen (chapters 1–2), this structural injustice involves two features: the abridgment of the basic human rights of a class of persons on inadequate grounds, and the rationalization of such treatment in terms of dehumanizing stereotypes supported by the denial of such rights. We have now seen that the grounds traditionally supposed to support the condemnation of homosexuality are not, in contemporary circumstances, the compelling secular

---

44. Justice Blackmun put the point acidly: "Like Justice Holmes, I believe that 'it is revolting to have no better reason for a rule of law than that so it was laid down in the time of Henry IV. It is still more revolting if the grounds upon which it was laid down have vanished long since, and the rule simply persists from blind imitation of the past.'" *Bowers,* 478 U.S. at 199 (quoting Oliver Wendell Holmes, "The Path of the Law," *Harvard Law Review* 10 [1897]: 457, 469).

45. See Leo Bersani, "Is the Rectus as a Grave?" in Douglas Crimp, *Cultural Analysis/Cultural Activism* (Cambridge: MIT Press, 1988), 211–12, 222.

46. I develop this argument at greater length in Richards, *Foundations of American Constitutionalism*, chap. 6; and in David A. J. Richards, "Constitutional Legitimacy and Constitutional Privacy," *New York University Law Review* 61 (1986): 800. See also Anne D. Goldstein, "History, Homosexuality, and Political Values: Searching for the Hidden Determinants of *Bowers v. Hardwick,*" *Yale Law Journal* 97 (1988): 1073; Nan D. Hunter, "Life after *Hardwick,*" *Harvard Civil Rights–Civil Liberties Law Review* 27 (1992): 531; Janet E. Halley, "Reasoning about Sodomy: Act and Identity in and after *Bowers v. Hardwick,*" *Virginia Law Review* 79 (1993): 1721; Anne B. Goldstein, "Reasoning about Homosexuality: A Commentary on Janet Halley's 'Reasoning about Sodomy: Act and Identity in and after *Bowers v. Hardwick,*'" *Virginia Law Review* 79 (1993): 1781; Kendall Thomas, "The Eclipse of Reason: A Rhetorical Reading of *Bowers v. Hardwick,*" *Virginia Law Review* 79 (1993): 1805.

purposes constitutionally required to justify basic human rights, including conscience, speech, intimate life, and work. The continuing force of such condemnation suggests the continuing power, in the case of homosexuals, of the pattern of structural injustice of racism and sexism earlier analyzed. Indeed, homophobia (as I shall call this structural injustice) today more conspicuously retains its traditional force than blatant racism and sexism, as we shall shortly see when we examine several cases, in addition to *Bowers,* of populist unjust aggression against the basic human rights of gays and lesbians.

To begin with, however, we may and should, on grounds of principle, extend our earlier analysis of moral slavery to the traditional reprobation of homosexuality. Homophobia reflects a cultural tradition of rights-denying moral slavery similar to and indeed overlapping with the American tradition of sexist degradation; the root of homophobia is, like sexism, a rigid conception of gender roles and spheres, only here focusing specifically on gender roles in intimate sexual and emotional life.[47] As my earlier analysis of the basis of the Western condemnation of homosexuality suggests (chapter 2), homophobia may be reasonably understood today as a persisting form of residual and quite unjust gender discrimination both in its object (stigmatizing homosexuality as inconsistent with gender identity, as a man or women) and in its grounds.

With respect to the latter, the nonprocreative character of homosexual sexuality may be of relatively little concern, but its cultural symbolism of disordered gender roles excites anxieties in a political culture still quite unjustly sexist in its understanding of gender roles; and indeed the condemnation of homosexuality acts as a reactionary reinforcement of sexism generally. The emergence of the modern conception of homosexual identity as intrinsically effeminate (in gay men) (and later mannish, in lesbians[48]) accom-

---

47. See Suzanne Pharr, *Homophobia: A Weapon of Sexism* (Inverness, Calif.: Chardon Press, 1988); Sylvia A. Law, "Homosexuality and the Social Meaning of Gender," *Wisconsin Law Review* 1988: 187; Young-Bruehl, *The Anatomy of Prejudices,* 35–36, 143–51; Okin, "Sexual Orientation and Gender: Dichotomizing Differences."

48. On the later development of lesbian identity, see Lillian Faderman, *Odd Girls and Twilight Lovers: A History of Lesbian Life in Twentieth-Century America* (New York:

panied the emergence of modern Western culture after 1700 and was associated with the reinforcement of the sexist definition of gender roles in terms of which the supposedly greater equality of men and women was interpreted.[49] Male homosexuals as such were thus symbolically understood as "effeminate members of a third or intermediate gender, who surrender their rights to be treated as dominant males, and are exposed instead to a merited contempt as a species of male whore"[50] (in the more overtly sexist and homophile ancient Greek world only the passive male partner would be thus interpreted[51]). Homosexuals as such—both lesbians and male homosexuals—are, on this persisting modern view, in revolt against what many still suppose to be the "natural" order of gender hierarchy: women or men, as the case may be, undertaking sexual roles improper to their gender—for example, women loving other women (independent of men[52]), and men, men, or dominance in women, passivity in men. It is plainly unjust to displace such sexist views, no longer publicly justifiable against heterosexual women or men, against a much more culturally marginalized and despised group—symbolic scapegoats of the feeble and cowardly sense of self that seeks self-respect in the unjust degradation of morally innocent people of good will.[53] It should also be clearly constitutionally condemned as a form of unjust gender discrimination, perpetuating unjustly rigid and impermeable gender stereo-

---

Columbia University Press, 1991); Carroll Smith-Rosenberg, *Disorderly Conduct: Visions of Gender in Victorian America* (New York: Knopf, 1985), 245–97.

49. See, in general, Randolph Trumbach, "Gender and the Homosexual Role in Modern Western Culture: The 18th and 19th Centuries Compared," in *Homosexuality, Which Homosexuality? International Conference on Gay and Lesbian Studies*, ed. Dennis Altman et al. (London: GMP Publishers, 1989), 149–69.

50. Ibid., 153. See also, in general, Trumbach, *Sex and the Gender Revolution*, vol. 1.

51. For a probing recent study, see Eva Cantarella, *Bisexuality in the Ancient World*, trans. Cormac O'Cuilleanain (New Haven: Yale University Press, 1992); but see also Boswell, *Same-Sex Unions in Premodern Europe*, 53–107.

52. For commentary on the sexism of heterosexism, see Adrienne Rich, "Compulsory Heterosexuality and Lesbian Existence," in Catharine R. Stimpson and Ethel Spector Person, *Women: Sex and Sexuality* (Chicago: University of Chicago Press, 1980).

53. On the antifeminism of anti-gay sectarian groups, see Didi Herman, *The Anti-gay Agenda: Orthodox Vision and the Christian Right* (Chicago: University of Chicago Press, 1997), 103–10; on their opposition, in general, to the agenda of civil rights in all areas, see ibid, 111–36, 140.

types (whether of women or men) that enforce their claims by indulging the dehumanization of any gender dissident (as a degraded or fallen woman or man).[54]

Homosexuals, because they violate these gender roles, are traditionally supposed to be outcasts from the human race as well, and thus incapable and indeed unworthy of being accorded what all persons are, on equal terms, owed: respect for their basic human rights to conscience, speech, intimate life, and work. A way of making this point is to observe that homophobic prejudice, like racism and sexism, unjustly distorts the idea of human rights applicable to both public and private life. The political evil of racism expressed itself in a contemptuous interpretation of black family life (enforced by segregation and antimiscegenation laws that confined blacks, as a separate species, to an inferior sphere).[55] The political evil of sexism expressed itself in a morally degraded interpretation of private life (to which women, as morally inferior, were confined as, in effect, a different species).[56] In similar fashion, the evil of homophobic prejudice is its degradation of homosexual love to the unspeakably private and secretive not only politically and socially, but intra-psychically in the person whose sexuality is homosexual; the intellectual reign of terror that once aimed to impose racism and anti-Semitism on the larger society and even on these stigmatized minorities themselves today aims to enforce homophobia at large and self-hating homophobia in particular on homosexuals as well.

Its vehicle is the denigration of gay and lesbian identity as a devalued form of conscience with which no one, under pain of ascribed membership in such a devalued species, can or should identify. Such degradation constructs not, as in the case of gender, merely a morally inferior sphere, but an unspeakably and inhu-

---

54. For important recent arguments along these lines, see Katherine M. Franke, "The Central Mistake of Sex Discrimination Law: The Disaggregation of Sex from Gender," *University of Pennsylvania Law Review* 144 (1995): 1; Mary Ann C. Case, "Disaggregating Gender from Sex and Sexual Orientation: The Effeminate Man in the Law and Feminist Jurisprudence," *Yale Law Journal* 105 (1995): 90.

55. See *Loving v. Virginia*, 388 U.S. 1 (1967) (antimiscegenation laws held unconstitutional expression of racial prejudice).

56. See Lillian Faderman, *Surpassing the Love of Men* (New York: William Morrow, 1981), 85–86, 157–58, 181, 236.

manly evil sphere, a culturally constructed and imagined diabolic hell to which gays and lesbians must be compulsively exiled on the same irrationalist mythological terms to which societies we condemn as primitive exiled devils and witches and werewolves;[57] homosexuals, self-consciously demonized (as devils) as they are by contemporary sectarian groups, must be kept in the sphere consistent with their inhumanity.[58] Gays and lesbians are thus culturally dehumanized as a nonhuman or inhuman species whose moral interests in love and friendship and nurturing care are, in their nature, radically discontinuous with anything recognizably human. The culture of such degradation is pervasive and deep, legitimating, as we shall shortly see, the uncritically irrationalist outrage at the very idea of gay and lesbian marriage,[59] which unjustly constructs the inhumanity of homosexual identity on the basis of exactly the same kind of viciously circular cultural degradation unjustly imposed on African Americans through antimiscegenation laws.[60] Groups, thus marked off as ineligible for the central institutions of intimate life and cultural transmission, are deemed subculturally nonhuman or inhuman, an alien species incapable of the humane forms of culture that express and sustain our inexhaustibly varied search, as free moral persons, for enduring personal and ethical meaning and value in living.

Both racism and sexism arose in the context of close living relationships between the hegemonic and oppressed groups, drew their potent political power from such allegedly loving relation-

57. On the imaginative processes that sustain such a sphere, see Alan E. Bernstein, *The Formation of Hell: Death and Retribution in the Ancient and Early Christian Worlds* (Ithaca: Cornell University Press, 1993); Elaine Pagels, *The Origin of Satan* (New York: Random House, 1996).

58. For the view of public identified gays and lesbians as, from within the perspective of sectarian theology, devils or demonic, see Didi Herman, *The Antigay Agenda: Orthodox Vision and the Christian Right* (Chicago: University of Chicago Press, 1997), 82–91, 143; for the similar sectarian view taken of Jews and the analogy to scapegoating homosexuals today, see Pagels, *The Origin of Satan*, 102–5.

59. For further development of this argument, see Richards, *Women, Gays, and the Constitution*, chap. 8.

60. See, for eloquent development of this point, Andrew Koppelman, "The Miscegenation Analogy: Sodomy Law as Sex Discrimination," *Yale Law Journal* 98 (1988): 145. See also Andrew Koppelman, *Antidiscrimination Law and Social Equality* (New Haven: Yale University Press, 1996), 146–76.

ships, and were rationalized accordingly as protections of intimate personal life. As James Madison saw in his constitutionally seminal elaborations of his theory of faction, factions are most powerful when they are most local and parochial.[61] Consistent with this view, racism and sexism are the prepotent forms of faction they are because they culturally arose and were sustained in the most local and personal of intimate relationships as forms of moral paternalism.

Homophobia shares a comparable cultural background of moral slavery. Heterosexuals and homosexuals lived together closely under the moral slavery of homosexuals,[62] but, as heterosexuals have now learned, in different worlds, one hegemonically and polemically assertive, the other resignedly withdrawn into a compulsory and silent servitude mistaken for consent. Homosexuals were not remitted to servile status as blacks and women were under their forms of moral slavery. Their moral slavery was, rather, more hegemonically absolute—servitude to an unjust moral paternalism that, based on crushing their basic rights (to conscience, speech, association, and work), exiled them from any legitimate space in public or private life into the realm of the unspeakable. Homosexuals were thus radically denied the very resources of self-respecting personal and ethical identity as homosexuals; and homophobia thus naturally takes, as its dominant contemporary form, the violent attack on the relatively recent development of conscientious moral claims to such a self-respecting identity either in public or private life.[63] The essentially hegemonic and subjugating force of

61. See Jacob E. Cooke, ed., *The Federalist* (Middletown, Conn.: Wesleyan University Press, 1961), No. 10, 56–65; for background and commentary, see Richards, *Foundations of American Constitutionalism*, 32–39.

62. For a powerful study of this phenomenon in renaissance England, see Alan Bray, *Homosexuality in Renaissance England* (London: Gay Men's Press, 1982).

63. For the history of this development in Great Britain, see Jeffrey Weeks, *Sex, Politics, and Society: The Regulation of Sexuality since 1800*, 2d ed. (London: Longman, 1989); Jeffrey Weeks, *Coming Out: Homosexual Politics in Britain from the Nineteenth Century to the Present*, rev. ed. (London: Quartet Books, 1990). For the American development of this movement, see John D'Emilio, *Sexual Politics, Sexual Communities: The Making of a Homosexual Minority in the United States, 1940–1970* (Chicago: University of Chicago Press, 1983); John D'Emilio and Estelle B. Freedman, *Intimate Matters: A History of Sexuality in America* (New York: Harper & Row, 1988).

this prejudice is shown in its insistence that homosexuality remain an unspeakably privatized debasement, tolerable only on terms of a servile, apologetic, and shrunken self-contempt, not on terms of respect for basic human rights (including the inalienable right to conscience) owed all persons, including lesbian and gay persons.

The oppression of homosexuals, like that of blacks and women under moral slavery, is, as we shall see, thus perversely rationalized as itself a protection of intimate life (family values), when it, in fact, wars on a legitimate form of intimate life. This marks the roots of the prejudice, like other forms of moral slavery, in the most intimately debasing forms of unjust moral paternalism (the totalizing assumption that the community legitimately can and should know and control the very heart and mind of another's most intimate resources of moral personality). Indeed, consistent with our earlier Madisonian observations, homophobia, directed at gender roles in intimate life, may be regarded as among the most intractable and virulent of factions, manifesting, as it does, an intrapsychic landscape of the gendered meaning of love based on sexist degradation in intimate life itself (as if, the equality traditionally understood to exist among men or among women could never be fertile soil for the garden of love).[64]

The common ground of our concern with racism, sexism, and homophobia is the radical political evil of a political culture, ostensibly committed to toleration on the basis of universal human rights, that unjustly denied a class of persons their inalienable human rights as persons with moral powers on the basis of the structural injustice of moral slavery. Liberal political culture, consistent with respect for this basic right, must extend to all persons the cultural resources that enable them critically to explore, define, express, and revise the identifications central to free moral personality;[65] the constitutional evil, condemned by suspect classification analysis under the Equal Protection Clause of the Fourteenth Amendment, is the systematic deprivation of this basic right to a

---

64. Cf. Okin, "Sexual Orientation and Gender: Dichotomizing Differences."

65. For development of this theme, see Will Kymlicka, *Liberalism, Community, and Culture* (Oxford: Clarendon Press, 1989), 162–78; Yael Tamir, *Liberal Nationalism* (Princeton: Princeton University Press, 1993), 13–56.

group of persons, unjustly degraded from their status as persons entitled to equal respect for the reasonable exercise of their free moral powers in the identifications integral to ethical life.[66]

To deny such a group, already the subject of a long history and culture of moral slavery, their culture-creating rights is to silence in them the very voice of their moral freedom, rendering unspoken and unspeakable the sentiments, experience, and reason that authenticate the moral personality that a political culture of human rights owes each and every person (including their moral powers to know and claim their basic rights and to protest injustice on such grounds). Sexual orientation is and should be a fully suspect classification because homosexuals are today victimized, in the same way claims to basic rights by African Americans and women are and have been, by irrational political prejudices rooted in this radical political evil, denying them the cultural resources of free moral personality.

Racism, sexism, and homophobia share a common background in moral slavery, which explains both the character and depth of the political evil they represent, in particular, its imposition of such injustice on the very terms of personal and moral identity both for the individuals afflicted by such injustice and the society at large. Both Du Bois and Friedan thus characterized the struggles, respectively, against racism and sexism in such terms, as a claim of African Americans and women to forge a new identity as blacks and as women but also of the role of race and gender in the constitution of American constitutional identity. By its very rights-based terms, such protest challenged the terms of moral slavery, whose unjust cultural force politically required abridgment of basic human rights of conscience and speech; the structural injustice thus under criticism attacked the very making of such criticism, as in, for example, the attempt in antebellum America to silence abolitionist dissent; it was not that such dissent was not conscientious or did not have a perceived basis in justice, but precisely because it was thus conscientious and perceived by many (including slave-

---

66. For further development and defense of this position, see, in general, Richards, *Women, Gays, and the Constitution.*

owners) as just that it was regarded as so dangerous (inciting slave revolts, for example).[67] Rights-based protests of the cultural terms of homosexuality has a similar character and has excited a similar repressive response, but one that attacks the very making of such claims as conscientious. Rights-based protests of racism and sexism both challenged and transformed identity, but identity which at least occupied a familiar if embattled cultural space in conscientious public opinion; such protests could be and were repressed as not only wrong but dangerously wrong. The structural injustice of homophobia imposes, however, a regime of unspeakability, that is, the denial of any acceptable terms of identity at all. The contemporary reactionary response to rights-based protest of such structural injustice is an attack on its ethical basis as a rights-based protest of the dehumanizing injustice of cultural unspeakability, invisibility, and marginalization.

A politics actuated by such injustice is not only suspect on the same structural grounds as race and gender, but on grounds of the first suspect classification under American public law, religion.[68] The essential terms of this argument have already been presented: claims of gay and lesbian identity are a form of ethically based conscientious conviction entitled to equal respect with other forms of such conviction under the religion clauses of the First Amendment, and there is no compelling secular basis in contemporary circumstances that could justify burdening or abridging this conviction as opposed to others. It remains, however, to complete this analysis, by showing that constitutional controversies currently in play correspond to the terms of the analysis proposed. In particular, many of these disputes are best understood as unconstitutionally sectarian attacks on gay and lesbian identity as a conscientious conviction entitled to equal respect. Three cases correspond closely to the terms of this identity-based analysis of the case for gay rights: anti-lesbian/gay initiatives, the exclusion of homosexuals

67. See, on this point, Richards, *Conscience and the Constitution,* 59.

68. See, on this point, Richards, *Foundations of American Constitutionalism,* 260, 280.

from the military, and the exclusion of gays and lesbians from the right to marriage. On analysis, all these cases involve the attempt to use public law to target sectarian condemnation on identity-based claims of conscience and are, as such, inconsistent with constitutional guarantees of equal respect for conscience.

ANTI-LESBIAN/GAY INITIATIVES

The organized opposition to gay rights recently successfully secured the adoption of Colorado Amendment Two, which not only repealed existing state laws that protect gay people from discrimination, but also banned all future laws that would recognize such claims by lesbians and gay men.[69] On May 20, 1996, Justice Kennedy, writing for the Supreme Court of the United States, 6–3, struck down Colorado Amendment Two on the ground that the classification in question was "so discontinuous with the reasons offered for it that the amendment seems inexplicable by anything but animus toward the class it affects; it lacks a rational relation-

---

69. See Amendment Two to Colo. Const. art. 2, § 2 (adopted Nov. 3, 1992). The full text of Amendment Two is as follows:

> Neither the State of Colorado, through any of its branches or department, nor any of its agencies, political subdivisions, municipalities or school districts, shall enact, adopt or enforce any statute, regulation, ordinance or policy whereby homosexual, lesbian or bisexual orientation, conduct, practices or relationships shall constitute or otherwise be the basis of, or entitle any person or class of persons to have or claim any minority status, quota preferences, protected status or claim of discrimination. This Section of the Constitution shall be self-executing.

The voters of Colorado approved Amendment Two by a vote of 53 percent to 47 percent on November 3, 1992. On July 19, 1993, the Colorado Supreme Court affirmed the grant of a preliminary injunction against the amendment. See *Evans v. Romer*, 854 P.2d 1270 (Colo.), *cert. denied*, 114 S. Ct. 419 (1993). On December 14, 1993, Judge H. Jeffrey Bayless granted a permanent injunction against the amendment, finding that, under the strict scrutiny standard applicable to the constitutional assessment of the amendment under *Evans*, the state failed to justify the amendment in terms of compelling state interests. See *Evans v. Romer*, 1993 WL 518586 (Colo. Dist. Ct. 1993), reprinted in *The Bill of Rights versus the Ballot Box: Constitutional Implications of Anti-Gay Ballot Initiatives*, Continuing Legal Education Materials, presented by the Gay-Lesbian Bisexual Law Caucus of The Ohio State University, March 12, 1994 (on file with *Ohio State Law Journal*), 23–32 (hereinafter cited as *CLE Materials*).

ship to legitimate state interests."[70] In effect, "Amendment 2 classifies homosexuals not to further a proper legislative end but to make them unequal to every else. This Colorado cannot do. A State cannot so deem a class of persons a stranger to its laws."[71] The application of the rational basis test in *Romer* is reminiscent of the first case in which the Supreme Court announced its skepticism about gender classifications, namely, *Reed v. Reed*.[72] The application of the rational basis standard with the consequence of invalidating such laws was in doctrinal tension with the many cases in which comparable laws with equally overinclusive and underinclusive legislative classifications had been upheld. *Reed* suggested what later cases made clear, that the Court had interpretively come to the view that some heightened level of constitutional scrutiny was owed gender classifications.[73] The same doctrinal criticism may be made of *Romer* as was earlier made of *Reed:* why was heightened scrutiny owed this as opposed to other classifications? If the decision is doctrinally problematic as a rational basis decision, we need to ask how it might better be understood, in particular, what the analogies might be that made this state law, in the words of Justice Scalia's bitter dissent, "as reprehensible as racial or religious bias."[74] In particular, Scalia questions the elabo-

70. *Romer,* 116 S. Ct. at 1627.

71. Id. at 1629. The Court of Appeals for the Sixth Circuit, instructed to reexamine its decision in *Equality Foundation of Greater Cincinnati, Inc. v. City of Cincinnati,* 54 F.3d 261 (6th Cir. 1995) (upholding an amendment of the City Charter of Cincinnati forbidding any special class treatment of sexual orientation in light of *Romer v. Evans* (*Equality Foundation of Greater Cincinnati v. City of Cincinnati,* 116 S. Ct. 2519 [1996]), upheld the charter amendment as, in contrast to Colorado Amendment Two, a local (not state-wide) provision that "merely prevented homosexuals, as homosexuals, from obtaining special privileges and preferences," *Equality Foundation of Greater Cincinnati, Inc. v City of Cincinnati,* 128 F.3d 289, 295 (6th Cir. 1997). In its recent denial of certiorari of review of this case, Justice Stevens, joined by Justice Souter and Justice Ginsburg, pointed out that such denial of review is not a ruling on the merits, noting that the construction of the city charter amendment by the Sixth Circuit differed significantly from the interpretation (as a prohibition of antidiscrimination protections only for gays and lesbians) ascribed to the amendment by petitioners, *Equality Foundation of Greater Cincinnati, Inc. v. City of Cincinnati,* 1998 U.S. LEXIS 6680 (Oct. 13, 1998).

72. 404 U.S. 71 (1971).

73. For further discussion of the judicial development and its background, see Richards, *Women, Gays, and the Constitution,* chap. 5.

74. See *Romer,* 116 S. Ct. at 1629.

ration of suspectness to sexual preference when the group in question is, in proportion to its numbers, quite politically powerful.[75] The strongest constitutional argument for constitutional limits on anti-lesbian/gay rights initiatives has been the one least explored: namely, the initiatives in question express constitutionally forbidden sectarian religious intolerance through public law against fundamental rights of conscience, speech, and association of lesbian and gay persons protected by America's first and premier civil liberty, liberty of conscience.[76] The ground for discrimination against gay and lesbian conscience, thus understood, is sectarian religious convictions—sectarian in the sense that they rest on perceptions internal to religious convictions not on public arguments reasonably available in contemporary terms to all persons.[77] This is confirmed, as I earlier argued, by the failure to extend to gay and lesbian persons public arguments (about the acceptability of nonprocreational sex and unacceptability of sexism) otherwise available to all persons on fair terms. The expression through public law of one form of sectarian conscience against another form of conscience, without compelling justification in public arguments available to all, is constitutionally invidious, and therefore constitutionally suspect, religious intolerance. It both unconstitutionally burdens conscience, inconsistent with free exercise principles, and unconstitutionally advances sectarian conscience, inconsistent with antiestablishment principles. Discrimination specifically directed against the claims of justice made by and on behalf of gay and lesbian conscience expresses such constitutionally forbidden intolerance.

75. Id. at 1637.

76. See, in general, William Lee Miller, *The First Liberty: Religion and the American Republic* (New York: Knopf, 1987); Thomas J. Curry, *The First Freedoms: Church and State in America to the Passage of the First Amendment* (New York: Oxford University Press, 1986); Leonard W. Levy, *The Establishment Clause: Religion and the First Amendment* (New York: Macmillan, 1986).

77. In its position paper, Colorado for Family Values, the sponsor of Colorado Amendment Two, invoked sectarian religious arguments to justify the initiative: "Gay behavior is what the Bible calls 'sin' because sin defines any attempt to solve human problems or meet human needs without regard to God's wisdom and solutions as found in Scripture and in His saving grace and mercy," cited in John F. Niblock, "Anti-Gay Initiatives: A Call for Heightened Judicial Scrutiny," *UCLA Law Review* 41 (1993): 157 n. 17.

If discrimination against persons on grounds of sexual preference expresses constitutionally forbidden religious intolerance, the
constitutional entrenchment of prohibitions on such discrimination (specifically naming a group in terms of the claims of justice
it makes) is unashamedly in service of such discrimination, and,
as such, an unconstitutional expression of religious intolerance
through public law. The character of the advocacy for such initiatives confirms the grounds for constitutional concern. As I more
fully argue below, advocacy groups standardly distort the true nature of their organizations, rely upon discredited experts and facts,
and conceal the true purpose of the proposed legislation.[78] Such
irrationalist distortion of facts and values, in polemical service of a
dominant orthodoxy now under reasonable examination, is at the
core of the political irrationalism (the paradox of intolerance) condemned, as a basis for law, by the argument for toleration central
to American constitutionalism.[79] In fact, advocacy of such initiatives appeals not to reasonable arguments consistently pursued,
but highly sectarian forms of controversial theological discourse
that regard publicly identified gays and lesbians as devils unworthy
of the most minimal standards of constitutional civility and respect.[80] If public law (on examination, as I argue) fails these standards (resting solely on a sectarian basis that uses public law in
service of sectarian wars of religion), it violates basic principles of
American constitutional law.

While the issue has usually been discussed in terms of the cases
dealing with constitutional entrenchment of laws forbidding racial
discrimination, the more exact analogy would be constitutional
entrenchment of prohibitions on claims of religious discrimination

78. See Note, "Constitutional Limits on Anti-Gay-Rights Initiatives," *Harvard
Law Review* 106 (1993): 1909. For important recent explorations of this reactionary
political movement and its power in contemporary American politics, see Chris Bull
and John Gallagher, *Perfect Enemies: The Religious Right, the Gay Movement, and the
Politics of the 1990's* (New York: Crown Publishers, 1996); Didi Herman, *The Antigay
Agenda: Orthodox Vision and the Christian Right* (Chicago: University of Chicago
Press, 1997).

79. See Richards, *Conscience and the Constitution*, 63–73.

80. For ample documentation, based on interviews with members of the Christian
Right, about the roots of their claims in Biblical inerrancy and premillennial theology,
see Herman, *The Antigay Agenda*.

made by groups most likely to be victimized in Christian America by such discrimination, i.e., Jews. To understand the force of this analogy between political anti-Semitism and homophobia (well supported in both historical and contemporary expressions of such sectarian intolerance[81]), we must remind ourselves about the nature of the constitutional evil of the expression of anti-Semitism through law, in particular, why such political anti-Semitism violates the argument for toleration of American traditions of religious liberty.[82] As I argued in chapter 1, such political anti-Semitism unjustly abridged basic rights of Jews, in violation of the argument for toleration, because their beliefs and ways of life raised reasonable doubts about the dominant religious orthodoxy. In order not to allow such reasonable doubts to be entertained, the dominant orthodoxy made itself the measure of tolerable belief and practice, abridging the basic rights of Jews to dissent by appealing to irrationalist stereotypes that dehumanized them (including the idea of Jews as the slaves of Christians[83]). I called the mechanism by which such an entrenched orthodoxy unjustly constructed the dehumanized status of dissidents from the dominant orthodoxy the paradox of intolerance: in effect, the views that dominant orthodoxy most reasonably needs to hear are those, paradoxically, savagely repressed on whatever irrationalist grounds sustain the embattled legitimacy of the dominant orthodoxy. American constitutional principles, reflecting the argument for toleration, forbid laws based on such sectarian intolerance.

In light of these reasons, we would and should immediately condemn constitutional entrenchment of political anti-Semitism (in the form of an initiative that forbade all laws protecting Jews as such against discrimination) as an unconstitutional expression of religious intolerance because such laws are in service of the forms of majoritarian religious intolerance that constitutional guar-

---

81. For historical support of the idea of Satan to condemn Jewish unbelief and the analogy of such scapegoating to homophobia, see Pagels, *The Origin of Satan*, 102–5; on the analogy between anti-Semitism and homophobia in the intolerance of the Christian Right, see Herman, *The Antigay Agenda*, 85–86, 125–28.

82. On the argument for toleration, see Richards, *Conscience and the Constitution*, 63–73; see also, in general, Richards, *Toleration and the Constitution*.

83. For citations and commentary, see Richards, *Women, Gays, and the Constitution*, 402–3, 419.

antees of religious toleration condemn as a basis for law. A state that entrenched such initiatives would, in clear violation of free exercise principles, unconstitutionally burden specifically named conscientious convictions in a blatantly nonneutral way,[84] and, in clear contradiction of the principles of our antiestablishment jurisprudence,[85] support a sectarian religious view as the one true church of Americanism to which all dissenters are encouraged to convert. A constitutional jurisprudence that questions the neutrality of unemployment compensation schemes imposing financial burdens on the convictions of Seventh Day Adventists[86] must condemn, *a fortiori*, laws that specifically target for focused disadvantage the convictions of a religion or form of conscience, and must regard as even worse the very naming of the group in question in the relevant law.[87] In effect, a state that entrenched such initiatives would itself be the unconstitutional agent of the political evil of intolerance, branding a religious group as heretics and blasphemers to American religious orthodoxy. American constitutionalism, which recognizes neither heresy nor blasphemy as legitimate expressions of state power,[88] must forbid exercises of state power, like the contemplated initiative, that illegitimately assert such a power, in this case, legitimating the dehumanizing evil of political anti-Semitism. The effect of such initiatives would be to enlist the state actively in the unconstitutional construction of a class of persons lacking the status of bearers of human rights, a status so subhuman

84. Cf. *Church of the Lukumi Babalu Aye, Inc. v. City of Hialeah*, 508 U.S. 520 (1993) (law forbidding animal sacrifice by the Santeria religion held violative of neutrality required in state burdens on religious practices by free exercise clause).

85. See, in general, Richards, *Toleration and the Constitution*, 146–62.

86. See *Sherbert v. Verner*, 374 U.S. 398 (1963), whose authority was reaffirmed in *Employment Division v. Smith*, 494 U.S. 872 (1990).

87. The imagined case is thus even worse than *Church of the Lukumi Babalu Aye, Inc. v. City of Hialeah*, 508 U.S. 520 (1993), in which the religion of Santeria was not specifically named in the statute found, on analysis, unconstitutionally to be directed against that religious group.

88. "Heresy trials are foreign to our Constitution," *United States v. Ballard*, 322 U.S. 78, 86 (1944) (Douglas, J., writing for the Court). On the unconstitutionality of blasphemy prosecutions under current American law of free speech and religious liberty, see Leonard W. Levy, *Blasphemy: Verbal Offense against the Sacred from Moses to Salman Rushdie* (New York: Knopf, 1993), 522–33, commenting, *inter alia*, on *Burstyn v. Wilson*, 343 U.S. 495 (1952) (censorship of movie, as sacrilege, held unconstitutional).

that they are excluded from the minimal rights and responsibilities of the moral community of persons. Political atrocity thus becomes thinkable and practical.

The case of anti-gay/lesbian initiatives is, as a matter of principle, exactly parallel. A dissenting form of conscience, on the grounds of its moral independence and dissenting claims for justice, is branded *for that reason* as heresy. The message is clear and clearly intended: persons should convert from this form of conscience that is wholly unworthy of respect to the only true religion of Americanism. The initiative is as much motored by sectarian religion and directed against dissenting conscience as the intolerably anti-Semitic initiative just discussed. Homosexuals are to late-twentieth-century sectarians what the Jews have traditionally been to sectarians in the Christian West throughout its history: intolerable heretics to dominant religious orthodoxy.[89]

The conception that homosexuality is a form of heresy or treason is both an ancient and modern ground for its condemnation.[90] In fact, there is no good reason to believe that the legitimacy of such forms of sexual expression destabilizes social cooperation. Homosexual relations are and will foreseeably remain the preference of small minorities of the population,[91] who are as committed

89. On the role that anti-Semitic ideology implicitly plays in the homophobia of the Christian Right, see Herman, *The Antigay Agenda*, 85–86, 116–28. On the historical background of such intolerance in ideas of Satan as the cause of Jewish unbelief and the analogy to contemporary homophobia, see Pagels, *The Origin of Satan*, 102–5.

90. Throughout the Middle Ages, homosexuals were persecuted as heretics and often burned at the stake on that ground. See Derrick S. Bailey, *Homosexuality and the Western Christian Tradition* (New York: Longmans, Green, 1955), 135. "Buggery," one of the names for homosexual acts, derives from a corruption of the name of one heretical group alleged to engage in homosexual practices. See ibid., pp. 141, 148–49. For a modern use of the idea of treason in this context, see Patrick Devlin, *The Enforcement of Morals* (London: Oxford University Press, 1965), 1–25. For rebuttal, see H. L. A. Hart, *Law, Liberty, and Morality* (Stanford: Stanford University Press, 1963); Hart, "Social Solidarity and the Enforcement of Morals," *University of Chicago Law Review* 35 (1967): 1.

91. The original Kinsey estimate that about 4 percent of males are exclusively homosexual throughout their lives is confirmed by comparable European studies. See Gebhard, "Incidence of Overt Homosexuality in the United States and Western Europe," *National Institute of Mental Health Task Force on Homosexuality*, ed. J. M. Livingood (Washington, D.C.: U.S. Government Printing Office, 1972), 22–29. The incidence figure remains stable even though many of the European countries do not apply the criminal penalty to consensual sex acts of the kind here under discussion. See

to principles of social cooperation and contribution as any other group in society at large; the issue, as with all suspect classes, is not one of increasing or decreasing the minority, but deciding whether we should treat such a minority justly with respect as persons or unjustly with contempt as unspeakably heretical outcasts. Indeed, the very accusation of heresy or treason brings out an important feature of the traditional moral condemnation in its contemporary vestments. It no longer appeals to generally acceptable arguments of necessary protections of the rights of persons to general goods; to the contrary, both the sexism and condemnation of nonprocreational sex of the traditional view are now inconsistent with the reasonable acceptability as general goods of both gender equality and nonprocreational sex.

Today, such condemnation appeals to arguments internal to highly personal, often sectarian religious decisions about acceptable ways of belief and life-style. When a moral tradition in this way abandons certain of its essential grounds in general goods, it may justly retain its legitimacy for those internal to the tradition, all the more so because it remains more exclusively constitutive of their tradition. But if those essential grounds are constitutionally necessary for the tradition coercively to enforce its mandates through the criminal law, the abandonment of those grounds must, *pari passu,* deprive the tradition of its constitutional legitimacy as a ground for enforcement though law. The tradition now no longer expresses nonsectarian ethical arguments that may fairly be imposed on all persons, but rather perspectives reasonably authoritative only for those who adhere to the tradition.

As we have seen, such reasonable attack has included criticism of this tradition both for its mandatory procreational demands and for its sexism; and both criticisms have, under American public law, significantly been expressed through constitutional principles of privacy and anti-discrimination for the benefit of the dominant heterosexual majority of both men and women. The entrenched

---

Walter Barnett, *Sexual Freedom and the Constitution* (Albuquerque: University of New Mexico Press, 1973), 293. Recent surveys indicate that as little as 2.8 percent of the population identify themselves as gay and less than half of that number as lesbian. See Robert T. Michael et al., *Sex in America: A Definitive Survey* (Boston: Little, Brown, 1994), 176.

orthodoxy is now much under reasonable critical attack in almost every imaginable aspect of heterosexual sexuality.[92] The orthodoxy, now in retreat in the domain of heterosexual sexuality, does not, however, extend such reasonable criticisms, as a matter of principle, to the examination of its traditional orthodoxy about homosexual sexuality. Rather, consistent with the paradox of intolerance (as in the case of Christian reasonable doubts about transubstantiation), it displaces its doubts from the reasonable doctrinal criticism of which it is most in need to the irrationalist scapegoating of a traditionally despised and culturally subjugated minority. It thus acquiesces in a war on homosexuals on sectarian grounds it would never accept in the other areas to which some sectarians extend their religious war (for example, on feminism, or on civil rights legislation in general).[93] To achieve such a constitutionally incoherent aim, its proponents suppress opposing views relevant to reasonable public argument, distort or misstate facts, disconnect values from ethical reasoning, indeed denigrate deliberation in politics in favor of a conception of politics that allegedly, as we shall see, *requires* the constitutional repression of dissent, a symbolic glorification of violence against claims of human rights.[94]

The arguments offered in support of Colorado Amendment Two exemplify all these features of the irrationalist politics associated with the paradox of intolerance. Six such arguments were examined and rejected, at the lower court level, by Judge Bayless in *Evans v. Romer*:[95] (1) the factionalized character of gay and lesbian identity,[96] (2) its militant aggression,[97] (3) the protection of ex-

---

92. See, for example, *Griswold v. Connecticut*, 381 U.S. 479 (1965); *Eisenstadt v. Baird*, 405 U.S. 438 (1972); *Roe v. Wade*, 410 U.S. 113 (1973); *Planned Parenthood of Southeastern Pennsylvania v. Casey*, 505 U.S. 833 (1992); *Frontiero v. Richardson*, 411 U.S. 677 (1973); *Craig v. Boren*, 429 U.S. 190 (1976).

93. On the antifeminism of the Religious Right, see Herman, *The Antigay Agenda*, 103–10; on their opposition to the civil rights agenda in general, see ibid., 111–36, 140.

94. Ibid., 76–80.

95. 1993 WL 518586 (Colo. Dist. Ct. 1993), reprinted in *CLE Materials*, to which reference is made hereafter in discussing this opinion. Judge Bayless examined the arguments in light of the standard of strict scrutiny required by the Colorado Supreme Court in *Evans v. Romer*, 854 P.2d 1270 (Colo. Sup. Ct. 1993), found them inadequate, and thus ordered that the preliminary injunction against Colorado Amendment Two be made permanent.

96. See *CLE Materials*, 25.

97. Ibid., 26.

isting suspect classes,[98] (4) privacy and religious rights of the heterosexual majority,[99] (5) not subsidizing political objections of interest groups,[100] and (6) protecting children.[101] All of them reflect the distortions of fact and value of the paradox of intolerance; I focus on the few that most dramatically illustrate the point. For example, Judge Bayless found the argument combating "militant gay aggression"[102] to be factually baseless.[103] As already observed, lesbians and gay men are a small minority of the American population. While relatively affluent[104] and sometimes influential,[105] their political gains have been comparatively small[106] and

98. Ibid., 27.
99. Ibid., 28.
100. Ibid., 29.
101. Ibid.
102. Ibid., 26.
103. Ibid., 27.
104. Marketing studies indicate gay and lesbian incomes are far in excess of the national average. See Joya L. Wesley, "With $394 Billion in Buying Power, Gays' Money Talks; and Corporate America Increasingly Is Listening," *Atlanta Journal,* December 1, 1991, p. F5. The 1990 census, measuring statistics for gay unmarried couples for the first time, showed gay male couples to have higher incomes than any other group, including heterosexual married couples. See Margaret S. Usdansky, "Gay Couples, By the Numbers—Data Suggest They're Fewer Than Believed, But Affluent," *USA Today,* April 12, 1993, p. 8A.
105. For a popular media account of gay power and influence, see, for example, Joni Balter, "Gay Power Brokers—Money, Stature and Savvy Give Leaders More Clout," *Seattle Times,* August 1, 1993, p. A1.
106. Only a handful of states and a comparatively tiny number of municipalities protect gays and lesbians from discrimination. Of the seventy-seven jurisdictions that have any sort of legislation or other government decree protecting lesbians and gay men, sixteen are merely resolutions, guidelines, or policy statements and are not fully binding. See Marc Wolinsky and Kenneth Sherrill, *Gays and the Military: Joseph Steffan versus the United States* (Princeton: Princeton University Press, 1993), 114. Only four states—Wisconsin, Massachusetts, Connecticut, and Hawaii—have any statewide legislation protecting the rights of homosexuals, while seven others have executive orders issued by governors. These executive orders are limited by the range of gubernatorial power and are rescinded more easily than legislation. Ibid. In twenty-five states, no jurisdiction whatsoever has *any* legislation or other governmental decree or policy which protects the rights of lesbians and gay men. Ibid. The importance of this legislation should not be overstated; as a recent *Harvard Law Review* study observes, "[V]ery little legislation protects gay men and lesbians from discrimination in the private sector. No federal statute prohibits discrimination by private citizens or organizations based on sexual orientation. Nor do the states provide protection: Only Wisconsin has a comprehensive statute barring such discrimination in employment." "Developments in the Law—Sexual Orientation and the Law," *Harvard Law Review* 102 (1989): 1508, 1667.

they remain radically underrepresented in key government positions.[107] Against this factual background, making an argument of "militant gay aggression" bespeaks a use of facts and values all too familiar in the history of intolerance, most grotesquely so in the late twentieth century.

Thus, the argument remarkably transforms the minority status of homosexuals, analogous to the similar irrationalist appeals of political anti-Semitism, into a secret and powerful conspiracy against which politics must be protected.[108] In effect, the very attempt by homosexuals or Jews to make any basic claims of equal citizenship and any small gains thus secured (including relative affluence and occasional influence) are irrationally interpreted as a murderous attack on dominant majorities. Normative outrage at the very idea of an outcast's claim of rights remakes reality to rationalize nullification of such rights. On this hallucinatory ground, aggression against basic rights of gay and lesbian persons is, as with Hitler's exactly comparable justification for his war on the Jews,[109] ideologically inverted into a reasonable "defensive measure"[110] of self-defense. No argument, offered in defense of Colorado Amendment Two, more starkly communicates the hermetically Manichean sectarian world view of its proponents—its polemical power to act as a distorting prism to remake reality in

107. In *Frontiero v. Richardson,* 411 U.S. 677 (1973), the Supreme Court found women as a class to be relatively politically powerless, despite the fact that then, as now, they constituted a majority of the electorate, because they were "vastly underrepresented in this Nation's decisionmaking councils." Id. at 686 n. 17. The Court based its conclusions on the fact that no woman had ever been elected president; that there had not yet been a woman Supreme Court Justice; that there were then no women in the United States Senate (although women had served as senators in the past); and that there were then only fourteen women in the House of Representatives. Id.

By this standard, lesbians and gay men are even more radically unrepresented. There has never been an openly gay president, nor Supreme Court Justice or even an openly gay federal court judge; there are no openly gay United States senators today, and there have never been any. Until 1984 there were no openly gay members of the United States House of Representatives, and while there are currently two gay House members, Congressmen Gerry Studds and Barney Frank, neither revealed his sexual orientation until after being elected. See Wolinsky and Sherrill, *Gays and the Military,* 20.

108. See, for an illuminating study of this argument, Herman, *The Antigay Agenda,* 116–28; on the analogy to anti-Semitism, see ibid., 85–86, 125–28.

109. For a characteristic example of the inversion of victims into aggressors and the compelling need to defend against them, see Adolf Hitler, *Mein Kampf* (New York: Reynal & Hitchcock, 1940), 824–27.

110. *CLE Materials,* 26.

its own ideological image of the wars of religion and to rationalize its conduct accordingly. Justice Scalia's critical remarks in his *Romer* dissent bespeak this perspective starkly. The persecutor is imaginatively transformed into the victim, thus rendering persecution innocent and indeed honorable. It is in such terms that good Germans acquiesced in Hitler's war on the Jews; it is in such terms that good Americans acquiesced in Colorado's war on gay and lesbian persons.[111]

Judge Bayless rejected the justification of Colorado Amendment Two, as protecting existing suspect classes, both because it lacked factual support and on the normative ground that fiscal concerns were inadequate to justify abridgement of basic rights and interests.[112] The alleged justification inverts a claim by gay and lesbian persons to basic equal justice, based on antidiscrimination principles available to all, into a claim for unequal, "special" rights subversive of guarantees of equality. Several courts have rejected as intrinsically distorting and manipulatively question-begging the wording of anti-gay/lesbian initiatives and referenda as opposing special laws for homosexuals.[113] But the implicit justification of such laws, as combating "special" rights, comes to the same thing. In effect, such polemics refuse to acknowledge what they are doing and mean to do: forbidding antidiscrimination laws. They do so by willfully suppressing the issues of principle common to all antidiscrimination laws, in effect, targeting an unpopular minority for making the same kind of claim that all other groups have made for such laws. Popular hostility is thus unreasonably directed at one form of antidiscrimination law by a rhetoric (confusing antidiscrimination with affirmative action) that irrationally stimulates unreflective social prejudice against a group precisely because it makes claims to antidiscrimination protections on grounds of principle.[114]

111. See, for example, Stephen Bransford, *Gay Politics vs. Colorado and America: The Inside Story of Amendment 2* (Cascade, Colo.: Sardis Press, 1994).

112. *CLE Materials*, 26.

113. See, for example, *Faipeas v. Municipality of Anchorage*, 860 P.2d 1214 (Ala. 1993); *Citizens for Responsible Behavior v. Superior Court*, 1 Cal. App. 4th 1013, 2 Cal. Rptr. 2d 648 (1992). Cf. *Mabon v. Keisling*, 856 P.2d 1023 (Or. 1993).

114. In effect, such rhetoric unreasonably confuses the case for antidiscrimination laws as such with the different though related case for affirmative action. Popular animus against affirmative action is thus unreasonably brought to bear on antidiscrimina-

Judge Bayless acknowledged that, in contrast to other alleged compelling state interests, the justification of Colorado Amendment Two in terms of protecting rights of personal, familial, and religious privacy at least articulated compelling state interests; but he denied that the amendment in question was, in light of its abridgment of the rights of homosexuals to nondiscrimination, sufficiently narrowly drawn to achieve these compelling interests.[115] But, "[i]n the present case, the religious belief urged by defendants is that homosexuals are condemned by scripture and therefore discrimination based on that religious teaching is protected within freedom of religion."[116] On this basis, discrimination against Jews, African Americans, and women could be similarly justified as protected by religious freedom since some sectarian interpretation of the Bible or its equivalent in other religious traditions could and would regard each of them as condemned. We would reject such an argument in these cases for the same reason we should reject it in the case of Colorado Amendment Two: under the basic terms of the American tradition of both free exercise and antiestablishment, let alone equal protection, the abridgment of basic rights requires a compelling, secular, nonsectarian justification.[117] The interpretation and justification of American religious liberty, enforced through Colorado Amendment Two, is, by its own admission, a sectarian interpretation of the Bible (with which many religious people in the Christian tradition disagree[118]), and, as such, an unconstitutional expression of religious intoler-

---

tion laws as such, when in fact strong proponents of antidiscrimination laws are sometimes skeptical of affirmative action. See, for example, Justice Powell's opinion in *Regents of University of California v. Bakke*, 438 U.S. 265 (1978).

115. *CLE Materials*, 28–29.

116. Ibid., 28.

117. For fuller development of this argument, see Richards, *Toleration and the Constitution;* Richards, *Conscience and the Constitution.*

118. See, for example, John Boswell, *Christianity, Social Tolerance and Homosexuality* (Chicago: University of Chicago Press, 1980); John J. McNeill, *The Church and the Homosexual* (Kansas City, Kan.: Sheed, Andrews & McMeel, 1976); cf. Derrick S. Bailey, *Homosexuality and the Western Christian Tradition* (New York: Longmans, Green, 1955); Bernadette J. Brooten, *Love between Women: Early Christian Responses to Female Homoeroticism* (Chicago: University of Chicago Press, 1996); Mark D. Jordan, *The Invention of Sodomy in Christian Theology* (Chicago: University of Chicago Press, 1997).

ance through public law.[119] In the Orwellian world of Colorado Amendment Two, sectarian religion has become the measure of respect for the inalienable right of conscience.

Judge Bayless also dismissed the defense of Colorado Amendment Two in terms of protecting children as unsupported by evidence, noting compelling evidence "that pedophiles are predominantly heterosexuals not homosexuals."[120] Colorado for Family Values, in its basic position paper on Amendment Two, had forthrightly espoused a range of such willful factual distortions by comparing homosexual orientation to "murder, theft, fraud, necrophilia, bestiality, and pedophilia."[121] In effect, elementary demands by lesbian and gay persons for equal treatment of their claims to the rights and responsibilities of adult public and private life have been transmogrified by advocates of Colorado Amendment Two, with no factual basic whatsoever, into bizarre claims to seduce and exploit the young as well as to murder and the like. We are, literally, in the same sectarian imaginative world as medieval anti-Semitism in which fantasies of cannibalism became the rationalizing measure of the massacre of the innocent and the just, or in the polemical world of modern anti-Semitism in which false conspiracies (by use of forged pamphlets like "The Protocols of the Elders of Zion") were manufactured; for example, such false conspiracies were concocted allegedly to show a comparable gay and lesbian conspiracy.[122] There are apparently no self-critical limits of accountability to fact or argument in a politics driven by the fantasies of sectarian religious intolerance as we know both from the history of anti-Semitism and from its more recent American expression, the religious war on gay and lesbian identity.[123] We need now, as much as ever, to remind ourselves of, to conserve, and to give effect to the American constitutional tradition of toleration that condemns, as indecent, a self-deceived and self-deceiving polemical

119. On the highly sectarian Biblical and theological basis for the war of the largely Protestant Christian Right on gays and lesbians (and its links with earlier attacks on Catholics, Jews, and communists), see, in general, Herman, *The Antigay Agenda.*

120. *CLE Materials,* 29.

121. Niblock, "Anti-Gay Initiatives," 170.

122. Herman, *The Antigay Agenda,* 85–86, 125–28.

123. For illuminating treatments, see Bull and Gallagher, *Perfect Enemies;* Herman, *The Antigay Agenda.*

politics that thus, through fantasy and fraud, creates a gargantuan appetite for the rights-denying evils that it monstrously feeds upon.

The perspective of the advocates of Colorado Amendment Two is that of a now much embattled religious orthodoxy on matters of sexuality and gender, one that frames its factual and normative distortions by the explanatory observation that homosexuals "often express deep hostility to traditional, Judeo-Christian moral beliefs and [family] values."[124] The terms of its homophobic agenda are self-consciously those of a larger, religiously sectarian "great cultural war."[125] What makes such a sectarian normative world both plausibly populist and so politically powerful is precisely the same dynamic that made political anti-Semitism plausible and powerful, namely, the paradox of intolerance.

The objection to homosexuals on the basis of their criticism of certain beliefs reveals this tangled political pathology. In fact, as we have seen, such traditional religious beliefs have been criticized, on religious and secular grounds, by a wide range of persons, most of them in fact heterosexual critics of a religion's indefensible insistence on procreational sexuality and its sexism;[126] criticisms of these sorts have, indeed, significantly shaped the interpretation of basic constitutional principles both of privacy and equal protection applicable to a wide range of issues relating to sexuality and gender.[127] Crucially, however, objection is not taken to such heterosexual critics, who would, as a matter of principle, be as logically prone to such sectarian condemnation as homosexual critics. However, the paradox of intolerance, in its nature, defies logic, suppressing internal critical doubts it might reasonably entertain (or, most probably, does entertain) about traditional religious views

124. See Niblock, "Anti-Gay Initiatives," 165 n. 70.
125. See, for example, Robert Sullivan, "An Army of the Faithful," *New York Times*, April 25, 1993, sec. 6 (magazine), p. 40.
126. For a useful history of such arguments in the area of the criticism of anticontraception laws, see Linda Gordon, *Woman's Body, Woman's Right: A Social History of Birth Control in America* (New York: Penguin, 1977).
127. See, for example, *Griswold v. Connecticut*, 381 U.S. 479 (1965); *Roe v. Wade*, 410 U.S. 113 (1973); *Planned Parenthood of Southeastern Pennsylvania v. Casey*, 505 U.S. 833 (1992); *Frontiero v. Richardson*, 411 U.S. 677 (1973); *Craig v. Boren*, 429 U.S. 190 (1976).

about heterosexual sexuality by singling out one group as the symbolic scapegoats of the embattled religious orthodoxy. Thus, among all the persons critical of traditional religious views, only one group is singled out by name by Colorado Amendment Two, one already the traditional object of unreasoning hatred and ignorance. The willful dynamics of the paradox of intolerance motor, as we have now seen at length, whatever rationalizing distortions of facts and values support its sectarian objective. The defense of the human rights of gay and lesbian persons becomes faction; arguments for such rights, unjust aggression; equality, inequality; sectarian convictions, the measure of the religious liberty; laws against discrimination, subsidizing an ideology; factual falsities, truths. Such insults to reason bespeak contempt for reason. Their appeal is at no point to arguments meeting impartial standards of epistemic and practical reason, which they blatantly flout. The nerve of their unreasonableness is their failure to extend such impartial standards to both a certain kind of claim and to the making of such a claim by gay and lesbian persons. Rather, their intrinsically irrationalist appeal turns on the manifold strategies of self-deception through which polemically entrenched convictions conceal from themselves and others their incoherence and their unreasonable willfulness when they are under reasonable criticism and debate both internally and externally in the larger society.[128] The motivational drive of such strategies gives rise to the grotesquely unreasonable interpretation accorded both the substance of the claims made and the making of such claims by gay and lesbian persons, in particular, substantive arguments of basic human rights claimed by gay and lesbian persons as bearers of human rights. The motivational drive behind the arguments they offer depends on distortions of fact or value that aim to rationalize to those already committed to the traditional orthodoxy its failure both to recognize the substance of such arguments and the right of gay and lesbian persons to make such arguments. The effort of reasonable justification is simply not recognized or acknowledged as owing to gay and lesbian persons, as persons. To the contrary,

---

128. For an illuminating philosophical study of these issues, see Denise Meyerson, *False Consciousness* (Oxford: Clarendon Press, 1991).

both the substance and the making of such rights-based claims, as normative claims, *must* be denied any factual or normative basis whatsoever.

The threat of gay and lesbian identity is, from this perspective, its expression of the powers of moral personality to originate legitimate claims of human rights. It is this perspective and only this perspective that can explain why claims of gay and lesbian identity have, as such, been inflated in the irrationalist terms of an aggressive threat, and why, in service of such irrationalism, the most minimal standards of intellectual and ethical responsibility in making political arguments have not been extended to lesbians and gay men as citizens and as persons. Such unreason violates the basic norms of civility central to the reasonable justification of political power in a constitutional democracy.[129] Its unreason strips political power of legitimacy, and renders it a work of willful political violence that shames our constitutionalism. As one court observed in striking down a comparable initiative: "All that is lacking is a sack of stones for throwing."[130]

Such arguments draw their irrationalist polemical power, in the same way anti-Semitism drew its political power, from a long history of cultural exclusion and degradation, in this case, of homosexuals from Western religio-moral community. An embattled religious orthodoxy chooses to suppress its own reasonable doubts about its tradition by choosing one small, traditionally despised group of such dissenters, and engages in a politics of identity, based on the paradox of intolerance, that effectively demonizes this group as heretics to moral value in living; the powerful political appeal of such polemics draws upon a long cultural tradition of moral slavery of the group in question, who, traditionally silenced and silent, are barely recognized as human and certainly not acknowledged as persons. In effect, a public opinion, formed on injustice, is polemically aroused to insist on its status as the measure of justice, and thus acquiesces in the degradation, as Colorado Amendment Two does degrade, dissenters to its injustice from the

129. See, in general, John Rawls, *Political Liberalism* (New York: Columbia University Press, 1993).

130. See *Citizens for Responsible Behavior v. Superior Court,* 1 Cal. App. 4th, 2 Cal. Rptr. 2d 648 (1992), passage cited in *CLE Materials,* 172.

very constitutional possibility of a person of conscience worthy of making elementary claims to justice. The constitutional evil of this initiative is transparently revealed in and by its very terms, that is, its constitutional entrenchment of a prohibition on precisely the claims of justice made by and on behalf of this group and only this group.

On this view, initiatives like Colorado Amendment Two unconstitutionally enlist the state as the agent of the political construction of intolerance. The fact of a long history of injustice, whether of Christian or anti-Christian anti-Semitism[131] or the subjection of women and homosexuals, cannot be the just measure of constitutional argument in this domain. In all these cases, the interpretive responsibilities imposed by constitutional guarantees of basic human rights like conscience must be critically to resist and repel the force of such history, precisely when such history is aggressively used against wholly just claims of constitutional rights made by and on behalf of a group of persons who has only recently reclaimed its rights of human nature against a tradition of repressive and subjugating moral slavery.[132]

The moral slavery of homosexuals may indeed today in America cut deeper and thus more unjustly into moral personality than that of African Americans, women, and Jews. For one thing, the moral slavery of these latter groups was usually rationalized in terms of some legitimate, albeit servile social space that the group might occupy; but, the social space occupied by homosexuals was and is that of the culturally unspeakable, which is the ultimate in cultural death and invisibility. For another, African Americans and women appeal to and elaborate a heritage of American antiracist and antisexist dissent at least as old as the abolitionist movement;[133] and Jewish Americans appeal both to a long historical tradition of learned dissent from Christian orthodoxy and the constitutional

131. On anti-Christian anti-Semitism, see Richards, *Conscience and the Constitution*, 156–57.

132. On the relatively recent emergence of a self-identified homosexual minority in the United States, see John D'Emilio, *Sexual Politics, Sexual Communities: The Making of a Homosexual Minority in the United States, 1940–1970* (Chicago: University of Chicago Press, 1983).

133. See, in general, Richards, *Conscience and the Constitution*; Richards, "Public Reason and Abolitionist Dissent."

principles of respect for dissenting conscience central to the American tradition of both free exercise and antiestablishment.[134]

The critical resources of the struggle for justice of lesbians and gay men are altogether more recent and fragile,[135] certainly not of a strength remotely commensurate to the strength of their arguments of justice. Indeed, the very making of such claims was, in contrast to such claims by African Americans and women, the object of repressive censorship in the United States until well after World War II. It is against this repressive background that the making of such claims is regarded today by many Americans as, at best, laughable, and, at worst, the object of vilifying unreason, reflecting a constitutionally decadent public opinion in which a lowest common denominator of unreflective majoritarian preferences is taken to be the measure of human and constitutional rights. A nation, in which majorities are thus demagogically persuaded, realizes the darkest nightmare of the tyrannical majority that worried America's constitutional Founders.[136]

Both the recency and fragility of the critical resources of gay and lesbian identity reflect not the merits of their case, but the extraordinary history of moral subjugation of homosexuals to which I have already made reference and the reality-shaping power that dehumanizing history evidently still so powerfully possesses for many Americans here and now in the late twentieth century. In effect, one of the gravest forms of constitutionally condemned traditions of moral slavery still flourishing in the late twentieth century is, in virtue of the power of the tradition of subjugation, the one most invisible to the complacent American public mind. Such a public mind is for this reason, in late twentieth century America, so uncritically and so easily polemically aroused to inflict with such guiltless self-righteousness the tyrannies that moral slavery wreaks on moral personality.

134. See, in general, Richards, *Toleration and the Constitution;* Richards, *Conscience and the Constitution.*

135. For an important recent study of some of these resources, see Jonathan Dollimore, *Sexual Dissidence: Augustine to Wilde, Freud to Foucault* (Oxford: Clarendon Press, 1991).

136. For Madison's worries about the tyrannical propensities of majority rule and the role of constitutionalism in limiting these propensities, see Richards, *Foundations of American Constitutionalism,* 107–9, 135, 180.

EXCLUSION FROM THE MILITARY

The issue of gay rights has recently come to national attention in two further contexts: President Clinton's initiation of a review of the current policy of exclusion of homosexuals from the military (leading to congressional adoption of Clinton's proposed change in policy, "Don't Ask, Don't Tell"), and congressional consideration of the Defense of Marriage Act (supported also by Clinton) that tries to limit the effect, under the Full Faith and Credit Clause of the United States Constitution,[137] of the possible legalization of same-sex marriage in Hawaii. In both cases, the legislation in question uses the classification of sexual preference (in particular, conscientious claims of gay and lesbian identity) in a constitutionally suspect way, and neither can survive the level of scrutiny in terms of compelling state secular purposes such laws must survive in order to be constitutional. I begin with the military exclusion question, then turn to same-sex marriage.

The pertinent law currently in constitutional dispute is 10 U.S.C. § 654, the popularly known "Don't Ask, Don't Tell" policy governing the participation of homosexuals in the military service, and the accompanying directives issued by the Department of Defence ("DoD") and the secretary of transportation. The background of this legislation lay in a debate, initiated by President Clinton, over whether homosexuals could any longer reasonably be excluded from service in the military.[138] In January 1993, Clinton directed the secretary of defense to review this policy, which led to such review and extensive hearings in both houses of Congress on the question of military service by homosexuals.[139] The President announced, several months later, a new policy which was the basis for section 654. In the legislation, Congress provided that a service member would be separated from the armed services,

---

137. See U.S. Const. art. IV, § 1.

138. For a good review of the historical background, see Lawrence J. Korb, "The President, the Congress, and the Pentagon: Obstacles to Implementing the 'Don't Ask, Don't Tell' Policy," in *Out in Force: Sexual Orientation and the Military*, ed. Gregory M. Herek, Jared B. Jobe, and Ralph M. Carney (Chicago: University of Chicago Press, 1996), 290–301.

139. See, for example, S. Rep. No. 112, 103d Cong., 1st sess. 269–70 (1993).

pursuant to regulations to be promulgated by the secretary of defense, in terms that generally tracked the previous policy (including, among the grounds for separation, gay sex acts and same-sex marriage) with the exception of the second ground for separation which now reads:

> (2) That the member has stated that he or she is a homosexual or bisexual, or words to that effect, unless there is a further finding, made and approved in accordance with procedures set forth in the regulations, that the member has demonstrated that he or she is not a person who engages in, or attempts to engage in, has a propensity to engage in, or intends to engage in homosexual acts.[140]

The regulations implementing the new policy state that its purpose is not aimed at the separation of homosexuals on status grounds alone.[141] In addition, the new policy sharply restricts the circumstances under which the military authorities may initiate an investigation of a service member: such an investigation may not be initiated without cause and a criminal investigation based on consensual gay sex acts must be based on credible evidence. Credible evidence of homosexual acts does not include "associational activity such as going to a gay bar, possessing or reading homosexual publications, associating with known homosexuals, or marching in a gay rights rally in civilian clothes. Such activity, in and of itself, does not provide evidence of homosexual conduct."[142] And applicants "shall not be asked or required to reveal whether they are heterosexual, homosexual, or bisexual."[143]

A number of constitutional difficulties could be raised about each of the grounds for exclusion under both the old and new policies: first, the ground of all homosexual sex acts in contrast to sexual relations or untoward sexual exploitation or harassment as such, heterosexual or homosexual, that prejudice legitimate mili-

140. 10 U.S.C. § 654(b). For the previous policy, see Richards, *Women, Gays, and the Constitution*, 413.

141. See DoD Directive No. 1332.14, encl. 3, pt. 1, at H.1b(2).

142. See Guidelines for Fact-Finding into Homosexual Conduct, Enclosure 4 to DoDD 1332.14, Enlisted Administrative Separations and Enclosure 8 to DoDD 1332.30, Separations of Regular Commissioned Officers, News Release No. 605-93, Office of Assistant Secretary of Defense (Public Affairs), Washington, D.C. 20231, December 22, 1993, 4-4.

143. See Directive No. 1304.26, encl. 1, at B.8.a.

tary interests; second, self-identifying speech as a homosexual; and third, same-sex marriage.

The exclusion on the basis of gay consensual sex may have been regarded as unproblematic when *Bowers v. Hardwick* was good law, but *Bowers* assumed the Court's acceptance of mere majoritarian moral opinion as the measure of constitutional toleration. If that were still acceptable, *Romer v. Evans* could arguably not have been decided as it was by six justices of the Supreme Court. The state's arguments in support of Colorado Amendment Two appealed to the strength of majoritarian moral opinion about homosexuality. When the Court found the amendment to lack a rational basis, it implicitly repudiated the force of such moral opinions as the measure of constitutional rights. If that is true in a case dealing with a state constitutional amendment forbidding antidiscrimination laws, it should apply, *a fortiori*, to the much deeper intrusion into moral sovereignty at stake in *Bowers*. *Bowers*, for this reason, should be regarded as no longer authoritative. If so, *Bowers* should no longer be regarded as good authority for the blunderbuss prohibition of gay sex as such in the exclusion policy.

If exclusion on the ground of gay sex simpliciter was problematic, the case for the unconstitutionality of the speech-based ground would be quite straightforward. Indeed, the new policy makes even clearer than the old policy that the speech-based ground is justified as good rebuttable evidence of gay sex acts. If such sex acts could not be crudely forbidden in the way both the new and old policies contemplate, both policies would be in doubt, the new policy quite clearly so. Even the ground of same-sex marriage might be problematic if the illegitimacy of *Bowers* was interpreted in terms of a sufficiently robust basic right of the person to moral independence in making decisions central to one's intimate life. I postpone further discussion of this last point until the discussion of the constitutional basis for same-sex marriage (in the next section), and turn here to constitutional discussion of the other grounds, in particular, self-identifying speech.[144]

144. For similar discussions, see Nan D. Hunter, "Life after *Hardwick*," in Duggan and Hunter, *Sex Wars*, 85–100; and "Identity, Speech, and Equality," in ibid., 123–43. See also David Cole and William N. Eskridge, Jr., "From Hand-Holding to Sodomy: First Amendment Protection of Homosexual (Expressive) Conduct," *Harvard Civil Rights–Civil Liberties Law Review* 29 (1994): 319.

The provision might be constitutionally problematic even if *Bowers* were good law, or at least good law in the military, if not the civilian context. The measure of free speech protection, under well-accepted American principles of free speech, is not limited to speech endorsing acts that are legal. In particular, the very core of the modern law of free speech is the protection of subversive advocacy—speech offering reasons for why current institutions are so fundamentally unjust that they should be rejected.[145] It is the speech that confronts American institutions with the most fundamental criticism (going to their basic worth) that most deserves judicial protection on grounds of free speech, not the speech that limits its criticisms to the measure of what is currently legal and acceptable. If so, constitutional protection of speech involving illegal acts would be called for though no one challenged the legitimacy of making such acts illegal.

In fact, of course, the moral and political reality of the exclusion policy is that there is enormous public controversy over the legitimacy of the traditional premise of the policy, one that condemned gay sex as immoral. Any discussion of the self-identifying speech ground, as an independent basis, must therefore be highly artificial, treating as a free speech issue what is as much an issue of legitimate criminalization. Indeed, as several commentators have critically observed, the new policy disingenuously confuses speech with conduct and conduct with speech in an unstable semiotics that may indulge, if not encourage, prejudiced enforcement by military authorities.[146] The issues are especially closely linked in the context of the military exclusion if, as I believe and will argue, the interlinked grounds for both exclusions are the normative con-

---

145. See *Brandenburg v. Ohio*, 395 U.S. 444 (1969) (speech advocating violent overthrown of government held protected and subject to demanding test of high probability of very grave harms not rebuttable in the normal course). For discussion and defense of this development in American public law, see Richards, *Toleration and the Constitution*, 178–87.

146. See Janet E. Halley, "The Status/Conduct Distinction in the 1993 Revisions to Military Anti-Gay Policy," *GLQ: A Journal of Lesbian and Gay Studies* 3 (1996): 159–252; Theodore R. Sarbin, "The Deconstruction of Stereotypes: Homosexuals and Military Policy," in *Out in Force*, ed. Herek, Jobe, and Carney, 189; Gail L. Zellman, "Implementing Policy Changes in Large Organizations: The Case of Gays and Lesbians in the Military," in ibid., 283.

ception of religious, racial, or gender roles that we have elsewhere, on grounds of constitutional principle, increasingly rejected as the measure of public rights and responsibilities. These constitutionally illegitimate purposes find fertile grounds in the military context because it, of all forms of state action, has been the one most traditionally associated with a defining, indeed constitutive sense of American nationality and citizenship that has historically unjustly excluded classes of persons, on constitutionally illegitimate grounds, from such a national identity as fully citizens. A constitutionally defective conception of national citizenship has been constructed on the basis of such exclusions.

Many of the great struggles for inclusion of such groups in American citizenship have thus been over access on equal terms to military service. Perhaps the best evidence of how constitutive such participation in the military has been of American nationality and citizenship is the African American experience in the Civil War.[147]

Until surprisingly late in the Civil War, Lincoln was considering various measures that would, after slavery had been decisively ended in the United States, colonize the freedmen and women abroad where they could establish their own national forms.[148] Lincoln, though morally opposed to slavery, could, no more than Jefferson (who was also antislavery), contemplate a national community that included on equal terms African Americans.[149] Under the pressure of abolitionist advocacy and military exigency, Lincoln authorized raising African American troops to serve in the war effort, and they played in important role in the Union victory.[150] Under the moral pressure of such participation (albeit in segregated regiments), Lincoln gradually came to the view that African Americans were now morally owed what he had once, like most Americans, assumed to be unthinkable, the radical abolition-

147. See James M. McPherson, *The Struggle for Equality: Abolitionists and the Negro in the Civil War and Reconstruction* (Princeton: Princeton University Press, 1964), 192–220.

148. See David Herbert Donald, *Lincoln* (New York: Simon & Schuster, 1995), 166–67, 343–48, 396–97.

149. For an important recent study of Jefferson and his racist legacy to America, see Paul Finkelman, *Slavery and the Founders: Race and Liberty in the Age of Jefferson* (Armonk, N.Y.: M. E. Sharpe, 1996), 105–67.

150. See James McPherson, *The Struggle for Equality*, 193–220.

ist dream of full inclusion of African Americans into the American political and moral community of equal rights and responsibilities.[151] Military service was the moralizing practice of equal responsibilities that gave birth to America's moral growth into at least the serious beginning of an American constitutional theory and practice of equal rights.

The later struggle of African Americans to serve in a racially integrated military culminated in President Truman's 1948 executive order calling for desegregation of the armed services, finally embraced by the military after the outbreak of the Korean War in June 1950.[152] That struggle was as important to the antiracist aims of the civil rights movement as integration in public education was. If integration in public education would make feasible a new public culture of inclusive educational and cultural opportunity, integration in the military would take the equally important step of forging a practice of the equal responsibilities of all citizens that would institutionalize as well a more profoundly rooted American sense of the equal rights of all Americans.

The struggle of African Americans to claim their basic rights as Americans was, as we have seen, in its nature a hard fought argument against a conception of national identity that had historically denationalized them as part of the American people; as Chief Justice Roger Taney put the point in *Dred Scott v. Sanford:*

> They [African Americans] had for more than a century before been regarded as beings of an inferior order, and altogether unfit to associate with the white race, either in social or political relations; and so far inferior, that they had no rights which the white man was bound to respect; and that the negro might justly and lawfully be reduced to slavery for his benefit. . . . It was regarded as an axiom in morals as well as in politics, which no one thought of disputing, or supposed to be open to dispute; and men in every grade and position in society daily and habitually acted upon it in their private

151. See Donald, *Lincoln,* 430, 456–57, 526–27, 556.
152. See Donald G. Nieman, *Promises to Keep: African-Americans and the Constitutional Order, 1776 to the Present* (New York: Oxford University Press, 1991), 139–42; Michael R. Kauth and Dan Landis, "Applying Lessons Learned from Minority Integration in the Military," in *Out in Force,* ed. Herek, Jobe, and Carney, 86–105.

pursuits, as well as in matters of public concern, without doubting for a moment the correctness of this opinion.[153]

Such denationalization depended on the dehumanizing abridgment of basic human rights (the basic equal rights of conscience, speech, intimate life, and work). After slavery, institutions of segregation and antimiscegenation laws maintained that dehumanized image and status by enforcing exclusion from the institutions of American cultural life and the exercise of culture-creating rights. Integration into these institutions advanced the aims of the civil rights movement because such access, on terms of respect for culture-creating rights, affirmed their rights-based constitutional claims as persons and as citizens.

Integration into the military had the focal significance that it did because such participation affirmed the status of African Americans as equal bearers of rights and responsibilities in the role of citizen-soldier historically important in the theory and practice of republican government.[154] In particular, American revolutionary constitutionalism, both in the wake of the American Revolution and of the Civil War, affirmed a constitutional theory and practice of respect for inalienable human rights, tested the legitimacy of political power in terms of such rights, and affirmed the right of persons and citizens to question and resist illegitimate such laws on constitutional grounds.[155] A theory and practice, thus based on respect for inalienable human rights, morally empowered persons freely to exercise their basic rights, including taking steps, when necessary, to assert and defend their rights.

One of the most insidious consequences of slavery under American revolutionary constitutionalism was that its racist rationalization required that African Americans be so dehumanized that they lacked such rights and thus the right to resist and, if necessary, revolt. Otherwise, the very foundations of American constitutionalism would legitimate the slave revolts that were the terror of the

---

153. *Dred Scott v. Sanford,* 60 U.S. (19 How.) 393, 407 (1857).

154. For illuminating discussion of this point from a skeptical feminist perspective, see Jean Bethke Elshtain, *Women and War* (New York: Basic Books, 1987), 47–91.

155. See, in general, Richards, *Foundations of American Constitutionalism;* Richards, *Conscience and the Constitution.*

American South.[156] Participation of African Americans in the Union armies was so transformative for American racist public opinion because it directly challenged the dehumanized image of African Americans as natural slaves. On the basis of such participation, American blacks laid claim to their human right and responsibility to resist the total abridgment of their rights that American slavery involved. Integration of African Americans into the American military powerfully made this deeper point in the deconstruction of American racism. It was important in this struggle that the sense of indignation at segregation in the military would become most intense after American participation in wars justified in terms of American rights-respecting republican values and principles, to wit, World War I and World War II.[157] The latter war, conceived in terms of the defeat of an aggressively racist power, particularly called for full integration of African Americans in the struggle against such a racist power.[158] It is striking, along these lines, that such integration should have taken place by order of President Truman in 1948,[159] and be followed in 1954 by *Brown v. Board of Education.*

Military service has a special character and role under American revolutionary constitutionalism as a public institution concerned to protect and defend rights-based constitutional institutions (of which the military itself is one). Accordingly, as the African American struggle makes abundantly clear, military service in the United States cannot be cordoned off from the larger struggles of rights-based justice under American constitutionalism. It is not and never has been a bystander to these struggles,

156. The black abolitionist, David Walker, had thus asked in his 1829 *Appeal:* "Now, Americans! I ask you candidly, was your sufferings under Great Britain, one hundredth part as cruel and tyrannical as you have rendered ours under you?" See David Walker, *Walker's Appeal, in Four Articles, Together with a Preamble, to the Coloured Citizens of the World,* in *A Documentary History of the Negro People in the United States,* ed. Herbert Aptheker (New York: Citadel Press Books, 1990), 1:97. For good general studies of the slave revolts, see Eugene D. Genovese, *From Rebellion to Revolution: Afro-American Slave Revolts in the Making of the Modern World* (Baton Rouge: Louisiana State University Press, 1979); Herbert Aptheker, *American Negro Slave Revolts* (New York: International Publishers, 1952).

157. See Nieman, *Promises to Keep,* 114–15, 139–40.

158. See Mary L. Dudziak, "Desegregation as a Cold War Imperative," *Stanford Law Review* 41 (1988): 61.

159. See Nieman, *Promises to Keep,* 141.

but itself has been, by its nature, involved in some of the nation's most disgraceful rights-denying exclusions and its most significant steps taken to remedy such constitutional evils. The claim that, by its nature, it must be immunized from civilian principles of constitutional analysis cannot reasonably be extended to rights-denying exclusions which, by their nature, compromise the very legitimacy of the role of the military under American rights-based constitutionalism. We must, rather, in each case inquire whether a ground for exclusion uncritically enforces a conception of national identity inconsistent with the demands of American constitutionalism.[160]

Issues of this sort arise in ongoing public discussions in the United States about the place and terms of the service of women, if any, in the military. Two issues should be distinguished: first, whether women may serve in the military at all; and second, assuming they may serve, whether they should be excluded from combat. The two issues are related in the following way: if women can reasonably be excluded from combat, the case for exclusion from the military as such may be stronger. For example, in *Rostker v. Goldberg*,[161] the Supreme Court considered the constitutionality of the exclusion of women from the requirement to register for the draft, and decided, 6–3, that the exclusion was constitutional. All justices assumed that the combat exclusion was legitimate. On that basis, it was easier for the majority to find the exclusion to be reasonable because considerably lesser numbers of women than men would be needed to serve in combat roles. Women now serve in the American military; indeed, there are more women in the military in the United States than any other country.[162] The main issue in dispute has been the legitimacy of the combat exclusion.[163]

The 1991 report[164] of a presidential commission on this matter

160. On the relevance of this experience to the integration of gays and lesbians into the military, see Kauth and Landis, "Applying Lessons Learned from Minority Integration in the Military."

161. 453 U.S. 57 (1981).

162. See Jean Bethke Elshtain, *Women and War* (New York: Basic Books, 1987).

163. See, in general, Nancy Loring Goldman, *Female Soldiers—Combatants or Non-combatants* (Westport, Conn.: Greenwood Press, 1982). But for general skepticism about service of women in the military at all, see Brian Mitchell, *Weak Link: The Feminization of the American Military* (Washington, D.C.: Regnery Gateway, 1989).

164. Presidential Commission on the Assignment of Women in the Armed Forces, *Women in Combat: Report to the President* (Washington, D.C.: Brassey's, 1991) (hereinafter *Women in Combat*).

unanimously recommended exclusion of women from ground combat (24–27), narrowly (8–7) recommended exclusion of women from service on aircraft in combat missions (28–30), and recommended (8–6, 1 abstention) that women be allowed to serve on combatant vessels except submarine and amphibious vessels (31–33). The grounds offered for the combat exclusion clustered in three categories: physical differences (bearing on "muscular strength and aerobic capacity" relevant to "tasks central to ground combat" [24]); unit cohesion factors (in particular, forced intimacy on the battlefield, paternalistic attitudes to women that undermine "such key ingredients [of unit cohesion] as mutual confidence, commonality of experience, and equitable treatment," and "dysfunctional relationships [e.g. sexual misconduct]"); and mistreatment of women after capture (which "could have negative impact on male captives") (25). None of these factors would reasonably justify exclusion in all cases; for example, the seven dissenters to the exclusion of women from combat aircraft have the stronger case for integration on the basis of the indisputable fact of "women's physical capability to perform in combat aviation" (81). Unit cohesion "is a function of leadership, shared purposes, and common risks and rewards" and should not be a bar when there is no demonstrated difference that would "be a contributing factor to the deterioration of unit performance" (81); and, as to worries about capture, it is not reasonable that "women who are willing to accept those risks should be restricted from competing for combat aviation assignments because of the protective tendencies of others" (83).

The force of arguments of rights-based feminism in this domain has recently been underscored by the Supreme Court's decision, 7–1, in *United States v. Virginia*.[165] In ruling that the exclusion on the basis of gender from Virginia Military Institute (VMI), a public military college, was unconstitutional, Justice Ginsburg, writing for the Court, critically examined the college's arguments of alleged gender differences in light of a constitutionally based skepticism about crude gender stereotypes that themselves reflect a history of unjust gender-based discrimination in basic rights and opportunities (2280–84). Ginsburg conceded, "for purposes of this

165. 116 S. Ct. 2264 (1996).

decision, that most women would not choose VMI's adversative method" (2280). But, in the same spirit of Justice Brennan's skepticism about giving effect to statistically significant factual differences between men and women rooted in unjust gender stereotypes in *Craig v. Boren* (see chapter 2), the Court denied that such differences can "constitutionally deny to women who have the will and capacity, the training and attendant opportunities that VMI uniquely affords" (2280).

In particular, the Court emphasized that women's integration into both federal military academies and the armed forces abundantly confirmed the equal competence of women as citizen-soldiers once they were afforded an equal opportunity (2281). Accordingly, any exclusion of women from a public military academy, on the grounds of cultural stereotypes of incapacity to be citizen-soldiers, must be held to a high standard of constitutional scrutiny in terms of an exceedingly persuasive justification; only such a level of heightened scrutiny can make sure that the operative generalization rested on compelling grounds independent of the rights-denying cultural stereotype. Such a justification was lacking here, and the exclusion was accordingly unconstitutional (2281–87).

Justice Ginsburg powerfully brings arguments of rights-based feminism to bear on the military domain, suggesting that gender integration in the military may be as important to the equality of women as racial integration was to African Americans.[166] Our earlier examination of the African American struggle for integration suggests why this should be so. Sexist, like racist, exclusion from the military affirms a dehumanized stereotype of servile dependence, certainly not the status of persons with moral powers that originate and demand claims of basic human rights, test the legitimacy of political power in those terms, and stand ready, if necessary, to uphold their basic rights, whether by self-defense, by resistance, or, if necessary, by revolution. Such defensive rights (to protect one's rights) dignify moral personality as a bearer of rights; it is, for this reason, that recognition of such rights (for groups previously subjugated) humanizes its members as, indeed, bearers

---

166. The Court indeed cites *Sweatt v. Painter*, 339 U.S. 629 (1950) (admitting African Americans to University of Texas Law School) as a relevant analogy.

of human rights (contesting the stereotype of subhumanity that subjugated them).[167] If Justice Ginsburg is correct on the importance to a rights-based constitutional feminism of gender integration in the military domain, the admission of women to the American volunteer military may now be regarded as constitutionally compelled. If that is so, then Jean Bethke Elshtain may be correct that "[t]here seems little point in maintaining the pretense of combat exclusion for 'their protection.' Nobody can be protected any longer in the old sense of being 'immune from possible destruction.' "[168]

In fact, perhaps reflecting the force of such arguments, incremental change in both congressional legislation and Department of Defense rules has substantially eroded the combat exclusion for women.[169] Both the integration of African Americans and of women into the military support the analogous case, on grounds of principle, for inclusion of gays and lesbians. The experience of such inclusion both in foreign militaries and in domestic police and fire departments suggests that appropriately articulated and enforced policies of integration are as reasonable and feasible as they have been in the cases of the integration of African Americans and women.[170]

It is certainly striking in this connection that the institutional

167. For an important exploration of this theme in terms of a normative argument for rights of resistance, by battered women, to violence from their spouses, see Jane Maslow Cohen, "Regimes of Private Tyranny: What Do They Mean to Morality and for the Criminal Law?" *University of Pittsburgh Law Review* 57 (1996): 757.

168. See Elshtain, *Women and War*, 244.

169. For a useful overview of these changes, see Madeline Morris, "By Force of Arms: Rape, War and Military Culture," *Duke Law Journal* 45 (1996): 732–38. For a recent expression of doubt by an anthropologist, see Anna Simons, "In War, Let Men Be Men," *New York Times*, April 23, 1997, p. A23.

170. *Out in Force*, ed. Herek, Jobe, and Carney, has many essays that expand on these ideas: see Kauth and Landis, "Applying Lessons Learned from Minority Integration in the Military," 86–105; Patricia J. Thomas and Marie D. Thomas, "Integration of Women in the Military: Parallels to the Progress of Homosexuals?" 65–85; Paul A. Gade, David R. Segal, and Edgar M. Johnson, "The Experience of Foreign Militaries," 106–30; Paul Koegel, "Lessons Learned from the Experience of Domestic Police and Fire Departments," 131–56; Robert J. MacCoun, "Sexual Orientation and Military Cohesion: A Critical Review of the Evidence," 157–76; Gail L. Zellman, "Implementing Policy Changes in Large Organizations: The Case of Gays and Lesbians in the Military," 266–89.

crucible for the development of the modern American movement for gay rights was the experience of gay men and lesbians in the military during World War II, including their resistance on grounds of justice to discrimination in the military.[171] The practice of gay rights in America, long before it had any publicly articulated theory, was thus formed around a sense of common identity in resisting injustice in the military service they rendered to the United States, as citizens, in perhaps the greatest struggle for human rights, against its self-conscious enemies, in human history. If participation in this struggle energized already existing claims of justice on behalf of African Americans, it literally forged the practice of making such claims of justice by American gay men and lesbians, who self-defined their previously unspeakable common identity in terms of making such claims.[172]

The distance gay men and lesbians traveled in this period was the distance from moral slavery to freedom, from submissive unspeakability to morally independent voice on grounds of the central rights-based principles of American constitutionalism. It would take time for such practices to become self-consciously political and to develop a sense of their place in the larger fabric of an emerging rights-based civil rights movement. But they first tested their moral voice in the military context because both its homosocial context, away from traditional ties and communities, and larger rights-based purposes made such a personal and political growth in moral consciousness factually and normatively possible;[173] for this reason, quite unsurprisingly, there may be a higher rate of same-gender sexual behavior in the military than in the general population.[174] Paradoxically, the institution that gave rise to and indeed sustained the practice of gay rights is now the state

171. See, in general, Allan Berube, *Coming Out under Fire: The History of Gay Men and Women in World War Two* (New York: Free Press, 1990).

172. See, in general, Berube, *Coming Out under Fire;* Randy Shilts, *Conduct Unbecoming: Gays and Lesbians in the U.S. Military* (New York: St. Martin's Press, 1993).

173. See, in general, Berube, *Coming Out under Fire.*

174. See, for relevant studies, Janet Lever and David E. Kanouse, "Sexual Orientation and Proscribed Sexual Behaviors," in *Out in Force,* ed. Herek, Jobe, and Carney, 22 (gay men); Thomas and Thomas, "Integration of Women in the Military," 72 (lesbians).

institution that most vigorously and self-consciously represses its claims, indeed makes the very assertion of such claims the ground for separation from military service.

It is against this background that we must constitutionally assess our current military policy on the exclusion of homosexuals, "Don't Ask, Don't Tell." Certainly, some aspects of the new policy are an advance over the previous policy. It clearly repudiates, for example, using sexual preference as such as a ground for separation, an aspect of the earlier policy that several federal courts have correctly found unconstitutional.[175] It carefully limits the kinds of evidence that may credibly be used to show homosexual acts, excluding, for example, going to gay bars or attending a gay rights parade (thus, protecting, to some degree, associational rights). It draws the line, however, at self-identifying oneself as gay or lesbian and, *a fortiori*, same-sex marriage, literally making such self-identifying exercises of speech a *per se* ground for separation. Once having made such a self-identifying statement, it is practically impossible to rebut the inference, which the policy requires one to rebut, namely, that one has a "propensity" to gay sex; as Judge Nickerson made clear in an opinion, later reversed, striking down the policy as unconstitutional, "propensity" here comes to the same thing as having a gay sexual orientation.[176] The ground for exclusion from the military under the new policy is thus the public assertion of one's identity as a gay and lesbian person. On the view earlier taken, this represents an unconstitutional abridgment by the state, at a minimum, of the central human rights of personal

175. See, for example, *Watkins v. United States Army,* 837 F.2d 1428 (9th Cir. 1988) (regulation barring gays violates equal protection by discriminating on basis of homosexual orientation); cf. *Watkins v. United States Army,* 875 F.2d 699 (9th Cir. 1989) (army estopped from barring soldier's enlistment solely because of his acknowledged homosexuality); *Cammermeyer v. Aspin,* 850 F. Supp. 910 (W.D. Wash. 1994) (national guard officer's discharge for sexual orientation violated equal protection); *Pruitt v. Cheney,* 963 F.2d 1160 (9th Cir. 1992) (discharged reverend's First Amendment rights not violated, but did state an equal protection claim [discrimination on grounds of sexual orientation] on which relief could be granted, so case remanded to district court); *Dahl v. Secretary of U.S. Navy,* 830 F. Supp. 1319 (E.D. Cal. 1993) (homosexual exclusion policy violated equal protection in that it could not be based on anything but illegitimate prejudice).

176. See *Able v. United States,* 880 F. Supp. 968, 974–75 (E.D.N.Y. 1995), *rev'd,* 1996 WL 391210 (2d Cir. 1996).

and ethical conscience and of speech, the capacity of a person to entertain and to express ethical convictions and identifications which give enduring meaning to personal and ethical life. The American military, an institution of legitimate government, thus unconstitutionally wars, like Colorado Amendment Two, on one form of conscientious personal and ethical identity, in effect, unconstitutionally enlisting the state on one highly sectarian side of our contemporary wars of religion among which the state must, as a matter of basic constitutional principle, be impartial.

A review of the new policy makes quite clear that the war is rather disingenuously on gay and lesbian identity much more than on gay sex acts. Even under a policy of full inclusion of gays and lesbians in the military, the evidence suggests that acknowledged homosexuals would be few in the military.[177] Against this background, the policy's focus on public statements of gay and lesbian identity appears all the more constitutionally problematic, targeting self-identifying speech acts (as gay or lesbian), rather than the sex acts that are the supposed evil against which the policy is directed. Circumspection about one's sex life should, under the policy, render one immune from separation from the military; associational acts, highly probative of gay sex like attending gay bars or gay rights demonstrations, are not to be regarded as credible evidence of such acts. The only things that are given such decisive probative weight are self-identifying speech acts as a gay and lesbian person, including undertaking same-sex marriage.

To rationalize the constitutionality of such a policy, federal circuit courts have implausibly either denied that it significantly restricts speech, or claimed that the restriction is in any event a reasonable way of pursuing the clearly justifiable purpose of limiting gay sex.[178] Analogies to support the speech claim, used by two of

177. See MacCoun, "Sexual Orientation and Military Cohesion," 165, 172; Zellman, "Implementing Policy Changes in Large Organizations," 281.
178. See *Able v. United States*, 1996 WL 391210 (2d Cir. 1996) (speech restriction of the policy not unconstitutional, but remanded for consideration of constitutionality of act restriction of policy and reconsideration of speech restriction in light of that analysis) and *Able v. United States*, 1998 WL 647142 (2d Cir. 1998) (act restriction held constitutional); *Thomasson v. Perry*, 80 F.3d 915 (4th Cir. 1996) ("Don't Ask, Don't Tell" policy subject to rational basis; there is no fundamental right to engage in homosexual acts, and there is legitimate interest in preventing them); *Philips v. Perry*,

the circuit courts, have included cases involving the regulation of obscene materials[179] or sexually harassing or provocative fighting words.[180] Neither opinion explains or attempts to explain how a self-identifying statement of one's homosexuality can reasonably be regarded as obscene or sexually harassing or fighting words. The statement, "I am gay," is not a hard-core pornographic representation of turgid genitals offensive to community values and lacking serious value under current judicial tests for the constitutionally obscene.[181] Nor is the statement in its nature sexually harassing or a provocative epithet like "damned Fascist."[182]

Judge Nickerson, in the lower court opinion reversed by the appellate court in one of these cases, observed a tendency, in the statute and regulations dealing with this policy, to indulge uses of language that are "nothing less than Orwellian."[183] We can see the same Orwellian distortions in the judicial opinions of these circuit courts. Self-identifying statements like "I am gay" are expressions of gay and lesbian moral identity that specifically protest the unjustly enforced tradition of moral slavery by asserting conscientiously a self-respecting moral identity that protests on grounds of justice the political and legal force that tradition has uncritically

---

1997 U.S. App. LEXIS 2646 (9th Cir. 1997) (policy, including restrictions on speech, has adequate basis in prohibiting sex acts).

179. See *Able v. United States* 1996 WL 391210, at *13 (2d Cir. 1996), citing *City of Renton v. Playtime Theatres, Inc.*, 475 U.S. 41 (1986) (scattering zoning of adult theatre held constitutional).

180. See *Thomasson v. Perry*, 80 F.3d 915, 930 (4th Cir. 1996), citing *Price Waterhouse v. Hopkins*, 490 U.S. 228 (1989) (discriminatory words may be basis for Title VII action), and *R.A.V. v. City of St. Paul*, 505 U.S. 377 (1992) (sexually derogatory fighting words may produce violation of Title VII).

181. See *Miller v. California*, 413 U.S. 15 (1973).

182. See *Chaplinsky v. New Hampshire*, 315 U.S. 568 (1942).

183. See *Able v. United States*, 880 F. Supp. 968, 974 (E.D.N.Y. 1995) (section of "Don't Ask, Don't Tell," which permitted removal of service members for self-identification as homosexuals, held violation of free speech), *rev'd and remanded*, 1996 WL 391210 (2d Cir. 1996). In a later decision on the remand from the Second Circuit, Judge Nickerson found the restrictions of the policy on acts (applying to a homosexual, but not a heterosexual, who "kisses or holds hands off base or in private or before entering the service") unconstitutional, *Able v. United States*, 1997 WL 369504, at *8 (E.D.N.Y. July 2, 1997), an opinion recently reversed by the Second Circuit in *Able v. United States*, 1998 WL 647142 (2d Cir. 1998).

enjoyed and continues to enjoy. To choose such an expression for detrimental state treatment is not only, in the terms of current constitutional principles of free speech, to censor a kind of speech (a content-based expression of speech), but to censor a point of view within one of the kinds of speech (conscientious dissent about issues of justice) that is one of the most clearly protected forms of speech.[184] This is, in short, the most blatant kind of unconstitutional censorship, to wit, of certain kinds of conscientious protests, namely, those that protest, on grounds of justice, the tradition of the unspeakability of homosexuality by, first, speaking of it at all, and second, speaking of it not as pathological or evil but as a self-affirming conscientious identity that gives meaning to personal and ethical life. The circuit courts, however, engage in Orwellian transformations of ethical claims into pornography, of dissent into sexual harassment, and of a challenge to dominant orthodoxy into fighting words. The measure of judicially protected speech has become, in this area, the entrenched sexual orthodoxy that such dissenters self-consciously challenge and mean to challenge. That cannot be an acceptable measure for the judicial protection of freedom of speech in a period when reasonable doubts about traditional conceptions of both gender and sexuality are very much in play, indeed fundamental to the growing judicial skepticism about both gender and sexual preference as suspect classifications.

The second judicial rationalization for the policy of exclusion on the ground of making self-identifying statements as a homosexual (namely, its rational basis in forbidding gay sex) is no more constitutionally reasonable. To begin with, as we have seen, such exclusion is a viewpoint-based discrimination about clearly protected speech. It is for this reason wholly inappropriate to apply to its constitutional analysis, as one circuit court has, the more deferential standards of review appropriate to time, place, and manner

---

184. On the centrality of both viewpoint-based and content-based restrictions as constitutional violations of free speech, see Geoffrey Stone, "Content Regulation and the First Amendment," *William & Mary Law Review* 25 (1983): 189. On conscientious dissent as the core of protected speech, see Richards, *Toleration and the Constitution*, 165–227.

regulations or symbolic speech;[185] and it is equally wrong doctrinally to analyze such a viewpoint-based restriction on distinctive forms of public speech, as another circuit court has, on the model of bias crimes or sexual harassment.[186]

Such crude doctrinal manipulations of the standard of review appropriate to viewpoint-based restrictions are constitutionally unprincipled in exactly the context that such evasions of principle work the most damage on traditionally stigmatized minorities subject to an unjust history of moral slavery, that is, they express and reinforce rights-denying cultural stereotypes that rationalize moral slavery. The nerve of the argument for the constitutionality of the new policy is along lines that the policy's concern for gay self-identifying speech targets not speech, but the gay sex acts of which such speech is highly probative.[187] But the new policy is aimed at identity, not acts, which is doubly constitutionally unreasonable.

First, public assertion of gay or lesbian identity is not, in its nature, a statement about sex acts any more than a comparable statement of dissenting religious or racial or gender identity is when made against the tradition of moral slavery. There has, in fact, in all these domains, been a long history of rights-denying dehumanization of persons, often in terms of politically enforced sectarian sexual mythologies of black or female sexuality or Jewish or gay femininity (Weininger). In particular, the culturally dominant Euro-American stereotype of homosexuals has been as a sexualized fallen woman (whether the feminization of gay men or the masculinization of lesbians). Against this background, to ascribe to the words "I am gay" a statement or even a prediction of sex acts

185. See *Able v. United States*, 1996 WL 391210, at *12–13 (2d Cir. 1996), citing, for example, *Madsen v. Women's Health Center, Inc.*, 114 S. Ct. 2516 (1996) (reviewing regulations of abortion protests under time, place, and manner standards), and related cases, and *United States v. O'Brien*, 391 U.S. 367 (1968) (upholding criminalizing draft-card burning as based on dominant conduct element).

186. See *Thomasson v. Perry*, 80 F.3d 915, 918 (4th Cir. 1996), citing *Wisconsin v. Mitchell*, 508 U.S. 476 (1993) (speech elements may be used in aggravation of bias crime); *Price Waterhouse v. Hopkins*, 490 U.S. 228 (1989) (discriminatory words in proper context may be used to prove discriminatory acts under Title VII).

187. See *Thomasson*, 80 F.3d at 931–32; *Able*, 1996 WL 391210, at *14–15.

is not fairly to hear what is being said but to degrade the speaker to the terms of a dehumanized and dehumanizing stereotype.

Such a self-ascribing claim of gay or lesbian identity makes, as we have seen, a claim of justice against a cultural tradition of moral slavery and the hegemonic political force its rights-denying cultural stereotypes have uncritically been allowed to enjoy. It claims what that tradition denied, speakability and moral voice, indeed, the basic human rights of conscience, speech, intimate life, and work, the moral powers rationally and reasonably to live a life founded in, among other things, convictions of the moral value of homosexual love and care and passion and the intimate identifications and personal and moral growth to which they give expression. These convictions express ethical arguments of justice, some of which reasonably interpret rights-based feminism as grounding a right to homosexual love as part of a just moral protest about compulsory heterosexuality. The lives that give expression to these convictions are as various as the people who claim such basic rights. There is no fundamentalist orthodoxy of sex acts integral to their moral claims, nor should there be. Rather, the resistance to any such orthodoxy is surely what may be most humane about its larger moral promise of emancipated moral imagination about love, as a basic human good, for the culture at large. Resistance to such stereotypes (including their sexualization as homosexuals) may indeed distinguish such claimants of gay and lesbian identity from other homosexuals who have accommodated themselves to what they cannot or will not challenge.[188]

Part of their challenge may be to insist, on grounds of justice like Whitman's, that homosexuality should no more be only about

---

188. See, on this conflict, Larry Gross, *Contested Closets: The Politics and Ethics of Outing* (Minneapolis: University of Minnesota Press, 1993); Michelangelo Signorile, *Queer in America: Sex, the Media, and the Closets of Power* (New York: Random House, 1993). The lowest rates of homosexuality are reported when people are asked whether they identify themselves as homosexuals, in contrast to attraction to the same sex or having had sex with members of the same sex. See Robert T. Michael et al., *Sex in America: A Definitive Survey* (Boston: Little, Brown, 1994), 174–76. Even within the group who identify themselves as homosexual in such a study, there will be differences between those who more publicly disclose their identity in contrast to those who do not.

sex than heterosexuality, challenging, on grounds of justice, the common assumption to the contrary.[189] Against this background, the judicial repetition as a kind of mantra that claims of homosexual identity equate to sex acts, is not made more reasonable by repetition;[190] rather, its appeal uncritically reflects the irrationalist force of a still largely uncontested and unchallenged stereotype of the sexualization of homosexuals (see chapter 4).

As Judge Betty Fletcher observed in her powerful dissent to her circuit court's disposition of this issue, the military's treatment of public statements of gay or lesbian identity ascribes to such statements, in the name of unit cohesion, an interpretation rooted in biases that cannot be tolerated under the laws.[191] Effectively, the discomfort of heterosexual men with homosexuality, as a kind of irrationalist sense of tribal pollution, is made the measure of unit cohesion. Unit cohesion, as a measure of the performance of groups, is most reasonably understood as a measure of task cohesion, not of generalized social cohesion, a critical understanding adopted in the integration of both African Americans and women into the military. Social discomfort, based on bias, cannot be a reasonable measure of task cohesion under properly stated and enforced policies of nondiscriminatory treatment in a military that, under such policies, has reasonably integrated African Americans and women. Sexist worries about sexuality, which were not adequate to bar the integration of African Americans or women into the military, cannot, in principle, bar the integration of gays and lesbians on similar terms of justice (including appropriate protections from sexual harassment, heterosexual or homosexual). Both the experience of foreign militaries and of domestic police and fire departments with such integration of homosexuals support the common grounds, methods, and success of such policies. In all these cases, clearly stated and appropriately enforced policies can

189. For support that this is the common assumption, see Gregory M. Herek, "Why Tell If You're Not Asked? Self-Disclosure, Intergroup Contact, and Heterosexuals' Attitudes Toward Lesbians and Gay Men," in *Out in Force*, ed. Herek, Jobe, and Carney, 203, 207–8.

190. See, for citation to other cases making the same mistake, *Able*, 1996 WL 391210, at *17; *Thomasson*, 80 F.3d at 930–31.

191. See *Philips v. Perry*, 1997 U.S. App. LEXIS 2646, at *52 (9th Cir. 1997).

enforce a professionally appropriate etiquette of disregard of sexual issues so that all persons may attend to their tasks ably and well. Judge Fletcher properly regards as homophobic the fear of heterosexuals that gays or lesbians could not (contrary to all evidence) appropriately observe such an etiquette in their professional lives (as they have done and continue to do in all professions); such bias, for bias it is, cannot be the constitutionally reasonable measure of service in the American military.[192]

Second, if the policy had been concerned with gay sex acts, it would not reasonably have gone about its business in the way, in fact, it did. Many of the courses of conduct expressly ruled out as probative of such sex acts (attending a gay bar or a gay rights rally or having homosexual friends) surely are probative of such acts, some of them much more probative than making a claim of gay identity. The structure of the new policy is hospitable to gay sex acts so long as they are clandestine, secretive, and, of course, discreet. The homage the new policy pays to the prohibition of gay sex acts is a matter of constitutional form, not substance: it is concerned with prohibiting gay sex only insofar as such concern is the necessary gesture to constitutional virtue that must be paid to rationalize its constitutional vice. Its real concern is to eliminate assertions of gay identity, a viewpoint-based discrimination against conscience and speech that should, as we have seen, have been subjected to much more demanding judicial scrutiny than it was. As it is, the dilution of such standards of review in this case indulges the hypocritical subterfuge that the new policy, in fact concerned with identity, targets acts, which it certainly does not. Such abuse of language is Orwellian indeed, and panders to the exigencies of politicians not measuring political power by arguments of

---

192. *Out in Force*, ed. Herek, Jobe, and Carney, covers many of these interpretations in depth: see Theodore R. Sarbin, "The Deconstruction of Stereotypes: Homosexuals and Military Policy," 181; Robert J. MacCoun, "Sexual Orientation and Military Cohesion: A Critical Review of the Evidence"; Patricia J. Thomas and Marie D. Thomas, "Integration of Women in the Military: Parallels to the Progress of Homosexuals?"; Michael R. Kauth and Dan Landis, "Applying Lessons Learned from Minority Integration in the Military"; Paul A. Gade, David R. Segal, and Edgar M. Johnson, "The Experience of Foreign Militaries"; Paul Koegel, "Lessons Learned from the Experience of Domestic Police and Fire Departments"; Lois Shawver, "Sexual Modesty, the Etiquette of Disregard, and the Question of Gays and Lesbians in the Military," 226–46.

integrity, rooted in deliberation of and about constitutional principles.

All the circuit courts put weight, perhaps decisively, on one last consideration: the deference the judiciary owes the expertise of the legislative and executive branches in running an orderly and effective military service.[193] *Rostker* is directly on point: the Supreme Court there applied the applicable standard of heightened scrutiny[194] deferentially in view of the judgment of the Congress that only men should be required to register for the draft. *Rostker*, decided in 1981, reflected acceptance by all justices of the legitimacy of the gender-based combat exclusion, and may have been superseded both by the erosion of the combat exclusion and by the heightened level of scrutiny that may now be applicable to such gender classifications in light of *United States v. Virginia*.[195] As I earlier suggested, there may now be a compelling constitutional argument why women could not be excluded from the current all-volunteer military.

Whatever may be the appropriate level of judicial scrutiny for constitutional issues involving military service in other contexts, there are, I believe, compelling arguments of principle why a higher level of scrutiny should be accorded exclusions which express and reinforce dehumanizing stereotypes that deprive whole classes of citizens of their equal rights of citizenship. The issue at stake here is nothing less that the constitutional conception of national citizenship, including the equal rights and responsibilities of rights-based, republican citizenship. That is not a conception on which the judgments of military leaders can be regarded as decisive in the way they might reasonably be regarded in other areas relating to issues of military discipline, organization, and readiness. Such judgments of national citizenship may uncritically reflect not impartial judgments of competence and merit in military

193. See *Thomasson*, 80 F.3d at 921–26; *Able v. United States*, 1996 WL 391210, at *11–12 (2d Cir. 1996); *Able v. United States*, 1998 WL 647142, at *3–8 (2d Cir. 1998); *Philips*, 1997 U.S. App. LEXIS 2646, at *13–20 (Rymer, J.), *30–39 (Noonan, J., concurring).

194. See *Craig v. Boren*, 429 U.S. 190 (1976) (intermediate level standard of review applicable to gender-based classification, in age at which beer may be sold to men and women, and classification found unconstitutional).

195. 116 S. Ct. 2264 (1996).

service, but the traditional military's sense of themselves as men, unjustly constructed, as racism and sexism surely are, on the unjust dehumanization of African Americans and women through long-standing traditions of racial or gender segregation.

All of the struggles marking our moral growth as a people under American revolutionary constitutionalism, have been over the insistence that the conditions of American citizenship must be rights-based, subjecting our religious, racial, ethnic, and most recently, gendered sense of our identities as Americans to critical scrutiny in terms of more demanding ethical principles. We cannot reasonably put such a strong conception of rights-based moral community at hazard by allowing uncritical conceptions of "true manhood," which may have no more basis than "Aryan brotherhood," to be the defining measure of American national identity. The analogy to Aryan brotherhood is, I believe, exact if the exclusion of conscientiously identified homosexuals from the military is, in principle, the same as excluding from such service a religious identity (Judaism) on that sectarian basis. We would reject such a constitutional outrage on grounds of constitutional principle that apply, in contemporary circumstances, to gays and lesbians as well.[196]

I would therefore propose that the appropriate standard of judicial review for such exclusions should scrutinize closely the grounds alleged in their support and, in particular, conclusory statements about the conditions of group solidarity, to examine whether such statements reflect, at bottom, prejudices expressive of a constitutionally condemned history of rights-denying dehumanization. Policies of exclusion, expressing such prejudices, should be constitutionally rejected. In fact, as our earlier discussion of the "Don't Ask, Don't Tell" policy makes clear, the grounds urged in its support, including those mentioned in the legislation itself, are essentially constitutionally suspect grounds about conditions of group

---

196. A different, perhaps closer case would be posed by a neutral military regulation requiring uniform dress regulations barring the wearing of headgear indoors (forbidding the wearing of a yarmulke by an Orthodox Jew). See *Goldman v. Weinberger*, 475 U.S. 503 (1986) (regulation held constitutional against free exercise challenge). Even *Goldman* may be a doubtful constitutional result as Congress apparently believed in reversing it. See 10 U.S.C. § 774 (1988) (granting relief from the regulation).

solidarity. Such exclusions should not be constitutionally tolerable.[197]

The American military, which gave birth to the modern American struggle for gay rights, has been among its most intransigent antagonists. Military life fostered this struggle because many gay men and lesbians found their lives to be validated by its demands and purposes (including a war against a power hostile, in principle, to the theory and practice of human rights). The rather homophobic attempts of the military to construct a difference between gay men and lesbians and all other persons in the military, including the rather rank record of persecution recorded by Randy Shilts in his important study of the post–World War II period,[198] attempts to deny what seems all too obvious: the demands and purposes of military life are, in fact, quite congenial to and supportive of gay and lesbian identity.[199]

Freud observed of anti-Semitism that its irrationalism was rooted in its heightening of small, morally irrelevant differences into Manichean stereotypical truths.[200] The analogy between homophobia and anti-Semitism, on which I earlier insisted, is again informative. The homophobia of the military builds upon small, morally irrelevant differences a dehumanized portrait of self-identified homosexuals as incapable of the responsible exercise of the duties of military service. The military could reasonably acknowledge what it clearly knows to be true (that homosexuals are as good soldiers as heterosexuals in republican military service judged

197. For a similar analysis, see Kenneth I. Karst, "The Pursuit of Manhood and the Segregation of the Armed Forces," *UCLA Law Review* 38 (1991): 499. See also Seth Harris, "Permitting Prejudice to Govern: Equal Protection, Military Deference, and the Exclusion of Lesbians and Gay Men from the Military," *New York University Review of Law & Social Change* 17 (1989–90): 171.

198. See Shilts, *Conduct Unbecoming*.

199. One severe critic of women in the military noted that, of the women in the military, lesbians were much the best soldiers. See Mitchell, *Weak Link*, 178–82. On the higher incidence of homosexuals in the military than in civilian life, see Lever and Kanouse, "Sexual Orientation and Proscribed Sexual Behaviors," 22 (gay men); Thomas and Thomas, "Integration of Women in the Military," 72 (lesbians).

200. On "the narcissism of small differences," see chapter 5 of Sigmund Freud, *Civilization and Its Discontents*, in *Standard Edition of the Complete Psychological Works of Sigmund Freud*, ed. and trans. James Strachey (London: Hogarth Press, 1961), 21:114; see also *Moses and Monotheism*, vol. 23 (1964), p. 91.

on the basis of merit and contribution). Instead, it self-destructively wars on its republican children, who have learned better than their parents the inward moral meaning of rights-based military service. We should not rest until they are fully satisfied in their wholly just quest for full republican citizenship on terms of equal respect.

SAME-SEX MARRIAGE

Another ground for the military exclusion is, of course, same-sex marriage, which, as itself a heightened expression of gay or lesbian identity, raises the same constitutional issues as the focus of the new policy on self-identified gay or lesbian identity as such. Certainly, claims for same-sex marriage, after they have been rejected on the constitutional merits, have then also been the basis for firing people on the ground of "flaunting" gay or lesbian identity, which have also usually been upheld.[201] If all such forms of state action discriminating against gay and lesbian identity are, as I have argued, presumptively unconstitutional, then these certainly should be as well.[202] If, however, there are compelling constitutional arguments why same-sex marriage itself may not be denied, that would afford an additional ground for the unconstitutionality of the military exclusion on that ground. We need to address on its merits

201. See *Singer v. Hara*, 522 P.2d 1187 (Wash. Ct. App. 1974) (statutory prohibition of same-sex marriage not violative of Washington Equal Rights Amendment), followed by *Singer v. United States Civil Service Commission*, 530 F.2d 247 (9th Cir. 1976) (federal government's firing of man who "flaunted" his homosexuality by, *inter alia*, commencing same-sex marriage suit did not violate First Amendment rights). See also *Baker v. Nelson*, 191 N.W.2d 185 (Minn. 1971) (same-sex couple not permitted to marry and denial not violative of constitutional provisions), followed by *McConnell v. Anderson*, 451 F.2d 193 (8th Cir. 1071) (university library permitted to withdraw offer to gay man because he had publicly applied for marriage license with another man).

202. One circuit court recently so held. See *Shahar v. Bowers*, 70 F.3d 1218 (11th Cir. 1995) (Georgia attorney general's withdrawal of job offer to attorney after learning of her plans for same-sex marriage held subject to heightened scrutiny based upon First Amendment claims), but the opinion was overruled by the en banc Court of Appeals for the Eleventh Circuit. *Shahar v. Bowers*, 114 F.3d 1097 (11th Cir. 1997) (en banc) (withdrawal of job offer subject to balancing test), *cert. denied*, 118 S. Ct. 693 (1998).

the latter question of the constitutionality of banning same-sex marriage.

The question has come very much to the forefront of national attention in light of the decision of the Hawaii Supreme Court in *Baehr v. Lewin*[203] and legislation approved by Congress and signed by the president to limit the force of that decision. I begin with the discussion of *Baehr* on its merits, and then turn to the legislation.

Baehr held, under the Hawaii state constitution, that the denial of marriage in Hawaii to same-sex couples must be subjected to strict scrutiny under Hawaii's Equal Rights Amendment (ERA). In reaching this result, the Hawaii Supreme Court declined to find that there was a fundamental right to gay marriage, a finding of which would also have subjected the case to demanding judicial scrutiny. The case was remanded for trial of the issue whether the denial of same-sex marriage could satisfy this demanding standard; unsurprisingly, the trial court found that the denial could not survive such scrutiny.[204] In response, an amendment to the Hawaii state constitution was recently approved that gives the legislature the authority to overturn *Baehr* and ban same-sex marriages.[205] *Baehr* will, however, continue to challenge the American constitutional conscience to the extent it raises valid issues of constitutional principle that must be responsibly addressed; another constitutional challenge, for example, is thus pending in Vermont.[206] The populist failure responsibly to address such issues may, if the arguments of basic principle are valid, measure the depth of the constitutional evil of moral slavery now so visibly at work in our constitutionally decadent politics.

Baehr v. Lewin is a pathbreaking departure from the usual interpretation of applicable constitutional principles in the area of same-sex marriage. Almost all American courts have held, both under state and federal constitutional law, that failure to recognize

203. 852 P.2d 44 (Haw. 1993).

204. See *Baehr v. Miike*, 1996 WL 694235 (Hawaii Cir. Ct.).

205. See Sam Howe Verhovek, "From Same-Sex Marriages to Gambling, Voters Speak," *New York Times*, Nov. 5, 1998, p. B1.

206. See Cheryl Wetzstein, "Gay Couples Sue Vermont for Refusing Marriage Licenses," *Washington Times*, July 23, 1997, p. A3.

same-sex marriage is not unconstitutional[207] and have, correlatively, failed to accord same-sex couples benefits like employee insurance coverage[208] or spousal rights under the law of wills,[209] the immigration laws,[210] or the law of veteran benefits.[211] *Baehr* suggests it may be timely to rethink this question fundamentally. Two important studies, one by William Eskridge[212] the other by Mark Strasser,[213] have to my mind argued cogently that the denial of same-sex marriage is presumptively unconstitutional not only on the suspectness ground urged in *Baehr,* but also on the independent ground of abridging the basic human right to intimate

207. See, for example, *Dean v. District of Columbia,* 653 A.2d 307 (D.C. 1995) (District of Columbia marriage law prohibits clerk from issuing marriage license to same-sex couple and does not unlawfully discriminate against couples under D.C. Human Rights Act or U.S. Constitution); *DeSanto v. Barnsley,* 476 A.2d 952 (Pa. Super. Ct. 1984) (man could not seek divorce from other man because same-sex common law marriages are not permitted in Pennsylvania); *Singer v. Hara,* 522 P.2d 1187 (Wash. Ct. App. 1974) (statutory prohibition of same-sex marriage not violative of Washington Equal Rights Amendment); *Jones v. Hallahan,* 501 S.W.2d 588 (Ky. Ct. App. 1973) (same-sex couple incapable of obtaining marriage license because same-sex marriage would not be a marriage); *Baker v. Nelson,* 191 N.W.2d 185 (Minn. 1971) (same-sex couple not permitted to marry and denial not violative of constitutional protections); *Anonymous v. Anonymous,* 325 N.Y.S.2d 499 (Sup. Ct. 1971) (marriage between males a nullity despite fact husband thought wife was a female at time of marriage and she subsequently underwent reassignment surgery). But see *M.T. v. J.T.,* 355 A.2d 204 (N.J. Super. Ct. 1976) (absent fraud, man not allowed to void marriage to postoperative transsexual female); *In re Matter of Marley,* 1996 WL 280890 (Del. Super. Ct. 1996).

208. See *Lilly v. City of Minneapolis,* 1994 WL 315620 (Minn. Dist. Ct. 1994) (registered domestic partners are not spousal dependents for purposes of extending employee insurance coverage).

209. See *In re Matter of Cooper,* 592 N.Y.S.2d 797 (App. Div. 1993) (surviving partner of same-sex relationship not entitled to spousal right of election against decedent's will).

210. See *Adams v. Howerton,* 673 F.2d 1036 (9th Cir. 1982) (an Australian and an American male citizen who had been married by minister in Colorado not married for purposes of Immigration and Nationality Act).

211. See *McConnell v. Nooner,* 547 F.2d 54 (8th Cir.) (spousal veteran benefits denied to same-sex partner of veteran who had gone through same-sex marriage ceremony).

212. See William N. Eskridge, Jr., *The Case for Same-Sex Marriage: From Sexual Liberty to Civilized Commitment* (New York: Free Press, 1996).

213. See Mark Strasser, *Legally Wed: Same-Sex Marriage and the Constitution* (Ithaca: Cornell University Press, 1997).

life, of which the right to marriage is an important institutional expression. If such statutes are subject to heightened scrutiny whether on the ground of their suspectness or their abridgment of a fundamental right, both scholars make clear that no compelling justification could constitutionally legitimate such invidious treatment.[214] I hope to complement their arguments by placing them in the context of the larger argument for gay rights that I offer here.

On the view I have taken, the moral slavery of homosexuals is as much constitutionally condemned by the Thirteenth Amendment as that of African Americans and women, and the correlative guarantees of the Fourteenth Amendment must be interpreted accordingly to give effect to this rights-based normative judgment in all its relevant dimensions. These dimensions include the abridgment of the basic human rights (conscience, speech, intimate life, and work) and the inadequate sectarian grounds on which such abridgments have been rationalized. These dimensions are, as we have seen in every area we have studied, systematically interconnected; and the rectification of such rights-denying evils has resulted in striking interpretive developments both recognizing such basic rights and in constitutional doctrines increasingly suspicious of the expression through public law of the dehumanizing prejudices that have traditionally abridged such rights. Even discrimination on grounds of sexual preference has now been acknowledged by the Supreme Court as a ground to some degree thus suspect.[215]

The right to intimate life has played an important role in each of these interpretive developments both because of the moral fundamentality of the right itself and because its abridgment has been so historically connected to the cultural formation and support of rights-denying dehumanizing prejudices and the political expres-

214. For example, as Eskridge argues, having children is not a constitutionally reasonable requirement for heterosexual marriage and, therefore, not having children could not be a compelling reason for excluding homosexuals from the institution. See, for a compelling rebuttal of a range of such arguments, Eskridge, *The Case for Same-Sex Marriage*, 127–52. See, for judicial support of the premise of Eskridge's argument, *Turner v. Safley*, 482 U.S. 78 (1987) (state bar to marriage by prison inmates, on ground could not procreate, held unconstitutional).

215. See *Romer v. Evans*, 116 S. Ct. 1620 (1996).

sion they have uncritically been permitted to enjoy through public law and policies. Antimiscegenation laws thus continued, long after the Civil War, the dehumanizing attitudes to African Americans that had, under slavery, deprived them of the basic rights to intimate life (including marriage and control of family relations) and thus dehumanized their treatment to the level of cattle and reduced to their utility (including reproductive fertility in producing further slaves) to the master class. As Lydia Maria Child first pointed out and Harriet Jacobs explored from the perspective of a former slave woman,[216] antimiscegenation laws abridged the basic human right of intimate life in a way that sustained the sectarian sexual mythology of the subhuman image of African Americans. As James Baldwin, a gay black man, observed of his own sexual exploitation at the hands of a white man, such a mythology could certainly easily sexualize and exploit African Americans, meeting their "enormous need to debase other men."[217] What they could not do was to dignify the lives of African Americans as persons capable of the free exercise of the moral powers of intimate life, including the right to marriage on whatever terms rationally and reasonably give expression to these powers for them in conferring enduring meaning on personal and ethical life. Abridgment of the right to intimate life was linked to this unjust dehumanization because the free exercise of this right advances enduring moral interests in loving and being loved, caring and being cared for, intimately giving value to the lives of others and having value given to one's own life; to be denied respect for such powers is, literally, to be deemed subhuman, incapable of the moral interests that give enduring value to living and sustain that value in others often over the generations.

In the case of women, as we have seen, the abridgment of all their basic rights was focally rationalized in terms of a sectarian mythology of mandatory gender roles that rationalized their moral slavery. To the extent such a mythology was uncritically sustained by suffrage feminism, it wreaked havoc on women's rights to inti-

216. See Richards, *Women, Gays, and the Constitution*, 55–56, 117–24.
217. See James Baldwin, *No Name in the Street* (New York: Dell, 1972), 63.

mate life in what I have elsewhere called the Wollstonecraft repudiation.[218] Indeed, suffrage feminists and their allies censored
reasonable public argument not only about the right to free love,
properly so called, but more concrete interpretations of that right,
including the right to contraception, abortion, and consensual homosexuality.[219] Recognition of these rights marked the emergence
and constitutionalization of rights-based feminism since World
War II not only because of their intrinsic fundamentality to moral
sovereignty, but also because their recognition reflected as well
constitutional skepticism about the traditional grounds for their
abridgment. No robust constitutional understanding of women's
human right to intimate life was possible as long as the political
orthodoxy of mandatory gender roles was the measure of such
rights. Nothing is, in my judgment, more ethically important in
the emancipatory meaning and promise of rights-based feminism
(building on and elaborating abolitionist feminism) than its skepticism about the political enforcement at large of such mandatory
gender roles, its insistence that women and men be accorded respect for their freedom and rationality in taking responsibility for
how and on what terms gender may or should play a role in fram-
ing their private and public lives. Such growing constitutional
skepticism about the legitimate enforcement through public law of
such sectarian conceptions of mandatory gender roles has cleared
normative space to acknowledge and respect not only women's
rights to intimate life, but all their basic human rights (both public
and private).

Rights-based feminism grounds as well, as I have argued, not
only respect for the basic human rights of homosexuals (to conscience, speech, intimate life, and work) but skepticism about the
traditional grounds for the abridgment of such rights (including
compulsory heterosexuality). Against the background of the distinctive moral slavery of homosexuals (their degraded unspeakability), the claim of any human rights at all must be regarded as an
outrageous heresy against traditional values, as it was by the ma-

218. On this point, see Richards, *Women, Gays, and the Constitution*, 141, 442.
219. Ibid., 155–82.

jority of Coloradans who approved Colorado Amendment Two. But the outrage is most polemically overwrought against self-respecting claims to gay and lesbian identity in contemplation of the recognition of the human right of homosexuals, on equal terms with heterosexuals, to intimate life and its reasonable corollary, the right to marriage. Such a right has the force it has, both for its proponents and opponents, because its acknowledgment, like the comparable right to marry of African Americans, so critically addresses the grounds of dehumanization that had excluded the stigmatized group from the moral community of equal rights.

The claim to the right to marriage thus takes on a public significance, which the right to consensual sex does not, as a heightened expression of gay and lesbian identity protesting the traditional terms of its unjust treatment. In the case of homosexuals, such dehumanization stigmatized them as fallen women, sexualized prostitutes incapable of exercising the powers of moral personality protected by basic human rights. The consequence of the unjust enforcement of this political epistemology is the common uncritical populist assumption that homosexuality, unlike heterosexuality, is exclusively about sex.[220] It is this assumption that is, I believe, the basis for the wounded sense of outrage surrounding even the suggestion of the legitimacy of extending the humane values of the institutions that protect the dignity of heterosexual intimate life to homosexuals. Homosexuals, on this view, no more can marry than animals.

There are two dimensions to any reasonable discussion of this matter: the nature and force of the constitutional right, and the appropriate constitutional burden of justification for any abridgment or regulation of such a right. On the first point, the basic right is, as we have seen, not only the right to intimate life, but the very making of rights-based protest to the terms of the moral slavery of homosexuals, that is, appealing to basic human rights (of conscience, speech, intimate life, and work) to bring to bear on public and private life one's ethical convictions about the good of homosexual love and care and to live a life rooted in such convic-

220. See, on this point, Herek, "Why Tell If You're Not Asked?" 203, 207–8.

tions and the relationships to which they give rise. At the level of the basic rights, basic human rights apply to all persons, including heterosexuals and homosexuals.

On the second point, any basic human right (like the right to intimate life) can only be abridged, consistent with the argument for toleration, on compelling grounds of public reason not themselves hostage to a sectarian view that, whatever may once have been the case in other historical circumstances, can no longer be regarded as justifiable to the public reason of all persons in the community. On this ground, the Supreme Court, as we have seen, correctly struck down both anticontraception and antiabortion laws. Anticontraception laws expressed, in contemporary circumstances, an unjustly sectarian view of mandatory procreational sexuality that many reasonable people no longer accept as the measure of sexual love; and antiabortion laws depend on a conception of fetal life in early pregnancy that cannot be legitimately enforced to abridge the reproductive autonomy of the many women who do not regard that conception of fetal life as a reasonable conception of moral personality. For the same reason, no compelling argument of public reason exists in contemporary circumstances that could justify the abridgment of the right to love of homosexuals. Neither of the two arguments, traditionally regarded as justifying such abridgment (the evil of nonprocreational sex, and the conception of homosexual love as lowering one party to the status of a woman, i.e. a degraded status), can be regarded as publicly reasonable today. The first argument was justly repudiated by the contraception cases; the second by the many cases repudiating the force of sexist stereotypes in public law. *Bowers v. Hardwick* was wrongly decided, and should be overruled; a reasonable interpretation of *Romer v. Evans* suggests implicitly that it has been.

A Catholic moral conservative like John Finnis has argued that, even if *Bowers* were properly overruled (as he suggests it should be), it would still be appropriate to make the exclusively procreational model of sexuality the measure of the right to marriage.[221] On this view, as another moral conservative put the point, the

221. See John Finnis, "Law, Morality, and 'Sexual Orientation,' " *Notre Dame Journal of Law, Ethics & Public Policy* 9 (1995): 11.

right to marriage is determined not solely by commitments arising from love as such, but by "the natural teleology of the body."[222] There is, however, no difference of principle between the sectarian character of such arguments in the one context (*Bowers*) as opposed to another (the right to marriage). Heterosexual couples who are childless, whether by design or by force of circumstances, are not for that reason disqualified from the right to marry, nor could they reasonably be.[223] If the natural teleology of the body made any sense as a basis for public law, such childlessness as much violates the natural teleology of the body as that of a homosexual couple. Yet the natural teleology of the body, whatever its legitimate force within sectarian moral and religious traditions, is not a publicly reasonable basis for law. The natural teleology of the body (like the teleology of nature more generally) cannot reasonably be a basis for public law in a morally and religiously pluralistic society which lacks any reasonable common ground to ascribe to such natural facts a politically enforceable normative purpose. We can no more reasonably impose such a normative conception on homosexual than on heterosexual intimate relations. In both cases, as free and rational persons, we may "employ our powers of mind and body to produce some innovation in the course of nature,"[224]

222. See Hadley Arkes, Testimony on the Defense of Marriage Act, 1996, Judiciary Committee, House of Representatives, 1996 WL 246693, at *11 (F.D.C.H.); see also Hadley Arkes, "Questions of Principle, Not Predictions," *Georgetown Law Journal* 84 (1995): 321; and, to similar effect, Robert P. George and Gerard V. Bradley, "Marriage and the Liberal Imagination," *Georgetown Law Journal* 84 (1995): 301. For cogent criticism, see Stephen Macedo, "Homosexuality and the Conservative Mind," *Georgetown Law Journal* 84 (1995): 261; and "Reply to Critics," *Georgetown Law Journal* 84 (1995): 329.

223. Cf. *Turner v. Safley*, 482 U.S. 78 (1987) (denial of marriage right to prison inmates, on ground could not procreate, held unconstitutional). For discussion, see Eskridge, *The Case for Same-Sex Marriage*, 128–30.

224. Arguments of such sorts are based on appeals to nature of the same sort that David Hume considered for similar reasons an illegitimate basis for public laws, including laws prohibiting suicide. The complete quotation is:

'Tis impious, says, the *French* superstition to inoculate for the small-pox, or usurp the business of providence, by voluntarily producing distempers and maladies. 'Tis impious says the modern *European* superstition, to put a period to our own life, and thereby rebel against our creator. And why not impious, say I, to build houses, cultivate the ground, and sail upon the ocean? In all these actions, we employ our powers of mind and body to produce some innovation

including taking pleasure in one another's bodies in whatever forms one gives or receives mutual pleasure in expressing and sustaining companionate sexual love as an end in itself. *Pace* Finnis, the illegitimacy of imposing such a sectarian view to forbid same-sex marriage may, if anything, be more unjustified than its imposition on same-sex relations simpliciter since abridgment of the right to marriage may play a more pivotally unjust role in the dehumanization of homosexuals, and is, to the extent, even more unjustified. Both are, of course, unjustified in principle.

The imposition of the model of mandatory procreational sex on either heterosexual or homosexual love is surely, in contemporary circumstances, constitutionally unjust, because it politically remakes reality in its own anachronistic sectarian image. In particular, it conspicuously fails to acknowledge what any reasonable understanding of modern life, not hostage to such a sectarian conception, must acknowledge: the force in human life of sexual love as an end in itself that sustains intimate relations of loving and being loved that give enduring meaning to personal and ethical life.[225] From this perspective, the political demand that human love, to be maritally legitimate, must conform to the natural teleology of the body usurps the moral sovereignty of the person over the transformative moral powers of love in intimate relations and the identifications that sustain personal and ethical value in living, in effect, dehumanizing human sexuality to its purely biological, reproductive aspect. As one Catholic critic of his church's condemnation of homosexuality recently put this point (against, among others, Finnis), it is extraordinary that so many branches of Christianity should have now degenerated into fertility cults; such a

---

in the course of nature, and in none of them do we any more. They are all of them, therefore, equally innocent or equally criminal.

David Hume, "Of Suicide," in *Essays Moral Political and Literary,* ed. Eugene F. Miller (1777; Indianapolis: LibertyClassics 1987), 585.

225. See, in general, Anthony Giddens, *The Transformation of Intimacy: Sexuality, Love, and Eroticism in Modern Societies* (Cambridge, U.K.: Polity, 1992); John D'Emilio and Estelle B. Freedman, *Intimate Matters: A History of Sexuality in America* (New York: Harper & Row, 1988), 239–360; Barbara Ehrenreich, Elizabeth Hess, and Gloria Jacobs, *Remaking Love: The Feminization of Sex* (New York: Anchor, 1986); Ann Snitow, Christine Stansell, and Sharon Thompson, eds., *Powers of Desire: The Politics of Sexuality* (New York: Monthly Review Press, 1983); Carole S. Vance, ed., *Pleasure and Danger: Exploring Female Sexuality* (Boston: Routledge & Kegan Paul, 1984).

view, dubious even today on internal religious grounds, can hardly reasonably be the measure of rights and responsibilities in a secular society.[226] The role of human sexuality in the plastic imaginative life and transformative moral passions and identifications of free personality would, by force of law, be unreasonably degraded to the procrustean sectarian measure of a purely animal sexuality.[227]

At bottom, the insistence on opposite sexes, as the legitimate measure of the right to marriage, indulges, as the *Baehr* court saw, constitutionally illegitimate gender stereotypes. Andrew Koppelman has persuasively explored, in this connection, the analogy of the antimiscegenation laws.[228] The prohibition of racial intermarriage was to the cultural construction of racism what the prohibition of same-sex marriage is to sexism and homophobia: "just as miscegenation was threatening because it called into question the distinctive and superior status of being white, homosexuality is threatening because it calls into question the distinctive and superior status of being male."[229] The condemnation of same-sex marriage is one of the crucial aspects of the cultural construction of the dehumanization of the homosexual as a sexualized fallen woman.

Such dehumanization retains popular appeal when brought

226. See Mark D. Jordan, *The Invention of Sodomy in Christian Theology* (Chicago: University of Chicago Press, 1997). "The Christian criterion of fertility, of parenting, of filiation, is not bodily. That much was worked out with painstaking care in the early Trinitarian debates." Ibid., 174.

227. For important studies of the differences between human and animal sexuality, see Clellan S. Ford and Frank A. Beach, *Patterns of Sexual Behavior* (New York: Harper & Row, 1951); Irenaus Eibl-Eibesfeldt, *Love and Hate: The Natural History of Behavior Patterns,* trans. Geoffrey Strachan (New York: Holt, Rinehart, and Winston, 1971). The insight is also central to Freud's exploration of the imaginative role of sexuality in human personality; see Sigmund Freud, " 'Civilized' Sexual Morality and Modern Nervous Illness," in *Standard Edition of the Complete Psychological Works of Sigmund Freud,* ed. and trans. James Strachey (London: Hogarth Press, 1961), 9:181, 187. "The sexual instinct . . . is probably more strong developed in man than in most of the higher animals; it is certainly more constant, since it has almost entirely overcome the periodicity to which it is tied in animals. It places extraordinarily large amounts of force at the disposal of civilized activity, and it does this in virtue of its especially marked characteristic of being able to displace its aim without materially diminishing its intensity. This capacity to exchange its originally sexual aim for another one, which is no longer sexual but which is physically related to the first aim, is called the capacity for sublimation."

228. See Andrew Koppelman, "The Miscegenation Analogy: Sodomy Laws as Sex Discrimination," *Yale Law Journal* 98 (1988): 145.

229. Ibid., 159–60.

into relation to claims for same-sex marriage because, consistent with Freud's observation of the narcissism of small differences, it enables a culture, with a long history of uncritical moral slavery of women and homosexuals, not to take seriously, let alone think reasonably, about the growing convergences of heterosexual and homosexual human love in the modern world. These include not only shared economic contributions to the household and convergent styles of nonprocreational sex and elaboration of erotic play as an end in itself, but the interest in sex as an expressive bond in companionate relationships of friendship and love as ends in themselves; several partners over a lifetime; when there is interest in children, only in few of them; and the insistence on the romantic love of tender and equal companions as the democratized center of sharing intimate daily life.[230] Indeed, some studies suggest that, if anything, homosexual relationships more fully develop features of egalitarian sharing that are more often the theory than the practice of heterosexual relations.[231]

The uncritical ferocity of contemporary political homophobia draws its populist power from the compulsive need to construct Manichean differences where none reasonably exist, thus reinforcing institutions of gender hierarchy perceived now to be at threat. In particular, as Whitman argued,[232] democratic equality in homosexual intimate life threatens the core of traditional gender roles and the hierarchy central to such roles. Consistent with the paradox of intolerance, the embattled sectarian orthodoxy does not explore such reasonable doubts, but polemically represses them by

230. See, on the continuities among heterosexual and homosexual forms of intimacy in the modern world, in general, Giddens, *The Transformation of Intimacy;* D'Emilio and Freedman, *Intimate Matters,* 239–360; Philip Blumstein and Pepper Schwartz, *American Couples* (New York: William Morrow, 1983), 332–545. On declining fertility rates, see Claudia Goldin, *Understanding the Gender Gap: An Economic History of American Women* (New York: Oxford University Press, 1990), 139–42; on childlessness, see May, *Barren in the Promised Land;* on rising divorce rates, see Carl N. Degler, *At Odds: Women and the Family in America from the Revolution to the Present* (New York: Oxford University Press, 1980), 165–68, 175–76.

231. On this point, see Susan Moller Okin, "Sexual Orientation and Gender: Dichotomizing Differences," in *Sex, Preference, and Family: Essays on Law and Nature,* ed. David M. Estlund and Martha C. Nussbaum (New York: Oxford University Press, 1997), 44–59.

232. See, for development of this point, Richards, *Women, Gays, and the Constitution,* 297–310.

remaking reality in its own sectarian image of marriage, powerfully deploying the uncritical traditional stereotype of the homosexual as the scapegoat of one's suppressed doubts (excluding the homosexual from the moral community of human rights, including the basic human right to intimate life). Homosexuals are the natural scapegoat for this uncritical backlash against feminism,[233] because they, unlike women, remain a largely marginalized and despised minority. Traditional sectarian orthodoxy objects as strongly to many of the achievements of the feminist movement (some to the decriminalization of contraception, others to that of abortion, still others to now mainstream feminist issues like ERA[234]), but they have lost many of these battles and the sectarian hard core of the orthodoxy, in fact hostile to feminism and civil rights measures in general,[235] takes its stand strategically where it still can against members of a traditionally stigmatized and silenced minority who are, like the Jews in Europe, easily demonized.[236]

A revealing historical analogy has been drawn upon in the resistance to contemporary same-sex marriage, namely, arguments taken from the antipolygamy movement of the nineteenth century.[237] Conservative commentators like George Will[238] and William Bennett[239] have thus questioned the allegedly conservative advocacy of same-sex marriage, by Andrew Sullivan among oth-

233. See, in general, Susan Faludi, *Backlash: The Undeclared War against American Women* (New York: Doubleday, 1991); Marilyn French, *The War against Women* (London: Penguin, 1992).

234. For some sense of the range of such views and their supporting reasons, see Sherrye Henry, *The Deep Divide: Why American Women Resist Equality* (New York: Macmillan, 1994); Elizabeth Fox-Genovese, *"Feminism Is Not the Story of My Life": How Today's Feminist Elite Has Lost Touch with the Real Concerns of Women* (New York: Doubleday, 1996); Elizabeth Fox-Genovese, *Feminism without Illusions: A Critique of Individualism* (Chapel Hill: University of North Carolina Press, 1991).

235. For its antifeminism, see Herman, *The Antigay Agenda*, 103–10; for its opposition to the civil rights agenda in general, see ibid., 111–36, 140.

236. On the analogy of such contemporary homophobia to anti-Semitism, see ibid., 82–91, 125–28; cf. Pagels, *The Origin of Satan*, 102–5. See also, for a useful study of the reactionary populist politics of this group, Bull and Gallagher, *Perfect Enemies*.

237. For fuller discussion, see Richards, *Women, Gays, and the Constitution*, 171–72.

238. See George Will, "And Now Pronounce Them Spouse and Spouse," *Washington Post*, May 19, 1996, p. C9.

239. See William Bennett, "Leave Marriage Alone" (legalizing same-sex marriage would tamper with centuries of tradition and demean the institution of marriage), *Newsweek*, June 3, 1996, p. 27.

ers,[240] as affording no limiting principle that would not extend the right to polygamy as well. Arguments against polygamy had two crucial features: a defense of monogamy as at the core of the values of Western civilization, and a critique of polygamy as reinforcing the unjust subjection of women. But the contemporary gay defense of same-sex marriage does not question monogamy, it insists on it;[241] and it does so, as I have argued here, on the basis of a forceful repudiation of sexist gender-roles in the name of the principles of rights-based feminism.[242] Polygamy, as traditionally understood, reinforced such unjust gender roles, and thus cannot be regarded as a constitutionally reasonable form of intimate life consistent with these principles. As Nancy Rosenblum recently observed:

> Despite rare exceptions, patriarchy has been the dominant form of polygamy. It has never had its basis in reciprocity or friendship, not even ideally. Its justification has never been the expansiveness of affection or cooperation. It has rested on ideological or spiritual accounts of male authority and female subjection, on status associated with numbers of wives, and of course on beliefs about male sexual power (or the need to temper women's sexual power) and male entitlements. It is doubtful that the known doctrinal supports for polygamy could be rehabilitated and made congruent with democratic sex.[243]

240. See, for example, Andrew Sullivan, "Here Comes the Groom: A (Conservative) Case for Gay Marriage," in *Beyond Queer: Challenging Gay Left Orthodoxy*, ed. Bruce Bawer (New York: Free Press, 1996), 252–58. See also Jonathan Rauch, "For Better or Worse?" *The New Republic*, May 6, 1996, pp. 18–23.

241. See Eskridge, *The Case for Same-Sex Marriage*. For a similar argument by a gay man defending the humane need within gay and lesbian culture for institutional incentives for fidelity, see Gabriel Rotello, *Sexual Ecology: AIDS and the Destiny of Gay Men* (New York: Dutton, 1997), 233–61.

242. For an argument that some forms of polygamy, if based on modern values giving "perfect freedom and independence to women in their relation to men," would be consistent with rights-based feminism, see Edward Carpenter, *Love's Coming of Age: A Series of Papers on the Relations of the Sexes* (1896; New York: Vanguard Press, 1926), 134. It would, on this view, be a factual question whether any such form of polygamy could reasonably be proposed in contemporary circumstances. Many advocates of gay marriage might reasonably deny, consistent with Nancy Rosenblum's view cited in the text, that it could be. See Eskridge, *The Case for Same-Sex Marriage*, 148–49.

243. See Nancy L. Rosenblum, "Democratic Sex: Reynolds v. U. S., Sexual Relations, and Community," in *Sex, Preference, and Family*, ed. Estlund and Nussbaum, 80.

The antipolygamy appeal is not then reasonably on point: the arguments for same-sex marriage do not support such an extension any more than they would justify spouse abuse or adultery or, for that matter, no fault divorce.[244] Compelling secular arguments of gender equality support the limitation of the right to marriage to monogamous couples.[245] But, the spirit of the antipolygamy movement is, I believe, very much in play in such appeals: an attempt, like demonizing Mormon polygamy, to insist on an uncritical conception of gender hierarchy in marriage, thus further immunizing the conventional theory of gender roles from much needed rights-based feminist critique (it was, on this ground, that John Stuart

244. For the debate in social science and law surrounding what this development factually comes to and what normative sense we should make of it, see Lenore J. Weitzman, *The Divorce Revolution: The Unexpected Social and Economic Consequences for Woman and Children in America* (New York: Free Press, 1985); Martha Albertson Fineman, *The Illusion of Equality: The Rhetoric and Reality of Divorce Reform* (Chicago: University of Chicago Press, 1991); Ira Mark Ellman, Paul M. Kurtz, Katharine T. Bartlett, eds., *Family Law: Cases, Text, Problems* (Charlottesville, Va.: Michie Co., 1991), 292–301; Howard S. Erlanger, ed., "Review Symposium on Weitzman's *Divorce Revolution,*" in *American Bar Foundation Research Journal* 4 (1986): 759–97; James B. McLindon, "Separate but Unequal: The Economic Disaster of Divorce of Women and Children," *Family Law Quarterly* 21 (1987): 351–409; Greg J. Duncan and Saul D. Hoffman, "A Reconsideration of the Economic Consequences of Marital Dissolution," *Demography* 22 (1985): 485; Judith A. Seltzer and Irwin Garfinkel, "Inequality in Divorce Settlements: An Investigation of Property Settlements and Child Support Awards," *Social Science Research* 19 (1990): 82; Susan Moller Okin, "Economic Equality after Divorce," *Dissent* (summer 1991): 383; Martha L. Fineman, "Implementing Equality: Ideology, Contradiction and Social Change, A Study of Rhetoric and Results in the Regulation of the Consequences of Divorce," *Wisconsin Law Review* 1983: 789; Jane Rutherford, "Duty in Divorce: Shared Income as a Path of Equality," *Fordham Law Review* 58 (1990): 539; Joan Williams, "Is Coverture Dead? Beyond a New Theory of Alimony," *Georgetown Law Journal* 82 (1994): 2227; Isabel Marcus, "Locked In and Locked Out: Reflections on the History of Divorce Law Reform in New York State," *Buffalo Law Review* 37 (1989): 375; Marsha Garrison, "Good Intentions Gone Awry: The Impact of New York's Equitable Distribution Law on Divorce Outcomes," *Brooklyn Law Review* 57 (1991): 621.

245. It is a different question whether such principles would justify, in contemporary circumstances, the use of criminal law against polygamous unions as such, and in particular, such unions undertaken in accord with religious conscience. Legitimate state purposes, that might be sufficiently powerful to disallow the extension of marriage to such unions, might not be sufficient, without more, to justify the use of criminal sanctions in this arena for the same reasons that one might reasonably believe adultery should no longer be condemned by the criminal law (such laws inflict a preponderance of harm over good in areas better regulated or addressed in other ways).

Mill, an advocate of feminist equality,[246] condemned the hypocrisy of the American persecution of the Mormons[247]).

The antipolygamy movement, like suffrage feminism and the temperance and purity movements, thus censored out from public debate and discussion important arguments of rights-based feminism, rationalizing the shrunken and decrepit thing suffrage feminism became. The ferocity of the populist attack on gay marriage has a similarly reactionary character and basis polemically to insist on a symbolism of marriage as an immovable rock (impermeable to reasonable doubt about gender roles) that is factually unreal and normatively unfair, using homosexuals as the normative scapegoat politically to reify gender hierarchy in marriage.

Same-sex marriage is not a threat to marriage, but a recognition of the deeper moral values in marriage and the principled elaboration of those values to all persons; the case for the legitimacy of gay marriage crucially affirms the value (real and symbolic) reasonably placed in our culture on marriage and family life, and argues, as a matter of principle, for fair extension of that value to all persons on fair terms. Homosexuality is no more exclusively about sex than heterosexuality. The culturally marked difference between them is the product of a culture of moral slavery, constructed in part by the unthinkability of extending the right to marriage (as aspect of the basic human right to intimate life) to homosexuals (because they are assumed to be subhuman, if not animalistic, in their intimate lives). Homosexuals thus justly resist the traditional terms of their dehumanization by insisting on their constitutional right to marriage as an aspect of the basic human right to respect for the dignity of intimate life, the transformative moral passion of mutual love and care in personal and ethical life.

Their argument gives, if you will, a distinctly liberal interpretation to the moral appeal of the argument for family values. The idea that gay marriage is a threat to marriage as such can barely be credited, as an argument, when an ethical wrong like adultery goes quite unmentioned in such ostensibly promarriage discourse. The

246. See John Stuart Mill and Harriet Taylor Mill, *Essays on Sex Equality*, ed. Alice S. Ross (Chicago: University of Chicago Press, 1970).
247. See John Stuart Mill, *On Liberty*, ed. Alburey Castell (1859; New York: Appleton-Century-Crofts, 1947), 92–94.

difference, of course, is that adultery is a reasonably popular heterosexual vice;[248] and there is no interest in tackling in a responsible way such serious ethical issues which require a challenge to be made to uncritical public opinion. Rather, same-sex marriage is demonized as a threat to marriage from within an embattled sectarian perspective on gender orthodoxy that still has a hold on uncritical public opinion. Arguments for same-sex marriage, which in fact depend on respect for the dignity of marriage, are thus irresponsibly but conveniently inverted into an attack on marriage, yet another instance of the paradox of forging irrationalist intolerance when public opinion most needs reasonable discussion and debate of real, not unreal ethical issues.

Such populist uncritical scapegoating is, I believe, quite clearly in play in congressional and presidential approval of the Defense of Marriage Act of 1996.[249] The act's purpose is to exercise federal power to limit the force of the possible legality of same-sex marriage in Hawaii, and it does so in two ways. First, it expressly excludes same-sex marriage from any of the benefits that accrue to married couples under federal law (thus, discouraging even Hawaii gay and lesbian couples from exercising their rights to marry). Second, it ordains that no other state shall be required to give effect to such same-sex marriage.[250] The purpose of the second provision is to limit any extraterritorial effect of the Hawaii legitimation of same-sex marriage under the Full Faith and Credit Clause of Article IV, section 1 of the U.S. Constitution.[251] Even assuming same-sex marriage were not a constitutional right, this provision would be constitutionally problematic since it claims for Congress a power over the substantive law of marriage that, under the federal system, it does not have; the recognition of Hawaiian same-

248. See, in general, Edward O. Laumann et al., *The Organization of Sexuality: Sexual Practices in the United States* (Chicago: University of Chicago Press, 1994), 172–224.

249. See 1 U.S.C.A. § 7, 28 U.S.C.A. § 1738C, as amended by Congress on September 21, 1996, Pub. L. No. 104-199, 110 Stat. 2419.

250. See Discussion Draft, May 2, 1996, H.R. 3396, 104th Cong., 2d sess.

251. Article IV, section 1, reads as follows: "Full faith and credit shall be given in each State to the public acts, records, and judicial proceedings of every other State. And the Congress may by general laws prescribe the manner in which such acts, records, and proceedings shall be proved, and the effect thereof."

sex marriages in other states is decisively a matter for state, not federal, law.[252] Since same-sex marriage is, however, a constitutional right, the first provision is unconstitutional as well, illegitimately exercising viewpoint discrimination with respect to a fundamental right.

On examination, current American populist sentiment against same-sex marriage is, I have argued, yet another example of sectarian condemnation of identity-based claims to conscience and, as such, inconsistent with constitutional guarantees of equal respect. The issue is such a reactionary rally point for the opponents of gay rights not because it is less but because it is, in its nature, more identity-based in ethical convictions and reasonable public argument that confront the American public mind with its uncritical assumptions of gender inequality as in the nature of things. The very popularity of this reactionary position indicates how far we have yet to go, as a people, in understanding either the legitimacy of the case for gay rights or the ethical demands of principle of our ostensible commitment to gender equality. To complete our understanding of the dimensions of the intellectual and ethical challenge of the case for gay rights, we need to bring our account to bear on the critical examination of how such populist views have been and are sustained.

252. See Laurence H. Tribe, "Toward a Less Perfect Union," *New York Times*, May 26, 1966, p. E11; letter of Laurence Tribe to Sen. Edward M. Kennedy, 142 Cong. Rec. S5931-01, at *S5932-3. See also Mark Strasser, "*Loving* the *Romer* Out for *Baehr:* On Acts in Defense of Marriage and the Constitution," *University of Pittsburgh Law Review* 58 (1997): 279.

FOUR

IDENTITY AND JUSTICE

I began my analysis of the three analogies for making the case for gay rights by putting the case for gay rights in the historical perspective of its development in the wake of the antiracist and antisexist movements and their legislative and judicial successes. I warned, however, that a relatively new human rights movement, like gay rights, must select with care among the strands of more long-standing human rights struggles that it takes as guides or models. Short-term strategic considerations, undertaken with the hope of fitting one's case to a settled precedent, exact a price not worth paying if the price distorts the legitimate claims of gay rights and the important link of those claims to the deeper understanding and elaboration of the struggles with which it is, as a matter of principle, allied. In light of the interpretive proposals I have made both for the case for gay rights and its analogical links to race, gender, and religion, we must now assess the possible merits of these proposals from both the perspective of the case for gay rights and the ways, if any, they illuminate the common constitutional principles that condemn racism, sexism, religious intolerance, and, as I have argued, homophobia.

These interpretive proposals define a normative scope and associated limits.[1] Not all basic constitutional values and rights can be understood in terms of these proposals, but some can be. In particular, my account points to unjust burdens on identity imposed by

---

1. For further discussion of the limits of these proposals, see David A. J. Richards, *Women, Gays, and the Constitution: The Grounds for Feminism and Gay Rights in Culture and Law* (Chicago: University of Chicago Press, 1998), 371–73.

a background structural injustice of history and culture with two features. First, a class of persons has been denied basic human rights of conscience, speech, intimate life, and work; second, such denial is rationalized in terms of dehumanizing stereotypes that, in a vicious circle of self-entrenching injustice, limit both discussion and speakers to the presumptively settled terms of the denial of basic rights. The model for both the understanding of basic rights and the burden of justification required for their just abridgment arises, I suggested, from the argument from toleration (which informs our understanding of both religious liberty and free speech); but, the understanding of the structural injustice I describe, while dependent on the argument for toleration, elaborates that argument to condemn an independent constitutional evil, one not limited to unjust abridgment of one right but abridgment of all rights on grounds that remove a class of persons from the category of bearers of human rights. Some cases of religious intolerance are rooted in this structural injustice as well (in my view, anti-Semitism and homophobia), but that fact requires special explanation in terms of a background history and culture of particularly focused and aggressively dehumanizing intolerance.

Both the burdens on identity and the background structural injustice inform a principled understanding of the constitutional condemnation of racism, sexism, extreme religious intolerance, and homophobia. In all these cases, the background structural injustice imposes unjust terms of identity on a subjugated group. Though the structural injustice may radiate out to encompass as well material and related disadvantages, merely remedying the latter disadvantages, without more, does not address the roots of the problem, which is a distinctive injury to moral personality.

The idea of identity, in the sense relevant to our concerns here, is not the philosophical problem of identity (in terms of the criteria of mind and/or body for identifying a person as the same over time and space) nor the broadly sociological question of our multiple roles and statuses, many of which are uncontroversially socially ascribed. It would, thus, trivialize the evil of burdens on identity to condemn any and all social ascriptions on identity. Rights-based struggle against structural injustice does not renegotiate all the terms of one's personal identity; one's identity, as a person, is never either infinitely malleable or even desirably regarded as entirely open to choice. Cultural assumptions must always be taken as given if any reasonable criticisms and reforms, including those based on rights-based protest of structural injustice, are to go forward sensibly.

But structural injustice, marked by the two features earlier described, inflicts an injury on aspects of our identity and identifications that organize features of our self-understanding of ourselves as persons and moral agents; this is the narrower sense of contestable and contested identity that is my concern. The pivotally important feature that structures the character of the injustice is its abridgment of basic human rights in general and inalienable rights to conscience and intimate life in particular, that is, denying the very moral powers in terms of which we come to understand and protest basic injustice. Abridgment of conscience and intimate life play the role they do in inflicting this evil because they are so intimately tied up with the sense of ourselves as persons embedded in and shaped by networks of relationships to other persons with the moral powers of rational choice and reasonable deliberation over the convictions and attachments that give shape and meaning to our personal and ethical lives, as lives lived responsibly from conviction. The dehumanization of people, on grounds of race or gender or religion or sexual orientation, imposes objectifying stereotypes of identity (as black or a woman or Jewish or homosexual) that deny these moral powers, indeed, that are rationalized in terms of this denial. In consequence, these stereotypes take on significance in our lives in terms dictated by the underlying injustice, reducing not only life chances but self-conceptions to their terms.

The depth of this genre of injustice is seen in the double consciousness that its most probing critics (like W. E. B. Du Bois, and Betty Friedan, anticipated by Sarah Grimke[2]) identified as among its worst consequences. The imposition of unjust stereotypes of race or gender thus rationalized the abridgment of conscience, imposing on the very terms of one's sense of oneself as an African American or a woman a devalued self-image of subhumanity. Such lack of free conscience rendered protesting thoughts

2. Ibid., 100.

unthinkable, which entrenched such stereotypes in the consciousness of oppressed and oppressor alike. The awakening sense of injustice was thus understandably articulated in the terms of double consciousness, the inward sense of oneself both in terms of the dominant stereotype and in yet undefined terms of oneself made possible by challenge to the uncritical force the stereotype had enjoyed. This new sense of identity, forged by rights-based protest to the terms of one's dehumanization, must in its nature affirm a basis for self-respect in exactly the moral complexity, experimental openness, and sense of variety and multiple options that dominant stereotypes deaden and stultify.

No small part of the political power of the enforcement of such stereotypes had been twofold: first, their denial of perspectives and voices that might challenge them; and second, their lack of reasonable standards in terms of which such injustice might even be understood, let alone protested by thought and action. A vicious circle thus locked human consciousness into a self-perpetuating repetition of unjust stereotypes as the measure of rights and responsibilities. A life lived to the full measure of such stereotypes must be as vacant of the consciousness of moral agency and responsibility as maintenance of the rigidity of the stereotypes required. Thankfully, even under circumstances of the most entrenched structural injustice, human beings are never entirely vacant of consciousness, even critical consciousness including the irony and sense of play and artistic genius of homosexuals over the centuries that invested life with enduring personal and ethical meaning in defiance of stereotypes.[3] However, culturally mandated accommodation to such unjust stereotypes exacted and exacts a heavy price.

Lack of protesting thoughts and the reasonable critical standards they make possible correspondingly distort emotional life in creatures, like ourselves, for whom the emotions have important connections to thoughts and beliefs.[4] The unjust force of this in-

---

3. See, for a sense of the range and variety of such cultural contribution and achievement over the centuries, Wayne R. Dynes, *Encyclopedia of Homosexuality*, 2 vols. (New York: Garland, 1990).

4. On the relation of beliefs and feelings, see David A. J. Richards, *A Theory of Reasons for Action* (Oxford: Clarendon Press, 1971), 70–71, 246–47, 252–55, 264–67, 308.

dignity is particularly stark in the case of homophobia. Under the structural injustice I call homophobia, the very experience of one's sexuality, as erotically drawn to those of the same sex, must often be experienced in terms of the dominant stereotypes that traditionally enforce homophobia, namely, as an unspeakable threat to one's gender identity let alone one's humanity, thus often as an object of panic and dread. The depth and importance of the human sexuality of sexual orientation may be analogized to that of the natural language we first acquire,[5] as fundamental to our sense of ourselves as a person formed by and living in affective social relationships to other persons. Under the structural injustice of homophobia, our sense of ourselves as homosexuals can barely connect to our wider beliefs and convictions, but must live in a psychic ghetto of the mind that corresponds to the cultural space of homophobically mandated unspeakability. One's homosexuality, an effectively forbidden language of sexual experience and sensual bonding, can hardly in such circumstances play the kind of role heterosexuality plays as a language that models and expresses love and friendship in ways that engage our central convictions about personal and ethical meaning in living. The enormously popular political reaction to claims of gay rights may be regarded as an attempt to maintain this culturally entrenched difference in the treatment of homosexuality and heterosexuality, a fact conspicuously shown by the focus, as we have seen, of many legal expressions of this attitude in the condemnation of assertions of gay and lesbian identity that protest this difference.

The depth of the problem is, if anything, compounded by the associated abridgment of the basic human right of intimate life, an abridgment also importantly constitutive of all the manifestations of structural injustice we have been concerned with. The right of intimate life plays so fundamental a role as a basic human right, on a par with the right to conscience, because such intimate relations and identifications structure one's sense of self as a person with creative moral powers formed, sustained, and transformed in

5. On this point, see John Money, *Gay, Straight, and In-Between: The Sexology of Erotic Orientation* (New York: Oxford University Press, 1988), 11–12, 54, 71, 74, 76, 80, 129–30.

relations to other persons dealing with many of the same issues of living (the meaning of birth, love, and death) addressed by the right of conscience. As I observed earlier in the discussion of the proper way of understanding the constitutional evil of racism (chapter 1), the nature of the evil of racism was understood and analyzed as very much active by those African American leaders who protested the evil even though they could have passed as white. For them, as for others afflicted by populist prejudices rooted in structural injustice, their protest was against unjust burdens on identifications with persons whom they love and respect; they refused to accept that it could ever be an acceptable condition of equal respect supinely to acquiesce in an unjust stigma placed upon distortions of one's history and heritage.

Their protest both broke the silence of such acquiescence and forged reasonable standards of critical assessment in terms of which such historical injustice might be understood, assessed, and protested. It is because American racism was so structured by abridgments of the right to intimate life both during and after slavery that it analogically illuminates the role of the abridgment of intimate life in the structural injustice that has been our concern here. Not to be deemed capable of choice of intimate relations (as in the denial of marriage and control of children under slavery) or such choice on equal terms (as under antimiscegenation laws) was to be deemed sexually subhuman or animalistic. As we earlier saw (chapters 1–2), similar such abridgments supported the structural injustice of sexism and anti-Semitism, rationalized in terms of objectifying stereotypes of sexuality and gender.

In contemporary circumstances, the most conspicuous example of a still largely intact structural injustice, arising from such abridgment of both the right to conscience and intimate life, is homophobia. The right to sexual intimacy between parties of the same-gender is not yet constitutionally recognized, and the right to marriage is disdained by large populist majorities and the demagogic politicians who pander to them.[6] As I earlier observed, the

6. For example, both Hawaii and Alaska recently approved constitutional amendments aimed to bar same-sex marriage. See Same Howe Verhovek, "From Same-Sex Marriages to Gambling, Voters Speak," *New York Times*, November 5, 1998, p. B1. Similar movements for such amendments are contemplated in other states. See Carol

abridgment of the right to conscience to gays and lesbians casts the pall of unspeakability over their intellectual and emotional life, and the further abridgment of the right to intimate life extends this pall beyond thought and emotion to ways of life. A group that, in just protest of the long-standing cultural tradition of their moral subjugation, most needs experimental space to exercise and test their creative moral powers of thought and action meets a reactionary attack on their very claims of justice and even their right to an intimate life. The extent of the injustice may be seen in two of its aspects that, in contrast to some other forms of structural injustice we have studied, remain largely intact.

First, the cultural pall of unspeakability falls not only on the intimate relations of gays and lesbians, but on their intimate relations to others, in particular, their families of origin. Gays and lesbians have as profound identifications with their families of origin as heterosexuals, and as much right to develop, reinterpret, and even deepen those identifications as a reasonable basis for sustaining enduring personal and ethical values in living. However, the terms of their cultural unspeakability often compel disruption of these bonds as the unjust price to be paid for gay and lesbian identity, inflicting a desolating homelessness as the price to be paid for integrity. No culture that claims (as ours proudly does) to respect the right to intimate life should put persons (either parents or children) to such an unjust, morally impoverishing choice. In fact, the kinds of unjust disruptions of family life (both in marriage and in relations of parents to children) that so repel us in the African American experience of slavery are today quite self-righteously inflicted on gays and lesbians by Americans who popularly rationalize such flagrant abridgments of the right to intimate life, in a forceful contemporary example of the irrationalist inversions and obfuscations wrought by the paradox of intolerance, by appeals to the very values (family values) they so aggressively attack.

Second, the discourse of African American, Jewish, and feminist protests of the terms of their moral slavery has now given rise

---

Ness, "Gay Marriage Foes Have Eyes on 2000 Ballot; With Voters on Two States Banning the Practice, California, Vermont Likely Are Next Battlefield," *San Francisco Examiner,* November 5, 1998, A-26.

to familiar and widely accepted traditions of dissent, many of whose claims now enjoy the status of established constitutional principles.[7] The claims of gay and lesbian identity, because so many of the terms of their moral slavery remain intact, are much more fragile, certainly lacking anything like the strength and durability of the now flourishing traditions of dissent that protest the vestiges of the other forms of moral slavery. In such a situation, gay and lesbian identity enjoys much less cultural support than the merits of its claims of justice would require, remaining exposed, as we have seen, to attacks triggered by its very making protests of the injustice of its terms of moral slavery. It remains largely marginal to the American sense of justice in matters of religion, race, and gender.[8]

In consequence, gay and lesbian identity remains conspicuously vulnerable in yet another way. Its culture of dissent is still so undeveloped and its moral slavery still so largely intact that the very terms of gay and lesbian identity are vulnerable to the stereotypes that have traditionally rationalized their subjugation. Their situation today is perhaps closer to the experience of double consciousness that Du Bois and Friedan discussed than any other group currently is that has historically suffered moral slavery. This may explain the temptation of some gay scientists and activists, earlier noted (chapter 1), to defend the case for gay rights in genetic or biological terms as if such explanations of sexual orientation, if true, would or should make any difference to the case for gay rights. But they are not true and are not harmlessly false, since they might be used to reimpose the objectifying stereotypes of sexuality and gender identity that the case for gay rights must and does protest. As I earlier observed (chapter 1), biological reductionism was used to rationalize the cultural degradation of African Americans and women as a separate species and will wreak comparable havoc on lesbians and gays today, as it did to earlier advocates of gay rights in the past, by confirming, rather than challenging, the unjust cultural stereotypes of the inferiority rooted in

7. For fuller discussion of these developments, see Richards, *Women, Gays, and the Constitution.*

8. See, in general, Alan Wolfe, *One Nation, After All* (New York: Viking, 1998), 72–81.

nature (in this case, biology). Lesbians and gays need responsibly to insist on and to demand our personal and moral identity as lesbian and gay persons, and to resist those unjust and objectifying stereotypes that have stripped us of our powers of free moral personality.

Whatever the etiology of sexual orientation, the normative question remains of what personal and ethical sense a person can reasonably make of such erotic thoughts and feelings and attachments, a quest that requires one to question a still largely intact cultural tradition of unspeakability that rules such a quest intrinsically unworthy of thought or discussion. The closest analogy to that quest is the religious analogy of the personal quest for reasonable conviction about ultimate values in living. This makes the case for gay rights not less based on established constitutional principles, but more so. The underlying structural injustice is of the same sort as that underlying racism and sexism (indeed, overlaps with aspects of the latter, chapter 2), and, its quest for justice, as we have seen (chapter 3), appeals as well to the oldest tradition of constitutional suspectness, namely, suspicion of sectarian political attempts to demean such a form of conscientious life without support in acceptably compelling secular state purposes.

Understood in this way, the case for gay rights advances understanding of the common constitutional principles that condemn racism, sexism, anti-Semitism, and homophobia. The evil in each case is directed at identity, and the ground for the evil is a structural injustice rooted in culture and history. The study of the case for gay rights, interpreted in this way, enables us to see clearly not only that immutability and salience are improper bases for constitutional suspectness, but illuminates as well the problematic motivations of this mistaken understanding. It is thus a common feature of all the constitutional evils, rooted in the structural injustice studied here, that the structural injustice, reflecting a history and tradition of subjugation (an essentially cultural wrong), is rationalized by alleged facts of nature (whether of race or gender or racialized religion or gendered sexual orientation). This is the origin of the intuition that these wrongs are importantly to be ascribed to an improper weight being placed on facts, more precisely, on immutable and salient facts. It is quite true that the resulting political prejudices self-rationalize themselves in terms of facts, but as we have seen, there is nothing factual in the traditions of moral subjugation we have examined, each of which inflicts a cultural constructed and maintained wrong. An adequate diagnosis of the problem must thus attend to the cultural conditions that construct and maintain the wrong, not, as it were, to preserve the wrong by maintaining the fiction that it is based on facts. The thesis of immutability and salience is thus in thrall to the view it claims to criticize, supposing that the wrong attaches to facts. The wrong, however, is marked not by its factual basis, but by its unjust construction of what counts as a factual basis, which may be quite remote from anything we would fairly want to describe as a rational basis rooted in a fact of nature. The motivation to such an account is thus itself tainted by attempting to preserve a factual basis for such wrongs, when the wrong is, as we have seen, cultural all the way down.

It is a virtue of the case for gay rights, from this perspective, that it does not easily or naturally fit the terms of the conventional understanding of suspect classification analysis in terms of immutability and salience. Of course, race and gender, on examination, don't fit the analysis either, but the case for gay rights more obviously fails to do so. It is, indeed, sometimes popularly condemned in these terms as involving choice in a way that, for example, race and gender do not.[9] The challenge for gay rights is not to fit itself to an analysis which is, in any event, inadequate, but to assist in forging a more adequate understanding both of its own claims and the related claims of the other manifestations of structural injustice.

It is not a disadvantage for such an account, like the one offered and defended here, to put the case for gay rights in terms of the choice of a gay and lesbian conscientious identity. The same Americans who popularly condemn gays reject any such condemnation of people of other faiths or even atheists,[10] a striking sociological fact that suggests a failure to understand that gay and lesbian identity operates at exactly the same level. My account thus has the

9. Ibid., 73–74, 77–78.
10. Ibid., 77.

virtue of pressing critical argument exactly where it should be pressed, on the crucial point that is popularly erased (the ethical convictions at the core of the case for gay rights) and on the structural injustice (the force of the tradition of unspeakability) that supports such erasure. Gay identity is, from this perspective, as much or as little chosen as any conventional religion; religion, the oldest suspect classification, involves the same kinds of choice and is nonetheless fully protected from sectarian burdens; and, on proper analysis, the suspectness of race and gender turn, like religion and sexual orientation, on unjust burdens placed on identity against a certain cultural background. It is a virtue of making the case for gay rights in the terms offered here that it compels us to identify these important common features, thus focusing analysis both on injuries to moral personality and on the cultural construction that motivates such injuries (including unjust popular failures to understand and give weight to these injuries).

There is a depth to such injustice that the theory of double consciousness attempts to articulate. The injustice imposes identifications that degrade essential impulses of moral freedom. The burdens of race, gender, religion, and sexual orientation all fall in this area, abridging, as we have seen, basic human rights. Burdens thus unjustly placed on our very consciousness of ourselves dehumanize because they attack our core humanity, living a life from rational and reasonable conviction. Life lived under the weight of such stereotypes must stultify and degrade moral personality. Accordingly, the protest of such structural injustice is, in terms of the self-originating claims of human rights through which we realize and indeed express our humanity, challenging in such empowering reasonable terms the stereotypical identifications that were unjustly imposed.

We need deeper critical understanding of the common grounds used to rationalize such dehumanization if we are to confront the force that it has enjoyed and continues to enjoy over public and private life. Two such important grounds are patterns of dehumanizing sexual stereotyping and the distortion of the public/private distinction. It is a virtue of the study of gay rights that it advances understanding of the role played by both grounds in the support of the structural injustice that is our concern here. Making the case for gay rights confronts and criticizes the role that stereo-typical images of sexuality and gender play not only in the dehumanization of homosexuals but in the rationalization as well of the structural injustice underlying racism, sexism, and anti-Semitism. The issue pervades all these forms of structural injustice in often interlinking ways.

American racism was constructed, as we have seen, in terms of dehumanized images of black sexuality expressed, under slavery, by laws abridging rights of marriage and custody of children, reducing black slaves to the terms of marketable cattle (reproduction being understood and defined in terms that advanced their market utility for the slaveowner). After slavery, laws against miscegenation were enforced to police the color line between black men and white women, but not between white men and black women, thus imposing, often through lynchings, a racialized conception of gender (the white women on her idealized pedestal, black women as sexually available prostitutes) that rationalized the dehumanization of African American men (as sexual predators) and women (as prostitutes).[11]

The same racialized conception of gender supported American sexism as well, a point cogently noted by Sojourner Truth in her famous speech pointing out that the alleged gender differences that supported unjust treatment of (white) women mythologically depended on an idealizing pedestal of delicacy that was belied by the experience of black women.[12] American feminism would only address this problem when, in the spirit of the abolitionist feminism of Sojourner Truth and others, it critically examined the unjust role uncritical conceptions of gender roles (including their racialized character) had been permitted to enjoy in determining the terms of public and private life. Importantly, this realization was crystallized for many American feminists by their own roles in forging stronger antiracist principles as participants in the civil rights movement.[13] Such interracial co-operation was, as we saw (chapter 2), interpreted by the parents of these white women as a

11. See, for full discussion of these points, Richards, *Women, Gays, and the Constitution*, 183, 224, 229, 244, 293, 423, 447.
12. For excerpts, see ibid., 116–17.
13. Ibid., 228.

degradation of their identities as white women (one such father angrily accused his daughter "of being a whore and chased her out of the house in a drunken rage, shouting that she was disowned"[14]).

Questioning images of gender and sexuality in this way naturally led as well to a comparable critical understanding of the unjust enforcement through law of gendered conceptions of sexuality that had abridged basic human rights of thought, speech, intimate life, and work. Such abridgments had been traditionally defended in terms of the idealizing pedestal of women's superior character and roles. In the wake of serious criticism of the racist character of the pedestal, criticism of its sexist character shortly followed. The pedestal was, from this perspective, a cage,[15] dehumanizing women in terms of stereotypical conceptions of their roles solely in terms of the sexual and reproductive interests of men. Second Wave feminism stated and elaborated the consequences of this criticism in terms of demands for equal respect for the basic human rights of women to conscience, speech, intimate life, and work, whose abridgment was not supported by compelling secular purposes.

Extreme forms of religious intolerance like anti-Semitism were rationalized in terms of images of sexuality and gender drawn from the roles of such stereotypes in both racist and sexist discourse. Religious intolerance was thus rationalized in racist terms of propensities to being a sexual predator or prostitute, and in sexist terms that feminized Jews in the same terms as homosexuals (as women, and fallen women at that).[16]

Introduction of the case for gay rights into serious study of the forms of such structural injustice compels attention to the pervasive force of such dehumanizing images of gender and sexuality in the rationalization of such injustice. The powerful populist resistance to this relatively new human rights struggle reflects a dehumanizing obsession with homosexuality solely in terms of a rather bleakly impersonal interpretation of same-gender sex acts in general, or, as Leo Bersani has observed (chapter 3), some such same-gender sex acts in particular (e.g., sexual penetration of a man), an

14. Evans, *Personal Politics*, 44.
15. See, on this point, Richards, *Women, Gays, and the Constitution*, 257, 462.
16. See ibid., 293, 333–34, 461.

interpretation that deracinates such sex acts from the life of a person that is recognizably human or humane. The background of such unjust sexualization was, as we earlier saw (chapters 2–3), the dominant stereotype of the homosexual as a fallen woman, as a prostitute; the terms of such stereotyping are, of course, unjust to sex workers,[17] but they are unjust to homosexuals as well.

In the case of homosexuals, such objectification of sex acts crucially isolates them from any of the familiar narratives through which we normally frame our understanding of the role and place of sex acts in a human life; I mean, of course, the narratives of romantic sexual attraction, quest, passion, and love as well as the narratives of connubial tender transparency and mutual support and nurture and those as well of patience in travail and care and solace in illness and before death. It is a mark of the astonishing injustice to homosexual life and experience that these and other humanizing narratives are, as if by fiat, not extended to homosexual eros. Rather, the culture limits the discussion of homosexuality, in contrast to heterosexuality, to one and only one genre, a clinical focus on sex acts historically associated with the trade of sex workers, namely, pornography.[18]

What can explain such injustice? As I earlier suggested, it cannot be the nonprocreative character of the sex acts that raises public concern, because nonprocreative sex for heterosexuals is now conventional and the right to it constitutionalized. The issue, rather, is its challenge to a highly gendered conception of sexuality as if, contrary to fact, sexual love between men or between women could not be or express passionate love and companionship, at the heart of reasonable conviction of what gives personal and ethical meaning to living, in the way it does for heterosexuals. Making the case for gay rights thus compels us to attend to a particularly entrenched form of gender stereotypy and to confront uncritical

17. See David A. J. Richards, "Commercial Sex and the Rights of the Person: A Moral Argument for the Decriminalization of Prostitution," *University of Pennsylvania Law Review* 127 (1979): 1195; on the scapegoating of prostitutes, see Richards, *Women, Gays, and the Constitution*, 164–71, 178, 296, 310, 321–22; on gender stereotyping of prostitutes, ibid., 175–76, 185, 295–96.

18. On these historical and related issues, see David A. J. Richards, "Free Speech and Obscenity Law: Toward a Moral Theory of the First Amendment," *University of Pennsylvania Law Review* 123 (1974): 45.

limits in our conventional understanding that gender stereotypy, whether of men or women, is now constitutionally suspect. If it is suspect, why isn't this entrenched form of it suspect as well? The force of an uncritical stereotype is shown by the ease with which it is indulged, a fact shown, as I earlier argued, not only by the willful nescience of the majority opinion in *Bowers v. Hardwick* but by the populist support for the many reactionary responses to the case for gay rights earlier discussed (chapter 3).

The case for gay rights thus compels us critically to attend to the continuing force of the enforcement of a kind of stereotype we now reject, as a matter of constitutional principle, in related areas of constitutional discourse. Indeed, if my earlier analysis of the case for gay rights is correct, we are compelled to attend to what, on analysis, are unprincipled limits in our understanding of now conventional constitutional principles that condemn the expression through public law of religious intolerance and of gender stereotypy, for the case for gay rights appeals justly to these and other such principles. The case for gay rights invites us, as well, to reflect on why stereotypical images of sexuality and gender so pervade support for the structural injustice that is our concern here.

The answer lies in important facts about human as opposed to animal sexuality, namely, the role of human sexuality in the plastic and symbolic imaginative life of persons not tied to the periodicities of the reproductive cycle.[19] Because of the imaginative depth of sexuality in the life of persons and in their intimate identifications with other persons, we understand our sexuality as a humane resource of transformative moral passion. As Ficino put the point,

> But when the loved one loves in return, the lover leads his life in him. Here, surely, is a remarkable circumstance that whenever two people are brought together in mutual affection, one lives in

19. For important studies of the differences between human and animal sexuality, see Clellan S. Ford and Frank A. Beach, *Patterns of Sexual Behavior* (New York: Harper & Row, 1951); Irenaus Eibl-Eibesfeldt, *Love and Hate: The Natural History of Behavior Patterns*, trans. Geoffrey Strachan (New York: Holt, Rinehart, and Winston, 1971). The insight is also central to Freud's exploration of the imaginative role of sexuality in human personality; see Sigmund Freud, " 'Civilized' Sexual Morality and Modern Nervous Illness," in *Standard Edition of the Complete Psychological Works of Sigmund Freud*, ed. and trans. James Strachey (London: Hogarth Press, 1961), 9:181, 187.

the other and the other in him. In this way they mutually exchange identities; each gives himself to the other in such a way that each receives the other in return. . . .

The truth must rather be that each has himself and has the other, too. A has himself, but in B; and B also has himself, but in A. When you love me, you contemplate me, and as I love you, I find myself in your contemplation of me; I recover myself, lost in the first place by own [*sic*] neglect of myself, in you, who preserve me. You do exactly the same in me. And then this, too, is remarkable: that after I have lost myself, as I recover myself through you, I have myself through you, and if I have myself through you, I have you sooner and to a greater degree than I have myself. I am therefore closer to you than I am to myself, since I keep a grasp on myself only through you as a mediary.[20]

Our erotic interests in love, as persons (whatever our sexual orientation), have this kind of imaginative depth whether or not they lead, in any particular case, to reproduction; indeed, the distinctive feature of our (as opposed to animal) sexuality is that we pursue such interests, when they are heterosexual, even in periods of the reproductive cycle when reproduction is not possible. The consequence of this important distinction between human and animal sexuality is that a class of persons may be significantly dehumanized by characterizing their sexuality as, in its nature, more animal than human.

The role of images of gender and sexuality in the rationalization of structural injustice may be understood as examples of this phenomenon. In each case, a group was dehumanized by means of stereotypical images (whether of blacks, women, or Jews) that rendered their sexuality more animal than human; in effect, groups

20. Marsilio Ficino, *Commentary on Plato's Symposium*, trans. Sears Reynolds Jayne (Columbia: University of Missouri, 1944), 144–45. This aspect of Ficino's account should be distinguished from other elements of it which are less defensible, including his sharp distinction of love from physical union (130) and his condemnation of the immoderate desire for copulation and unnatural sex (143). On Ficino's as well as Pico della Mirandola's possible motives in legitimating forms of homosexual love, see Giovanni Dall'Orto, " 'Socratic Love' as a Disguise for Same-Sex Love in the Italian Renaissance," in Kent Gerard and Gert Hekma, *The Pursuit of Sodomy: Male Homosexuality in Renaissance and Enlightenment Europe* (New York: Harrington Park Press, 1989), 37–38, 41–44.

were stripped of their humanity by imposing on them mandatory stereotypes of sexuality and gender whose force turned on denial to them of respect for their moral powers (including the exercise of those powers in sexual love), on this ground rationalizing abridgment of their basic human rights. The means of such dehumanization is a kind of stereotypical sexualization: ascribing to a class of persons exclusively and obsessionally sexual or reproductive interests incapable of self-direction in terms of our wider moral powers. Making the case for gay rights brings this general issue into sharp analytical focus because the long-standing cultural tradition it addresses so dramatically exemplifies the irrationalist enforcement of such sexualization. On the one hand, the tradition includes a doctrine of personal love, like Ficino's (interpreting a similar doctrine in Plato[21]), that suggests, if anything, that loving bonds between men realize the full moral meaning of reciprocal human love between equals, as, in Ficino's words, "they mutually exchange identities." On the other, the same tradition (Ficino, again following Plato) condemns as unnatural, indeed unspeakable, same-sex relations as such. For Ficino (like Plato), the issue was resolved apparently by the acceptability, indeed idealization of homoerotic love, as the model for love, but not of sex. In our own much more homophobic age, the issue is not even addressed because the dominant stereotype of homosexuality (as a fallen woman, a prostitute) denies even the thinkability of love, let alone sexual love, between men and between women.

The case for gay rights demands that the issue be addressed particularly since the two traditional grounds for the condemnation of same-sex relations (derived from Plato) are no longer con-

---

21. See Plato, *Phaedrus*, in *Collected Dialogues of Plato*, ed. Edith Hamilton and Huntington Cairns, trans. R. Hackworth (New York: Pantheon, 1961), 476; Plato, *Symposium*, in *Collected Dialogues*, ed. Hamilton and Cairns, 527. Plato appears to have had a highly developed, idealized concept of romantic homosexual love which required that it rarely, if ever, be consummated. Plato, himself homosexual and a celebrant of aim-inhibited romantic homosexual love, appears to have condemned actual homosexual relations, introducing, for the first time anywhere, philosophical arguments for its unnaturalness. Plato, *Laws*, trans. A. E. Taylor, bk. 8, *835d-42a, in *Collected Dialogues*, ed. Hamilton and Cairns, 1226, 1401–6. See Gregory Vlastos, "The Individual as an Object of Love in Plato," in *Platonic Studies* (Princeton: Princeton University Press, 1973), 3, 22–28.

stitutionally acceptable, in principle, at least when enforced against heterosexual men and women. If they cannot be legitimately enforced against heterosexuals, they cannot be legitimately enforced, in principle, against homosexuals either. If same-sex relations cannot, for this reason, be legitimately criminalized, then the Plato-Ficino tradition (endorsing homosexual love but not sex) has lost its requisite support; we would have to endorse both homosexual love and sex. But we are living, as I observed, in a much more homophobically irrationalist period, which avoids even thinking about such issues (like the distinctive nature of human love, whatever its sexual object or orientation) by accepting and enforcing the stereotype of homosexuality as, in its nature, animalistic, expressed obsessionally in a bleakly impersonal interpretation of gay sex acts as if they were not, indeed could not be, expressions of human personality.

The images of gender and sexuality, once so aggressively enforced against African Americans, women, and Jews, today retain much of their traditional force when popularly enforced against homosexuals. If we want to understand, in stark contemporary terms, the historical power of racism, sexism, and anti-Semitism, we have at hand a useful example for study and comparison, namely, the response of modernist homophobia to claims for gay rights. Such claims include both demands for basic human rights of conscience, speech, intimate life, and work and skeptical scrutiny of laws and policies expressing homophobia rooted in structural injustice. From this perspective, homosexuality is no more exclusively about sex than heterosexuality, as deeply rooted in our humanity and as expressive, on just terms, of our moral powers.

The homophobic response to such claims is to distort them in ways that illustrate the force of the paradox of intolerance in contemporary terms. For example, the defense of the human rights of gay and lesbian persons is called faction; arguments for such rights, unjust aggression (inverting, like Hitler's anti-Semitism, victims into aggressors); claims for equality, claims of inequality (special rights); sectarian convictions, the measure of human liberty; laws against discrimination, subsidizing any ideology; factual falsities (sexual abuse of the young), truths (chapter 3). The underlying rationale of such injustice is the sexualization of gay and lesbian identity in a dehumanizing way in terms of objectified sex acts with no ostensible connection to human life and personality.

The ideological force of this stereotypical objectification is the erasure of what was so clear to Ficino and Plato, namely, that homoeroticism could and did express our imaginative moral powers of mutual love and friendship in ways that engaged and elevated our creative intelligence and sense of enduring personal and ethical value in living. The modernist scapegoating of the homosexual can only self-rationalize such appalling injustice by suppressing the very views and speakers that contest its crassly stereotypical sexualization of homosexuals, thus attacking, as we have seen, the very making of rights-based claims by gays and lesbians (chapter 3). Gays and lesbians must not, from this perspective, speak from and to conscience and a sense of justice. They must be what homophobic ideology requires them to be, not persons but sex acts and only sex acts. The homophobic degradation that James Baldwin experienced as a black gay man at the hands of a white Southerner (chapter 1) was of a piece with the degradation of Southern white women participating in the civil rights movement, as prostitutes (chapter 2). Such ideological sexualization of protests of structural injustice remains powerfully operative against claims of gay and lesbian identity today. As we earlier saw, many of the arguments against claims of gay and lesbian rights (chapter 3) turn on an uncritical public common sense shaped by structural homophobia (out gays and lesbians in the military thus are sexual predators, and gays and lesbians can no more have the right to marry than animals). What Baldwin learned about the role of homophobia in fulfilling men's "enormous need to debase other men"[22] remains, perhaps because of the progress we have made against the evil of such sexualization in so many other areas of structural injustice, *painfully* evident today in the popular discourse dismissing gay rights as a heresy to true American values.

There is another feature of the various forms of structural injustice usefully clarified by the case for gay rights. A structural injustice, like racism and sexism, is an affront to human rights both in the public and private spheres that is often rationalized in terms

---

22. James Baldwin, *No Name in the Street* (New York: Dell, 1972), 63.

of protecting the values of intimate personal life (one's slave or one's wife as intimately oneself).[23] The sphere of women was thus defined as fixed and limited to private life, and the sphere of African Americans segregated to an appropriately servile sphere, not extending to public rights and responsibilities. There is an intimacy to the kinds of despotic control thus rationalized, for the control was often over intimate services in the home, including sexual availability. Such structural injustice was constructed in terms of a distorted interpretation of the public/private distinction, and its remedy required a recasting of the public/private distinction. For example, issues previously regarded as private (like spouse and child abuse) importantly became matters of legitimate public concern.[24]

The structural injustice of homophobia raises the same general issue, but at another, perhaps deeper level that advances understanding of the political dynamics that support structural injustice in general. Homophobia does not limit homosexuality to a private sphere (as with gender) or to a servile sphere (race), but to no legitimate sphere of activity at all—a sphere defined by its unspeakability. Such structural injustice inflicts a deeper injury to moral personality even than race and gender in the sense that no legitimate cultural space at all is allowed to the thoughts, feelings, and actions, that express spontaneous erotic feelings and attachments deeply rooted in one's sense of self as a person, let alone to integration of that sense of self into the fabric of convictions about enduring personal and ethical value in living.

Homosexuals, acculturated to the mandate of such unspeakability, live in intimate relation to heterosexuals, both in and outside their families of origin, but under a ban of thoughts, feeling, and action in public and private life that would rightly be regarded as intolerable by contemporary heterosexuals. Under this regime, ho-

23. For fuller discussion, see Richards, *Women, Gays, and the Constitution,* 253, 273–74, 347–48, 367–68.

24. See, for example, *People v. Liberta,* 474 N.E.2d 567 (N.Y. Ct. App. 1984) (rape in marriage no longer exempt from criminal liability). See, for an important exploration of the normative considerations that motivate growing legal concern with violence in private life, Jane Maslow Cohen, "Regimes of Private Tyranny: What Do They Mean to Morality and for the Criminal Law?" *University of Pittsburgh Law Review* 57 (1996): 757.

mosexuals and homosexual activity exist but as a culturally mandated family secret at the intimate heart of a persisting pattern of gender hierarchy in marriage. As I earlier observed, modernist homophobia (based on scapegoating the homosexual as a fallen woman) arose as an aspect of the cultural construction of gender differences in ostensibly companionate marriage in reactionary response to emerging claims of gender equality. Culturally constructed gender differences were thus rationalized as natural to women and men, including the complementarity of such differences that would mandate gender hierarchy in and outside marriage. In particular, the legitimate terms of intimate life (both love and sex) were defined in terms of the opposite gender of the parties, terms of inequality construed as just in virtue of the gender differences natural to intimate life. Men or women, who violated this orthodoxy of love and sex, were necessarily regarded as, respectively, not true men (but women) or not true women (but men). Not only must sex between parties of the same gender be rendered unspeakable, but, more remarkably (in view of the distinguished philosophical tradition on the nature of love between men tracing to Plato and Ficino), love between persons of the same gender. Such love must be excluded from any cultural legitimacy because the parties to it (men, or women, as the case may be) were, within the terms of the gender orthodoxy, equals (an idea repugnant to the orthodoxy of legitimate love and sex as exclusively between unequals).

The consequence of such unspeakability was the enforcement through law of a conception of family life built upon structural injustice; importantly, the very legitimacy of the unequal terms of companionate marriage, in avowedly egalitarian America, required the total erasure of those forms of intimate relations (between men or between women) that would challenge the terms of inequality in marriage as not mandated by the nature of things. To achieve this ideological end, the privatization of homosexuality was more radically total than that endured by women or African Americans, inflicting on homosexuality not limitation to a devalued private sphere, but erasure as the unspeakable secret on which the legitimacy of private life, as conventionally understood, depended. The sense of intimacy of homophobia thus arises, as does sexism and racism, from an embattled sense of protecting the legitimate terms of intimate life, here, however, requiring a more extreme privatization of the aggrieved group (homosexuals) in order ideologically to enforce the terms of the devalued private sphere of women. The issue of homosexuality is intimately constitutive of the sense of conventional gender identity, of the sense, for example, of protection of one's wife as self-defense of one's self. The force of such structural injustice is shown by the only way it can permit itself to construe the unspeakable challenge to the conventional terms of gender identity, namely, as a degradation of gender identity to what is supposed to be the impersonal sex acts of a prostitute that are chosen for perverse and ostensibly superficial reasons (thus, the emphasis in contemporary homophobia on a consumerist model of the choice of sex acts as having the superficiality of a choice of soap).[25] In particular, homophobia requires that such sex acts cannot, in their nature, have the kinds of deep personal roots of fantasy and longing and moral competence for loving and being loved that dignify the intimate lives among heterosexuals in all their variegated moral complexity. In consequence, homosexuality is equated with the conventional stereotype of prostitution, namely, as objectified consumerist sex acts. It is striking that early modern advocates of gay rights insisted on understanding gay sexuality in terms of some humanizing understanding of the role of homoeroticism in the lives and histories of persons.[26] We may and should critically recognize the degree to which their interpretation of personality was much too much in thrall to the gender stereotypes they should have contested,[27] but their argument surely compels respect when properly understood, as it should be,[28] as a way

25. See Alan Wolfe, *One Nation, After All* (New York: Viking, 1998), 73–74, 77–78.

26. See, for further development of this theme, Richards, *Women, Gays, and the Constitution*, chap. 6.

27. On male homosexuality as a congenitally abnormal male who is a female "third sex," see ibid., 305–6, 313–17, 322, 332, 369.

28. Michel Foucault's critical account of the resulting pathologization of homosexuality, while certainly true, lacks, in my judgment, interpretive charity of the humanizing impulses behind many of the early gay rights advocates. Foucault thus observed: "The sodomite had been a temporary aberration; the homosexual now was a species." See Michel Foucault, *The History of Sexuality*, trans. Robert Hurley (New York: Pantheon, 1978), 1:43.

of challenging the dehumanizing objectification of gay and lesbian sexuality.

The contemporary case for gay rights challenges both the terms and consequences of the traditional unspeakability of homosexuality, thus reframing yet again our understanding of the public/private distinction. It challenges its terms by rights-based demands for voice and the reasonable discourse that voice makes possible; it challenges its consequences by insisting on a new conversation in which the choice of homosexuality is no longer homophobically a gratuitous choice of animalistic debasement, but a moral choice of a legitimate form of private and public life on terms of gender equality.

The contemporary case for gay rights has available to it a normative resource only incompletely available, at best, to the first generation of advocates of gay rights, namely, rights-based feminism. A case for gay rights, drawing on rights-based feminism, had certainly been made notably by Walt Whitman and developed by Emma Goldman and Edward Carpenter in the ways they sought common grounds between arguments for rights-based feminism and gay rights.[29] But the case for rights-based feminism had been morally compromised by its strategic alliances (with the temperance and purity movements) based on reinforcing gender stereotypy as part of the development of suffrage feminism.[30] Figures like Goldman, for example, were notably marginalized by most American feminists of her day. Even Carpenter's remarkably prophetic attempt to unite rights-based feminism with arguments for gay rights was flawed by the ways in which his arguments indulged and sometimes reinforced the unjust gender stereotypy of both woman and homosexuals, and other advocates of gay rights were aggressively misogynistic.[31] Contemporary rights-based feminism has, however, carried its analysis of the role of gender stereotypy in rationalizing injustice to women far enough reasonably to acknowledge lesbianism as a legitimate feminist alternative.[32] The case for gay rights may, in ways I earlier suggested, deepen this

---

29. See Richards, *Women, Gays, and the Constitution,* 173–78, 297–310, 317–30.
30. For fuller discussion of this point, see ibid., chap. 4.
31. See, on these points, ibid., 322–23, 326, 329–37, 358.
32. See, on this point, ibid., 342–46, 352.

analysis to criticize, on feminist grounds of principle, the role that gender stereotypy uncritically continues to play in the oppression of both gay men and lesbians.[33]

Indeed, from this perspective, the struggle for gay rights may reasonably be regarded as at the cutting edge of an important criticism of the sexist terms in which family life continues largely to be understood. As we earlier saw (chapter 3), the dehumanization of homosexuals retains popular appeal when brought into relation to claims for same-sex marriage because, consistent with Freud's observation of the narcissism of small differences, it enables a culture, with a long history of uncritical moral slavery of women and homosexuals, not to take seriously, let alone think reasonably about, the growing convergences of heterosexual and homosexual human love in the modern world (for example, the insistence on the romantic love of tender and equal companions as the democratized core of sharing intimate daily life).[34] Indeed, some studies suggest that, if anything, homosexual relationships more fully develop features of egalitarian sharing that are more often the theory than the practice of heterosexual relations.[35] The uncritical ferocity

33. See, for further development of this argument, ibid., chap. 6.

34. See, on the continuities among heterosexual and homosexual forms of intimacy in the modern world, in general, Anthony Giddens, *The Transformation of Intimacy: Sexuality, Love, and Eroticism in Modern Societies* (Cambridge, U.K.: Polity, 1992); John D'Emilio and Estelle B. Freedman, *Intimate Matters: A History of Sexuality in America* (New York: Harper & Row, 1988), 239–360; Philip Blumstein and Pepper Schwartz, *American Couples* (New York: William Morrow, 1983), 332–545. On declining fertility rates, see Claudia Goldin, *Understanding the Gender Gap: An Economic History of American Women* (New York: Oxford University Press, 1990), 139–42; on childlessness, see, in general, Elaine Tyler May, *Barren in the Promised Land: Childless Americans and the Pursuit of Happiness* (New York: Basic Books, 1995); on rising divorce rates, see Carl N. Degler, *At Odds: Women and the Family in America from the Revolution to the Present* (New York: Oxford University Press, 1980), 165–68, 175–76. See also Barbara Ehrenreich, Elizabeth Hess, and Gloria Jacobs, *Remaking Love: The Feminization of Sex* (New York: Anchor, 1986); Ann Anitow, Christine Stansell, and Sharon Thompson, eds., *Powers of Desire* (New York: Monthly Review Press, 1983); Carol S. Vance, ed., *Pleasure and Danger: Exploring Female Sexuality* (Boston: Routledge & Kegan Paul, 1984).

35. On this point, see Susan Moller Okin, "Sexual Orientation and Gender: Dichotomizing Differences," in *Sex, Preference, and Family: Essays on Law and Nature*, ed. David M. Estlund and Martha C. Nussbaum (New York: Oxford University Press, 1997), pp. 44–59.

of contemporary political homophobia (targeted destructively on same-sex marriage) draws its populist power from the compulsive need to construct Manichean differences where none reasonably exist, thus reinforcing institutions of gender hierarchy perceived now to be at threat. In particular, as Whitman argued,[36] democratic equality in homosexual intimate life threatens the core of traditional gender roles and hierarchy. The sectarian political reaction to the growing constitutional success of claims of gender equality acknowledges this threat when it takes its stand strategically where it still can against members of a traditionally stigmatized and silenced minority who are, like the Jews in Europe, easily demonized.[37]

From this perspective, the choice of gay and lesbian identity elaborates the terms of gender equality on deeper grounds of principle. Their experiments in living are of interest not only to them but to the larger culture increasingly concerned, as it is and should be, to forge a conception of both public and private life more consistent with principles of gender equality. Such choice of gay and lesbian identity is, in its nature, an empowering ethical protest of conventional gender stereotypy that enables homosexuals, like heterosexuals, to live as individuals with hearts and minds authentically open to the grace of love. The most illuminating understanding of the distinctive character of this choice is to be drawn from the religious analogy, the right to choose gay and lesbian identity as a matter of conscience.

We understand such issues of conscience in terms of an inalienable right of liberty and the argument for toleration not because we choose our convictions any more than our beliefs in general, but because responsibility for our deepest convictions about value

36. See, for development of this point, Richards, *Women, Gays, and the Constitution*, 297–310.

37. On the analogy of such contemporary homophobia to anti-Semitism, see Didi Herman, *The Antigay Agenda: Orthodox Vision and the Christian Right* (Chicago: University of Chicago Press, 1997), 82–91, 125–28; cf. Elaine Pagels, *The Origin of Satan* (New York: Random House, 1996), 102–5. See also, for a useful study of the reactionary populist politics of this group, Chris Bull and John Gallagher, *Perfect Enemies: The Religious Right, the Gay Movement, and the Politics of the 1990's* (New York: Crown Publishers, 1996).

in living expresses the appropriate attitude of respect for the free moral powers of persons. Such responsibility empowers persons to live a life from reasonable conviction, exploring as much as organizing their experience of what gives enduring value to personal and ethical life. The right to liberty of conscience, in the terms protected by the argument for toleration, ensures the requisite moral independence rationally and reasonably to undertake and meet this responsibility free from the unjust imposition of sectarian views. The right to choose gay and lesbian identity is grounded on the right to conscience, thus understood, because only respect for this right ensures the required moral independence in taking responsibility, free of unjust sectarian views unsupported by compelling secular reasons, for convictions about homosexual love as deeply rooted in life experience and personality and the sense of enduring values in living as those about heterosexual love.

It is in the nature of this kind of right that respect is accorded for our moral responsibility, as persons, for our reasonable convictions, whatever they are. That persons are thus acknowledged as morally responsible in this arena allows persons to understand, discover, explore, express, develop, revise, and sometimes change their convictions on whatever reasonable terms move them as a matter of conscience; persons are to this extent respected as free to address these issues independent of unjust sectarian impositions that compel or burden such exercise of our moral powers. It does not follow, of course, that the exercise of such freedom of conscience is itself experienced as a gratuitous matter of consumerist whim. More often, our convictions speak with authority, tell us what must be done, sometimes even erupt with the force of a power greater than ourselves. For this reason, the very point of guaranteeing such freedom is the experience of conscience as the source of reasonable demands or even imperatives of moral personality with an ultimate claim on our convictions. The case for gay rights calls for such responsible freedom for gays and lesbians to confront and meet such demands on terms of justice.

The case for gay rights thus appeals to the moral idea of responsibility for self in the theory and practice of rights-based constitutional law and government. Both the substantive and procedural guarantees of American constitutional law may reasonably be understood as in service of this moral idea.[38] The moral sense and role of this idea may be sharply drawn and appreciated by contrasting this idea to the picture of human life, as dictated by natural hierarchy, that it criticizes. Such natural hierarchy embeds human lives in prescribed statuses whose force depends on the denial of the moral idea of responsibility for self.

The connection between respect for human rights and the idea of responsibility for self may be clarified in terms of two ways that values of human rights protest natural hierarchy. First, human rights ground self-originating claims that challenge the very terms of such hierarchy, in which one's role is externally dictated as exhaustive of meaning in living. Second, such claims of human rights also make possible reasonable criticism of the unjust political construction that has rendered such hierarchy ostensibly natural and uncontroversial. I have already discussed the force of such criticism both in terms of the argument for toleration and the theory of structural injustice. The theory of structural injustice thus is a criticism of certain ways in which unjust claims of natural hierarchy have been rationalized, for example, in terms of race or gender. The criticism of such hierarchy, as a naturalization of injustice, affirms the moral idea and value of responsibility for self, claiming one's reasonable moral powers against the stereotypical impositions of natural hierarchy that have blighted critical moral freedom. The case for gay rights, which draws both upon the argument for toleration and the theory of structural injustice, affirms such responsibility for self of gays and lesbians. In particular, such claims protest the traditional naturalization of injustice to homosexuals in terms of dehumanizing stereotypes of the depraved nature of homosexuality. In this way, gays and lesbians take responsibility for defining their personal and ethical lives on terms of justice.

The choice of gay and lesbian identity derives its moral sense and political and constitutional significance as the condition for exercising this kind of responsibility for self. That sense of responsibility ethically empowers thoughts, feelings, and convictions that

---

38. For extended defense of this view, see David A. J. Richards, *Foundations of American Constitutionalism* (New York: Oxford University Press, 1989).

challenge the naturalization of the structural injustice of homophobia, including the cultural meaning ascribed to one's homosexuality. Feelings need no longer be held in uncritical contempt nor regarded as an affliction, but interpreted as the basis for a confident and self-respecting sense of self, an identity, as a moral agent and person. Such a new interpretive attitude to self is made possible by and fosters moral powers to protest the structural injustice that had silenced such powers. The attempt thus to forge a sense of identity, not flawed by the repressive tradition of unspeakability, integrates one's understanding of sexual orientation with ethical convictions about the meaning and place of love and friendship, of intimacy and community, of justice in private and public life. Such integration insists on connection where cultural homophobia compelled isolation, making possible an interpretation of homoerotic sexual feeling and passion as a constructive moral resource, as Whitman urged,[39] for a more just understanding of the promise of American democratic community on terms of principle. As I have suggested, such promise includes advances in moral and constitutional understandings from which all Americans will benefit, in particular, contesting the political enforcement of unjust gender roles in public and private life that stultify the just range of liberty and opportunity that should be available to all Americans.

Such a new sense of gay and lesbian identity must, in its nature, be contested and contestable in ways similar to the debates among African Americans, women, and Jews about how the terms of personal and ethical identity, forged against structural injustice, should be understood. There is an interpretive depth and complexity to all such disputes that resist any simplistic reduction to tribalizing slogans and rhetoric, let alone any reduction of them to the stereotypical terms (as a simple fact) that rationalized the injustice. The range of views on these questions among gays and lesbians is at least as broad and various as those among other similarly situated groups. What actuates such debates is resistance to any reductively stereotypical view of homosexuality as an uninterpreted simple fact and a corresponding common sense of interpretive possibility

---

39. For development of this point, see Richards, *Women, Gays, and the Constitution*, 297–310.

and responsibility that the struggle for human rights against structural injustices, in all its forms, opens in terms of a new space for free moral imagination to explore. We can, in terms of that space, give a moral sense and interpretation to the idea of the legitimate invention of self. The invention of self is not always and everywhere a good thing; indeed, in some notorious cases, such invention (as by fascist demagogues appealing to the chauvinistic authenticity of national identity) has been at the heart of our twentieth century's moral heart of darkness. But, the invention of self, in protest of structural injustice, is a humane moral need—indeed, as I understand it, an imperative of justice. It is that important fact about it (as an imperative of justice) that makes contemporary claims of gay and lesbian identity at the core, not the periphery, of the most principled constitutional understanding of the inalienable human right of conscience and related rights. They remind us, in the voice of their recovered moral powers, of the deepest principles and values of our constitutional tradition. We best respect those principles not when they are not at threat, but when they evidently are.

Finally, the case for gay rights invites closer attention to yet another pervasive feature of all the forms of structural injustice studied here, namely, the injuries inflicted on identity are very much supported, on the other side, by the sense of identity (for example, in racism, of whites as superior; or, in sexism, of conventional heterosexual men as superior). The political power of structural injustice importantly depends on its constitutive power in the formation of such identity in intimate life. Identity, thus formed in intimate relations (as sexism clearly is), has a personal intimacy that, when under attack, construes the attack as a direct threat to self, in particular, invoking the protection of family values. Study of the case for gay rights, from this perspective, confirms the political power of this dynamic. As I have suggested, gender identity has been formed in intimate relations on terms that enforce gender hierarchy as the measure of intimate life in ostensibly egalitarian America (thus, ideologically compelling the unspeakability of homosexual love); in consequence, the populist reactionary response to the case for gay rights takes the form of resisting alleged unjust aggression against a threatened sense of self, appealing, paradoxically, to family values. As an argument, there is no factual basis for it, and indeed decisive objections to its irrationalism (ideologically transforming, consistent with the paradox of intolerance, victims into aggressors). But the populist appeal of the claim requires explanation. The explanation is the continuing political power of homophobia, as a structural injustice—the tangled sexist ideology that rationalizes this injustice as an ideological support for gender hierarchy in contemporary circumstances.

The absorbing interest of the case for gay rights, in contemporary circumstances, is that it confronts a form of structural injustice that, unlike the other forms we have studied, remains very largely intact. The constitutional principles that now liberally condemn conspicuous forms of racism, sexism, and anti-Semitism, have enjoyed only limited, quite recent application to condemn homophobia.[40] What makes this so striking is that basic constitutional principles both of conscience and of intimate life and of antidiscrimination fully apply to the laws that continue to disadvantage gay and lesbian people. In particular, the constitutional principles that now condemn unjust gender stereotypy disadvantageous to both men and women, condemn, as a matter of principle, the important role of gender stereotypy in modernist homophobia. That these issues are barely seen, let alone acted on, suggests the continuing power of the structural injustice of homophobia, which, as it were, exempts—without explanation or any sense of a need for an explanation—gays and lesbians from the principles now aggressively extended to protect the basic rights of all other Americans.

This gap in principles raises larger questions about the integrity of a cluster of constitutional principles, preoccupied with the role of structural injustice in American history and tradition, that are among the principles that inform our sense of ourselves as a people capable of transformative moral growth under the rule of law—a people that struggled constitutionally with itself to understand and remedy the evils of slavery, racism, sexism, and anti-Semitism. The struggle for the rights of gay and lesbians is the retelling in contemporary circumstances of perhaps our most valuable narra-

40. See *Romer v. Evans*, 116 S. Ct. 1620 (1996).

tive of the struggle to come to know, understand, and act on one's human rights in protest of dehumanizing traditions that have denied one's status as even a bearer of human rights. Such rights-based protest of the terms of one's dehumanization makes the case for gay rights, in its contemporary nature, a struggle to forge a self-respecting identity on terms of justice in the best American tradition of morally transformative constitutional discourse aimed at our most entrenched and popular structural injustices.

The case for gay rights, thus understood, must engage any one seriously interested in the continuing power and authority of American constitutionalism to address fundamental injustices in American public and private life inflicted by the complacent populist tyrannies of democratic majorities that so darkly worried James Madison, our constitutional founder most profoundly engaged by the normative demand to structure legitimate political power to respect the inalienable human right of conscience.[41] Like the related antiracist and antisexist struggles, the struggle for gay and lesbian identity will, as it proceeds, transform American identity as well, deepening and widening the advances we have made on the rights-based grounds of principle that are the birthright of all Americans. Respect for such rights-based protest of the terms of an identity constructed on injustice best defines the American people, as Lincoln believed,[42] as a moral people because capable of moral growth on reasonable terms of constitutional principle. Consistent with this tradition, Americans should embrace the case for gay rights as calling on the best in themselves—a moral competence, tested by history yet freshly alive to humane experience, for the rebirth of freedom as the ethical responsibility of freedom in light of the basic human rights due all Americans under the rule of law.

41. See, for exploration of this issue, Richards, *Foundations of American Constitutionalism*, 107–30, 147–48, 175–82.

42. For Lincoln's appeal to "the light of reason and the love of liberty in this American people," see Robert W. Johannsen, ed., *The Lincoln-Douglas Debates* (New York: Oxford University Press, 1965), 67.

BIBLIOGRAPHY

Abelove, Henry, Michele Aina Barale, and David M. Halperin, eds. *The Lesbian and Gay Studies Reader.* New York: Routledge, 1993.

Ackerman, Bruce. "Beyond *Carolene Products.*" *Harvard Law Review* 98 (1985): 713.

Amsterdam, Anthony G. "Thurgood Marshall's Image of the Blue-Eyed Child in *Brown.*" *New York University Law Review* 68 (1993): 226.

Ahlstrom, Sydney E. *A Religious History of the American People.* New Haven: Yale University Press, 1972.

Altman, Dennis, et al. *Homosexuality, Which Homosexuality? International Conference on Gay and Lesbian Studies.* London: GMP Publishers, 1989.

Aptheker, Herbert. *American Negro Slave Revolts.* New York: International Publishers, 1952.

————, ed. *A Documentary History of the Negro People in the United States,* 4 vols. New York: Citadel Press Books, 1990.

Aquinas, Thomas. *On the Truth of the Catholic Faith: Summa Contra Gentiles.* Translated by Vernon Bourke. New York: Image, 1956.

Arendt, Hannah. *The Origins of Totalitarianism.* New York: Harcourt Brace Jovanovich, 1973.

Arkes, Hadley. "Questions of Principle, Not Predictions." *Georgetown Law Journal* 84 (1995): 321.

————. Testimony on the Defense of Marriage Act, 1996. Judiciary Committee, House of Representatives, 1996 WL 246693, at *11 (F.D.C.H.).

Augustine. *The City of God.* Translated by Henry Bettenson. Harmondsworth: Penguin, 1972.

Bailey, Derrick S. *Homosexuality and the Western Christian Tradition.* New York: Longmans, Green, 1955.

Bailey, J. Michael, and Richard C. Pillard. "A Genetic Study of Male Sexual Orientation." *Archives of General Psychiatry* 48 (1991): 1089.

Baldwin, James. *No Name in the Street.* New York: Dell, 1972.

————. *The Price of the Ticket: Collected Nonfiction, 1948–1985.* New York: St. Martin's, 1985.

Balter, Joni. "Gay Power Brokers—Money, Stature and Savvy Give Leaders More Clout." *Seattle Times,* August 1, 1993, p. A1.

Barkan, Elazar. *The Retreat of Scientific Racism: Changing Concepts of Race in Britain and the United States between the World Wars.* Cambridge: Cambridge University Press, 1992.

Barnett, Walter. *Sexual Freedom and the Constitution.* Albuquerque: University of New Mexico Press, 1973.

Bawer, Bruce, ed. *Beyond Queer: Challenging Gay Left Orthodoxy.* New York: Free Press, 1996.

Beattie, James. *An Essay on the Nature and Immutability of Truth.* New York: Garland Publishing, Inc. 1983.

————. *Elements of Moral Science.* Delmar, N.Y.: Scholars' Facsimiles & Reprints, 1976.

Beauvoir, Simone de. *The Second Sex.* Translated by H. M. Parshley. 1953. New York: Vintage, 1974.

Bell, Alan P., Martin S. Weinberg, and Sue K. Hammersmith. *Sexual Preference.* New York: Simon & Schuster, 1978.

Benedict, Ruth. *Race: Science and Politics.* New York: The Viking Press, 1945.

Bennett, William. "Leave Marriage Alone." *Newsweek,* June 3, 1996, p. 27.

Bernstein, Alan E. *The Formation of Hell: Death and Retribution in the Ancient and Early Christian Worlds.* Ithaca: Cornell University Press, 1993.

Berube, Allan. *Coming Out under Fire: The History of Gay Men and Women in World War Two.* New York: Free Press, 1990.

Blackstone, William. *Commentaries on the Laws of England 1765–1769.* Vol. 4. Edited by Thomas A. Green. Chicago: University of Chicago Press, 1979.

Blumstein, Philip and Pepper Schwartz. *American Couples.* New York: William Morrow, 1983.

Boas, Franz. *The Mind of Primitive Man.* 1911. Rev. ed., Westport, Conn.: Greenwood Press, 1983.

Boswell, John. *Christianity, Social Tolerance and Homosexuality.* Chicago: University of Chicago Press, 1980.

————. *Same-Sex Unions in Premodern Europe.* New York: Villard Books, 1994.

Branch, Taylor. *Parting the Waters: Martin Luther King and the Civil Rights Movement, 1954–1963.* London: Papermac, 1990.

Bransford, Stephen. *Gay Politics vs. Colorado and America: The Inside Story of Amendment 2.* Cascade, Colo.: Sardis Press, 1994.

Bray, Alan. *Homosexuality in Renaissance England.* London: Gay Men's Press, 1982.

Brooten, Bernadette J. *Love between Women: Early Christian Responses to Female Homoeroticism.* Chicago: University of Chicago Press, 1996.

Brown, Peter. *The Body and Society: Men, Women, and Sexual Renunciation in Early Christianity.* New York: Columbia University Press, 1988.

Bull, Chris, and John Gallagher. *Perfect Enemies: The Religious Right, the Gay Movement, and the Politics of the 1990's.* New York: Crown Publishers, 1996.

Bushnell, Horace. *Women Suffrage: The Reform against Nature.* New York: Charles Scribner and Co., 1869.

Calhoun, Emily. "The Thirteenth and Fourteenth Amendments: Constitutional Authority for Federal Legislation against Private Sex Discrimination." *Minnesota Law Review* 61 (1977): 313.

Cantarella, Eva. *Bisexuality in the Ancient World.* Translated by Cormac O'Cuilleanain. New Haven: Yale University Press, 1992.

Carpenter, Edward. *Love's Coming of Age: A Series of Papers on the Relations of the Sexes.* 1896. New York: Vanguard Press, 1926.

Case, Mary Ann C. "Disaggregating Gender from Sex and Sexual Orientation: The Effeminate Man in the Law and Feminist Jurisprudence." *Yale Law Journal* 105 (1995): 90.

Cash, W. J. *The Mind of the South.* New York: Vintage Books, 1941.

Chafe, William H. *The Paradox of Change: American Women in the 20th Century.* New York: Oxford University Press, 1991.

———. *Women and Equality: Changing Patterns in American Culture.* New York: Oxford University Press, 1977.

Chamberlain, Houston Stewart. *The Foundations of the Nineteenth Century.* Translated by John Lees. 2 vols., London: John Lane, 1911.

Chesler, Ellen. *Woman of Valor: Margaret Sanger and the Birth Control Movement in America.* New York: Anchor, 1992.

Churchill, Wainwright. *Homosexual Behavior among Males.* New York: Hawthorn, 1967.

Cobb, Thomas R. R. *An Inquiry into the Law of Negro Slavery in the United States of America.* 1858. New York: Negro Universities Press, 1968.

Cohen, Jane Maslow. "Regimes of Private Tyranny: What Do They Mean to Morality and for the Criminal Law?" *University of Pittsburgh Law Review* 57 (1996): 757.

Cole, David, and William N. Eskridge, Jr. "From Hand-Holding to Sodomy: First Amendment Protection of Homosexual (Expressive) Conduct." *Harvard Civil Rights–Civil Liberties Law Review* 29 (1994): 319.

Continuing Legal Education Materials. *The Bill of Rights versus the Ballot Box: Constitutional Implications of Anti-Gay Ballot Initiatives.* Presented by the Gay-Lesbian Bisexual Law Caucus of The Ohio State University, March 12, 1994.

Cooke, Jacob E., ed. *The Federalist.* Middletown, Conn.: Wesleyan University Press, 1961.

Cooper, Anna Julia. *A Voice from the South.* Edited by Mary Helen Washington. 1892. New York: Oxford University Press, 1988.

Crimp, Douglas. *Cultural Analysis/Cultural Activism.* Cambridge: MIT Press, 1988.

Curry, Thomas J. *The First Freedoms: Church and State in America to the Passage of the First Amendment.* New York: Oxford University Press, 1986.

Davis, F. James. *Who Is Black? One Nation's Definition.* University Park: Pennsylvania State University Press, 1991.

Degler, Carl N. *At Odds: Women and the Family in America from the Revolution to the Present.* New York: Oxford University Press, 1980.

———. *In Search of Human Nature: The Decline and Revival of Darwinism in American Social Thought.* New York: Oxford University Press, 1991.

D'Emilio, John, and Estelle B. Freedman. *Intimate Matters: A History of Sexuality in America.* New York: Harper & Row, 1988.

———. *Sexual Politics, Sexual Communities: The Making of a Homosexual Minority in the United States, 1940–1970.* Chicago: University of Chicago Press, 1983.

"Developments in the Law—Sexual Orientation and the Law." *Harvard Law Review* 102 (1989): 1508.

Devlin, Patrick. *The Enforcement of Morals.* London: Oxford University Press, 1965.

Dollimore, Jonathan. *Sexual Dissidence: Augustine to Wilde, Freud to Foucault.* Oxford: Clarendon Press, 1991.

Donald, David Herbert. *Lincoln.* New York: Simon & Schuster, 1995.

Dover, Kenneth J. *Greek Homosexuality.* London: Duckworth, 1978.

———. *Greek Popular Morality in the Time of Plato and Aristotle.* Oxford: Basil Blackwell, 1974.

———. *The Greeks and Their Legacy.* Oxford: Blackwell, 1988.

Duberman, Martin. *Stonewall.* New York: Plume, 1994.

Du Bois, W. E. B. *Black Reconstruction in America, 1860–1880.* 1935. New York: Atheneum, 1969.

Dudziak, Mary L. "Desegregation as a Cold War Imperative." *Stanford Law Review* 41 (1988): 41.

Duncan, Greg J., and Saul D. Hoffman. "A Reconsideration of the Economic Consequences of Marital Dissolution." *Demography* 22 (1985): 485.

Dworkin, Ronald. *Law's Empire.* Cambridge: Harvard University Press, 1986.

———. *Life's Dominion: An Argument about Abortion, Euthanasia, and Individual Freedom.* New York: Knopf, 1993.

Dynes, Wayne R. *Encyclopedia of Homosexuality.* 2 vols. New York: Garland, 1990.

Ehrenreich, Barbara, Elizabeth Hess, and Gloria Jacobs. *Remaking Love: The Feminization of Sex.* New York: Anchor, 1986.

Eibl-Eibesfeldt, Irenaus. *Love and Hate: The Natural History of Behavior Patterns.* Translated by Geoffrey Strachan. New York: Holt, Rinehart, and Winston, 1971.

Elliot, Jonathan. *The Debates in the Several State Conventions on the Adoption of the Federal Constitution.* Vol. 2. Washington, D.C.: Printed for the Editor, 1836.

Ellman, Ira Mark, Paul M. Kurtz, and Katharine T. Bartlett, eds. *Family Law: Cases, Text, Problems.* Charlottesville, Va.: Michie Co., 1991.

Elshtain, Jean Bethke. *Women and War.* New York: Basic Books, 1987.

Ely, John Hart. *Democracy and Distrust: A Theory of Judicial Review.* Cambridge: Harvard University Press, 1980.

Erlanger, Howard S., ed. "Review Symposium on Weitzman's *Divorce Revolution.*" *American Bar Foundation Research Journal* 4 (1986): 759–97.

Eskridge, Jr., William N. *The Case for Same-Sex Marriage: From Sexual Liberty to Civilized Commitment.* New York: Free Press, 1996.

Estlund, David M., and Martha C. Nussbaum, eds. *Sex, Preference, and Family: Essays on Law and Nature.* New York: Oxford University Press, 1997.

Evans, Sara. *Personal Politics: The Roots of Women's Liberation in the Civil Rights Movement and the New Left.* New York: Vintage, 1980.

Faderman, Lillian. *Odd Girls and Twilight Lovers: A History of Lesbian Life in Twentieth-Century America.* New York: Columbia University Press, 1991.

Faderman, Lillian. *Surpassing the Love of Men.* New York: William Morrow, 1981.

Faludi, Susan. *Backlash: The Undeclared War against American Women.* New York: Doubleday, 1991.

Faust, Drew Gilpin, ed. *The Ideology of Slavery: Proslavery Thought in the Antebellum South, 1830–1860.* Baton Rouge: Louisiana State University Press, 1981.

Ficino, Marsilio. *Commentary on Plato's Symposium.* Translated and introduced by Sears Reynolds Jayne. Columbia: University of Missouri, 1944.

Fineman, Martha Albertson. "Implementing Equality: Ideology, Contradiction and Social Change, A Study of Rhetoric and Results in the Regulation of the Consequences of Divorce." *Wisconsin Law Review* 1983: 789.

———. *The Illusion of Equality: The Rhetoric and Reality of Divorce Reform.* Chicago: University of Chicago Press, 1991.

Finkelman, Paul. *Slavery and the Founders: Race and Liberty in the Age of Jefferson.* Armonk, N.Y.: M. E. Sharpe, 1996.

Finnis, John. "Law, Morality, and 'Sexual Orientation.'" *Notre Dame Journal of Law, Ethics, & Public Policy* 9 (1995): 11.

Foner, Philip S., ed. *The Life and Writings of Frederick Douglass.* 5 vols. New York: International Publishers, 1975.

Ford, Clellan S., and Frank A. Beach. *Patterns of Sexual Behavior*. New York: Harper & Row, 1951.

Foucault, Michel. *The History of Sexuality*. Vol. 1. Translated by Robert Hurley. New York: Pantheon, 1978.

Fox-Genovese, Elizabeth. *"Feminism Is Not the Story of My Life": How Today's Feminist Elite Has Lost Touch with the Real Concerns of Women*. New York: Doubleday, 1996.

———. *Feminism without Illusions: A Critique of Individualism*. Chapel Hill: University of North Carolina Press, 1991.

Franke, Katherine M. "The Central Mistake of Sex Discrimination Law: The Disaggregation of Sex from Gender." *University of Pennsylvania Law Review* 144 (1995): 1.

Frankenberg, Ruth. *The Social Construction of Whiteness: White Women, Race Matters*. Minneapolis: University of Minnesota Press, 1993.

Franklin, John Hope. *The Militant South, 1800–1861*. Cambridge: Harvard University Press, Belknap Press, 1956.

Fredrickson, George M. *The Black Image in the White Mind: The Debate on Afro-American Character and Destiny, 1817–1914*. Middletown, Conn.: Wesleyan University Press, 1971.

Freeman, Jo. *The Politics of Women's Liberation: A Case Study of an Emerging Social Movement and Its Relation to the Policy Process*. New York: Longman, 1975.

French, Marilyn. *The War against Women*. London: Penguin, 1992.

Friedan, Betty. *The Feminine Mystique*. 1963. London: Penguin, 1982.

Garrison, Marsha. "Good Intentions Gone Awry: The Impact of New York's Equitable Distribution Law on Divorce Outcomes." *Brooklyn Law Review* 57 (1991): 621.

Genovese, Eugene D. *From Rebellion to Revolution: Afro-American Slave Revolts in the Making of the Modern World*. Baton Rouge: Louisiana State University Press, 1979.

———. *Roll, Jordan, Roll: The World the Slaves Made*. New York: Vintage Books, 1974.

George, Robert P., and Gerard V. Bradley. "Marriage and the Liberal Imagination." *Georgetown Law Journal* 84 (1995): 301.

Gerard, Kent, and Gert Hekma. *The Pursuit of Sodomy: Male Homosexuality in Renaissance and Enlightenment Europe*. New York: Harrington Park Press, 1989.

Giddens, Anthony. *The Transformation of Intimacy: Sexuality, Love, and Eroticism in Modern Societies*. Cambridge, U.K.: Polity, 1992.

Giddings, Paula. *When and Where I Enter . . . : The Impact of Black Women on Race and Sex in America*. New York: William Morrow, 1984.

Gilman, Sander L. *Jewish Self-Hatred: Anti-Semitism and the Hidden Language of the Jews*. Baltimore: Johns Hopkins University Press, 1986.

Goldin, Claudia. *Understanding the Gender Gap: An Economic History of American Women*. New York: Oxford University Press, 1990.

Goldman, Nancy Loring. *Female Soldiers—Combatants or Noncombatants*. Westport, Conn.: Greenwood Press, 1982.

Goldstein, Anne B. "History, Homosexuality, and Political Values: Searching for the Hidden Determinants of *Bowers v. Hardwick*." *Yale Law Journal* 97 (1988): 1073.

———. "Reasoning about Homosexuality: A Commentary on Janet Halley's 'Reasoning about Sodomy: Act and Identity in and after *Bowers v. Hardwick*.'" *Virginia Law Review* 79 (1993): 1781.

Gordon, Linda. *Woman's Body, Woman's Right: A Social History of Birth Control in America*. New York: Penguin, 1977.

Gossett, Thomas F. *Race: The History of an Idea in America*. New York: Schocken Books, 1965.

Gould, Stephen J. *The Mismeasure of Man*. New York: W. W. Norton, 1981.

Grant, Madison. *The Passing of the Great Race or The Racial Basis of European History*. New York: Charles Scribner's Sons, 1919.

Green, Peter. *Classical Bearings: Interpreting Ancient History and Culture*. New York: Thames and Hudson, 1989.

Green, Richard. *Sexual Science and the Law*. Cambridge: Harvard University Press, 1992.

Greenberg, Jack. *Crusaders in the Courts: How a Dedicated Band of Lawyers Fought for the Civil Rights Revolution*. New York: BasicBooks, 1994.

Greenberg, Kenneth S. *Masters and Statesman: The Political Culture of American Slavery*. Baltimore: The Johns Hopkins University Press, 1985.

Gross, Larry. *Contested Closets: The Politics and Ethics of Outing*. Minneapolis: University of Minnesota Press, 1993.

Gutman, Herbert G. *The Black Family in Slavery and Freedom, 1750–1925*. New York: Vintage Books, 1976.

Halley, Janet E. "Reasoning About Sodomy: Act and Identity in and after *Bowers v. Hardwick*." *Virginia Law Review* 79 (1993): 1721.

———. "Sexual Orientation and the Politics of Biology: A Critique of the Argument from Immutability." *Stanford Law Review* 46 (1994): 503.

———. "The Status/Conduct Distinction in the 1993 Revisions to Military Anti-Gay Policy." *GLQ: A Journal of Lesbian and Gay Studies* 3 (1996): 159–252.

Halperin, David M. *One Hundred Years of Homosexuality: And Other Essays on Greek Love*. New York: Routledge, 1990.

Halperin, David M., John J. Winkler, and Froma I. Zeitlin, eds. *Before Sexuality: The Construction of Erotic Experience in the Ancient Greek World*. Princeton: Princeton University Press, 1990.

Hamer, Dean H., et al. "A Linkage between DNA Markers on the X Chromosome and Male Sexual Orientation." *Science*, 16 July 1993, pp. 321–27.

Hamilton, Edith, and Huntington Cairns, eds. *The Collected Dialogues of Plato.* New York: Pantheon, 1961.

Harris, Seth. "Permitting Prejudice to Govern: Equal Protection, Military Deference, and the Exclusion of Lesbians and Gay Men from the Military." *New York University Review of Law & Social Change* 17 (1989–90): 171.

Hart, H. L. A. *Law, Liberty, and Morality.* Stanford, Calif.: Stanford University Press, 1963.

———. "Social Solidarity and the Enforcement of Morals." *University of Chicago Law Review* 35 (1967): 1.

Henry, Sherrye. *The Deep Divide: Why American Women Resist Equality.* New York: Macmillan, 1994.

Herek, Gregory M., Jared B. Jobe, and Ralph M. Carney. *Out in Force: Sexual Orientation and the Military.* Chicago: University of Chicago Press, 1996.

Herman, Didi. *The Antigay Agenda: Orthodox Vision and the Christian Right.* Chicago: University of Chicago Press, 1997.

Hilberg, Raul. *The Destruction of the European Jews.* 3 vols. New York: Holmes & Meier, 1985.

Hirsch, Marianne, and Evelyn Fox Keller. *Conflicts in Feminism.* New York: Routledge, 1990.

Hitler, Adolf. *Mein Kampf.* New York: Reynal & Hitchcock, 1940.

Hole, Judith, and Ellen Levine. *Rebirth of Feminism.* New York: Quadrangle, 1971.

Honoré, Tony. *Sex Law.* London: Duckworth, 1978.

hooks, bell. *Ain't I a Woman: Black Women and Feminism.* Boston: South End Press, 1981.

———. *Feminist Theory: From Margin to Center.* Boston: South End Press, 1984.

Horowitz, Daniel. *Betty Friedan and the Making of "The Feminine Mystique."* Amherst: University of Massachusetts Press, 1998.

Huggins, Nathan, ed. *W. E. B. Du Bois.* New York: Library of America, 1986.

Hume, David. *Essays Moral Political and Literary.* Edited by Eugene F. Miller. Indianapolis: LibertyClassics, 1987.

Hunter, Nan D. "Identity, Speech, and Equality." *Virginia Law Review* 79 (1993): 1695.

———. "Life after *Hardwick.*" *Harvard Civil Rights–Civil Liberties Law Review* 27 (1992): 531.

Hutcheson, Francis. *A System of Moral Philosophy.* 2 vols. 1755. New York: Augustus M. Kelley, 1968.

Hutchinson, George. *The Harlem Renaissance in Black and White.* Cambridge: Harvard University Press, 1995.

Johannsen, Robert W., ed. *The Lincoln-Douglas Debates.* New York: Oxford University Press, 1965.

Jordan, Mark D. *The Invention of Sodomy in Christian Theology.* Chicago: University of Chicago Press, 1997.

Kalven, Jr., Harry. *The Negro and the First Amendment.* Chicago: University of Chicago Press, 1965.

Karst, Kenneth I. "The Pursuit of Manhood and the Segregation of the Armed Forces." *UCLA Law Review* 38 (1991): 499.

Klineberg, Otto. *Race Differences.* New York: Harper & Brothers, 1935.

Koppelman, Andrew. *Antidiscrimination Law and Social Equality.* New Haven: Yale University Press, 1996.

———. "The Miscegenation Analogy: Sodomy Laws as Sex Discrimination." *Yale Law Journal* 98 (1988): 145.

Kymlicka, Will. *Liberalism, Community, and Culture.* Oxford: Clarendon Press, 1989.

Langmuir, Gavin I. *History, Religion, and Antisemitism.* Berkeley and Los Angeles: University of California Press, 1990.

Law, Sylvia A. "Homosexuality and the Social Meaning of Gender." *Wisconsin Law Review* 1988: 187.

Laycock, Douglas. "Free Exercise and the Religious Freedom Restoration Act." *Fordham Law Review* 62 (1994): 883.

Leeming, David. *James Baldwin.* New York: Knopf, 1994.

Lerner, Michael. *The Socialism of Fools: Anti-Semitism on the Left.* Oakland, Cal.: Tikkun Books, 1992.

LeVay, Simon. "A Difference in Hypothalamic Structure between Heterosexual and Homosexual Men." *Science,* August 30, 1991, pp. 1034–37.

Levy, Leonard W. *Blasphemy: Verbal Offense against the Sacred from Moses to Salman Rushdie.* New York: Knopf, 1993.

———. *The Establishment Clause: Religion and the First Amendment.* New York: Macmillan, 1986.

Lewis, David Levering. *W. E. B. Du Bois: Biography of a Race, 1868–1919.* New York: Henry Holt, 1993.

Livingood, J. M., ed. *National Institute of Mental Health Task Force on Homosexuality.* Washington, D.C.: U.S. Government Printing Office, 1972.

Lofgren, Charles A. *The Plessy Case.* New York: Oxford University Press, 1987.

Macedo, Stephen. "Homosexuality and the Conservative Mind." *Georgetown Law Journal* 84 (1995): 261.

———. "Reply to Critics." *Georgetown Law Journal* 84 (1995): 329.

Mansbridge, Jane J. *Why We Lost the ERA.* Chicago: University of Chicago Press, 1986.

Massey, Douglas S., and Nancy A. Denton. *American Apartheid: Segregation and the Making of the Underclass.* Cambridge: Harvard University Press, 1993.

Marcus, Isabel. "Locked In and Locked Out: Reflections on the History of Divorce Law Reform in New York State." *Buffalo Law Review* 37 (1989): 375.

Mathews, Donald G., and Jane Sherron De Hart. *Sex, Gender, and the Politics of ERA: A State and the Nation.* New York: Oxford University Press, 1990.

Matthews, Glenna. *"Just a Housewife": The Rise and Fall of Domesticity in America.* New York: Oxford University Press, 1987.

May, Elaine Tyler. *Barren in the Promised Land: Childless Americans and the Pursuit of Happiness.* New York: BasicBooks, 1995.

McGlen, Nancy E., and Karen O'Connor. *Women's Rights: The Struggle for Equality in the Nineteenth and Twentieth Centuries.* New York: Praeger, 1983.

McLindon, James B. "Separate but Unequal: The Economic Disaster of Divorce of Women and Children." *Family Law Quarterly* 21 (1987): 351–409.

McNeil, Genna Rae. *Groundwork: Charles Hamilton Houston and the Struggle for Civil Rights.* Philadelphia: University of Pennsylvania Press, 1983.

McNeill, John J. *The Church and the Homosexual.* Kansas City, Kan.: Sheed, Andrews & McMeel, 1976.

McPherson, James M. *The Struggle for Equality: Abolitionists and the Negro in the Civil War and Reconstruction.* Princeton: Princeton University Press, 1964.

Meyerson, Denise. *False Consciousness.* Oxford: Clarendon Press, 1991.

Michael, Robert T., John H. Gagnon, Edward O. Laumann, and Gina Kolata. *Sex in America: A Definitive Survey.* Boston: Little, Brown, 1994.

Mill, John Stuart. *On Liberty.* Edited by Alburey Castell. 1859. New York: Appleton-Century-Crofts, 1947.

Mill, John Stuart, and Harriet Taylor Mill. *Essays on Sex Equality.* Edited by Alice S. Ross. Chicago: University of Chicago Press, 1970.

Miller, William Lee. *The First Liberty: Religion and the American Republic.* New York: Knopf, 1987.

Millett, Kate. *Sexual Politics.* New York: Avon, 1969.

Mitchell, Brian. *Weak Link: The Feminization of the American Military.* Washington, D.C.: Regnery Gateway, 1989.

Money, John. *Gay, Straight, and In-Between: The Sexology of Erotic Orientation.* New York: Oxford University Press, 1988.

Money, John, and Anke A. Ehrhardt. *Man & Woman, Boy & Girl.* Baltimore: Johns Hopkins University Press, 1972.

Money, John, J. G. Hampson, and J. L. Hampson. "An Evidence of Some Basic Sexual Concepts: The Evidence of Human Hermaphroditism." *Bulletin of Johns Hopkins Hospital* 97 (1955): 301.

Morris, Madeline. "By Force of Arms: Rape, War and Military Culture." *Duke Law Journal* 45 (1996): 651.

Murphy, Francis, ed. *Walt Whitman: The Complete Poems.* Harmondsworth: Penguin, 1975.

Murphy, Timothy F. *Gay Science: The Ethics of Sexual Orientation Research.* New York: Columbia University Press, 1997.

Myrdal, Gunnar. *An American Dilemma: The Negro Problem and Modern Democracy.* 2 vols. 1944. New York: Pantheon Books, 1972.

Ness, Carol. "Gay Marriage Foes Have Eyes on 2000 Ballot." *San Francisco Examiner,* November 5, 1998, p. A-26.

Niblock, John F. "Anti-Gay Initiatives: A Call for Heightened Judicial Scrutiny." *UCLA Law Review* 41 (1993): 153.

Nieman, Donald G. *Promises to Keep: African-Americans and the Constitutional Order, 1776 to the Present.* New York: Oxford University Press, 1991.

Note. "Constitutional Limits on Anti-Gay-Rights Initiatives." *Harvard Law Review* 106 (1993): 1905.

Note. "Jones v. Mayer: The Thirteenth Amendment and the Federal Anti-Discrimination Laws." *Columbia Law Review* 69 (1969): 1019.

Note. "The 'New' Thirteenth Amendment: A Preliminary Analysis." *Harvard Law Review* 82 (1969): 1294.

Okin, Susan Moller. "Economic Equality after Divorce." *Dissent* (summer 1991), p. 383.

———. *Justice, Gender, and the Family.* New York: Basic Books, 1989.

Olsen, Frances. "Statutory Rape: A Feminist Critique of Rights Analysis." *Texas Law Review* 63 (1984): 387.

Pagels, Elaine. *The Origin of Satan.* New York: Random House, 1996.

Percy III, William Armstrong. *Pederasty and Pedagogy in Archaic Greece.* Urbana: University of Illinois Press, 1996.

Perry, Michael J. "Modern Equal Protection: A Conceptualization and Appraisal." *Columbia Law Review* 79 (1979): 1023.

Pharr, Suzanne. *Homophobia: A Weapon of Sexism.* Inverness, Cal.: Chardon Press, 1988.

Presidential Commission on the Assignment of Women in the Armed Forces. *Women in Combat: Report to the President.* Washington, D.C.: Brassey's. U.S., 1991.

Rauch, Jonathan. "For Better or Worse?" *The New Republic,* May 6, 1996, pp. 18–23.

Rawls, John. *Political Liberalism.* New York: Columbia University Press, 1993.

Reed, Jr., Adolph L. *W.E.B. Du Bois and American Political Thought: Fabianism and the Color Line.* New York: Oxford University Press, 1997.

Richards, David A. J. *A Theory of Reasons for Action.* Oxford: Clarendon Press, 1971.

————. "Commercial Sex and the Rights of the Person: A Moral Argument for the Decriminalization of Prostitution." *University of Pennsylvania Law Review* 127 (1979): 1195.

————. *Conscience and the Constitution: History, Theory, and Law of the Reconstruction Amendments.* Princeton: Princeton University Press, 1993.

————. "Constitutional Legitimacy and Constitutional Privacy." *New York University Law Review* 61 (1986): 800.

————. *Foundations of American Constitutionalism.* New York: Oxford University Press, 1989.

————. "Free Speech and Obscenity Law: Toward a Moral Theory of the First Amendment." *University of Pennsylvania Law Review* 123 (1974): 45.

————. "Public Reason and Abolitionist Dissent." *Chicago-Kent Law Review* 69 (1994): 787.

————. *Sex, Drugs, Death, and the Law: An Essay on Human Rights and Overcriminalization.* Totowa, N.J.: Rowman and Littlefield, 1982.

———— "Sexual Autonomy and the Constitutional Right to Privacy: A Case Study in Human Rights and the Unwritten Constitution." *Hastings Law Journal* 30 (1979): 957.

————. *Toleration and the Constitution.* New York: Oxford University Press, 1986.

————. "Unnatural Acts and the Constitutional Right to Privacy: A Moral Theory." *Fordham Law Review* 45 (1977): 1281.

————. *Women, Gays, and the Constitution: The Grounds for Feminism and Gay Rights in Culture and Law.* Chicago: University of Chicago Press, 1998.

Rose, Kenneth D. *American Women and the Repeal of Prohibition.* New York: New York University Press, 1996.

Rosenberg, Gerald N. *The Hollow Hope: Can Courts Bring About Social Change?* Chicago: University of Chicago Press, 1991.

Rosenberg, Rosalind. *Beyond Separate Spheres: Intellectual Roots of Modern Feminism.* New Haven: Yale University Press, 1982.

Rotello, Gabriel. *Sexual Ecology: AIDS and the Destiny of Gay Men.* New York: Dutton, 1997.

Ruddick, Sara. *Maternal Thinking: Towards a Politics of Peace.* Boston: Beacon Press, 1989.

Ruse, Michael. *Homosexuality.* Oxford: Basil Blackwell, 1988.

Rutherford, Jane. "Duty in Divorce: Shared Income as a Path of Equality." *Fordham Law Review* 58 (1990): 539.

Seligman, Edwin R. A., ed., *Encyclopaedia of the Social Sciences.* Vol. 7. New York: Macmillan, 1937.

Seltzer, Judith A., and Irwin Garfinkel. "Inequality in Divorce Settlements:

An Investigation of Property Settlements and Child Support Awards."
Social Science Research 19 (1990): 82.

Shaw, Brent D. "A Groom of One's Own?" *The New Republic,* July 18 and
25, 1994, pp. 33–41.

Shilts, Randy. *Conduct Unbecoming: Gays and Lesbians in the U.S. Military.*
New York: St. Martin's Press, 1993.

Signorile, Michelangelo. *Queer in America: Sex, the Media, and the Closets of
Power.* New York: Random House, 1993.

Simons, Anna. "In War, Let Men Be Men." *New York Times,* April 23, 1997,
p. A23.

Smith-Rosenberg, Carroll. *Disorderly Conduct: Visions of Gender in Victorian
America.* New York: Knopf, 1985.

Snitow, Anne, Christine Stansell, and Sharon Thompson, eds. *Powers of Desire.* New York: Monthly Review Press, 1983.

Sollors, Werner. *Beyond Ethnicity: Consent and Descent in American Culture.*
New York: Oxford University Press, 1986.

Southern, David W. *Gunnar Myrdal and Black-White Relations: The Use and
Abuse of an American Dilemma, 1944–1969.* Baton Rouge: Louisiana State
University Press, 1987.

Stampp, Kenneth M. *The Peculiar Institution.* New York: Vintage, 1956.

Stanton, William. *The Leopard's Spots: Scientific Attitudes toward Race in
America, 1815–1859.* Chicago: University of Chicago Press, 1960.

Stimpson, Catharine R., and Ethel Spector Person. *Women: Sex and Sexuality.* Chicago: University of Chicago Press, 1980.

Stocking, Jr., George W., ed. *A Franz Boas Reader: The Shaping of American
Anthropology, 1883–1911.* Chicago: University of Chicago Press, 1974.

———. *Race, Culture, and Evolution: Essays in the History of Anthropology.*
New York: Free Press, 1968.

Stone, Geoffrey. "Content Regulation and the First Amendment." *William &
Mary Law Review* 25 (1983): 189.

Strachey, James, ed. and trans. *Standard Edition of the Complete Psychological
Works of Sigmund Freud.* London: Hogarth Press. Vol. 9: 1959. Vol. 21:
1961. Vol. 23: 1964.

Strasser, Mark. *Legally Wed: Same-Sex Marriage and the Constitution.* Ithaca:
Cornell University Press, 1997.

———. *"Loving* the *Romer* Out for *Baehr:* On Acts in Defense of Marriage
and the Constitution." *University of Pittsburgh Law Review* 58 (1997):
279.

Sullivan, Robert. "An Army of the Faithful." *New York Times,* April 25, 1993,
sec. 6 (magazine), p. 40.

Sundquist, Eric J. *To Wake the Nations: Race in the Making of American Literature.* Cambridge: Harvard University Press, Belknap Press, 1993.

Tamir, Yael. *Liberal Nationalism*. Princeton: Princeton University Press, 1993.

Tavris, Carol. *The Mismeasure of Woman*. New York: Simon & Schuster, 1992.

tenBroek, Jacobus. *Equal under Law*. New York: Collier, 1969.

———. "Thirteenth Amendment to the Constitution of the United States: Consummation to Abolition and Key to the Fourteenth Amendment." *California Law Review* 39 (1951): 171.

Thomas, Kendall. "The Eclipse of Reason: A Rhetorical Reading of *Bowers v. Hardwick*." *Virginia Law Review* 79 (1993): 1805.

Tribe, Laurence H. Letter of Laurence Tribe to Sen. Edward M. Kennedy, 142 Cong. Rec. S5931-01, at *S5932-3.

———. "Toward a Less Perfect Union." *New York Times*, May 26, 1966, p. E-11.

Tripp, C. A. *The Homosexual Matrix*. New York: McGraw-Hill, 1975.

Trumbach, Randolph. *Sex and the Gender Revolution: Heterosexuality and the Third Gender in Enlightenment London*. Vol. 1. Chicago: University of Chicago Press, 1998.

Tushnet, Mark V. *Making Civil Rights Law: Thurgood Marshall and the Supreme Court, 1956–1961*. New York: Oxford University Press, 1994.

———. *The NAACP's Legal Strategy against Segregated Education, 1925–1950*. Chapel Hill: University of North Carolina Press, 1967.

Tussman, Joseph, and Jacobus tenBroek. "The Equal Protection of the Laws." *California Law Review* 37 (1949): 341.

Usdansky, Margaret S. "Gay Couples, By the Numbers—Data Suggest They're Fewer Than Believed, but Affluent." *USA Today*, April 12, 1993, p. 8A.

Vance, Carole S., ed. *Pleasure and Danger: Exploring Female Sexuality*. Boston: Routledge & Kegan Paul, 1984.

Verhovek, Sam Howe. "From Same-Sex Marriages to Gambling, Voters Speak." *New York Times*, November 5, 1998, p. B1.

Vlastos, Gregory. *Platonic Studies*. Princeton: Princeton University Press, 1973.

Walters, Ronald G. *The Antislavery Appeal: American Abolitionism after 1830*. New York: W. W. Norton, 1978.

Washington, James Melvin, ed. *A Testament of Hope: The Essential Writings of Martin Luther King, Jr.* 1963. New York: Harper & Row, 1986.

Weeks, Jeffrey. *Coming Out: Homosexual Politics in Britain from the Nineteenth Century to the Present*. Rev. ed. London: Quartet Books, 1990.

———. *Sex, Politics, and Society: The Regulation of Sexuality Since 1800*. 2d ed. London: Longman, 1989.

Weininger, Otto. *Sex and Character*. London: William Heinemann, 1907.

Weitzman, Lenore J. *The Divorce Revolution: The Unexpected Social and Eco-*

nomic Consequences for Woman and Children in America. New York: Free Press, 1985.

Weld, Theodore. *American Slavery As It Is.* 1839. New York: Arno Press, 1968.

Wesley, Joya L. "With $394 Billion in Buying Power, Gays' Money Talks; and Corporate America Increasingly Is Listening." *Atlanta Journal,* December 1, 1991, p. F5.

West, Donald J. *Homosexuality.* Chicago: Aldine, 1968.

Wetzstein, Cheryl. "Gay Couples Sue Vermont for Refusing Marriage Licenses." *Washington Times,* July 23, 1997, p. A3.

Will, George. "And Now Pronounce Them Spouse and Spouse." *Washington Post,* May 19, 1996, p. C9.

Williams, Joan. "Is Coverture Dead? Beyond a New Theory of Alimony." *Georgetown Law Journal* 82 (1994): 2227.

Witherspoon, John. *Lectures of Moral Philosophy.* Edited by Jack Scott. East Brunswick, N.J.: Associated University Presses, 1982.

Wolfe, Alan. *One Nation, After All.* New York: Viking, 1998.

Wolinsky, Marc, and Kenneth Sherrill, *Gays and the Military: Joseph Steffan versus the United States.* Princeton: Princeton University Press, 1993.

Young-Bruehl, Elisabeth. *The Anatomy of Prejudices.* Cambridge: Harvard University Press, 1996.